REMEMBER WHY YOU PLAY

REMEMBER WHY YOU PLAY

Faith, Football, and a Season to Believe

DAVID THOMAS

Tyndale House Publishers, Inc.

CAROL STREAM, ILLINOIS

Visit Tyndale's Web site at www.tyndale.com.

Visit the author's Web site at www.RememberWhyYouPlay.com.

TYNDALE and Tyndale's quill logo are registered trademarks of Tyndale House Publishers, Inc.

Remember Why You Play: Faith, Football, and a Season to Believe

Designed by Ron Kaufmann

The author is represented by Chip MacGregor of MacGregor Literary, 2373 NW 185th Avenue, Suite 165, Hillsboro, OR 97124.

Library of Congress Cataloging-in-Publication Data

Thomas, David, date.
　　Remember why you play : faith, football, and a season to believe / David Thomas.
　　　　p. cm.
　　Includes bibliographical references.
　　ISBN 978-1-4143-3727-2 (sc)
　　1. Faith Christian High School (Grapevine, Tex.)—Football—History. I. Title.
　　GV958.F36T46 2010
　　796.332′6209764531—dc22　　　　　　　　　　　　　　2010025041

Printed in the United States of America

16　15　14　13　12　11　10
7　6　5　4　3　2　1

To Ashlin and Tyson, my two favorite athletes.

Remember why you play.

TABLE OF CONTENTS

Introduction

It is late January 2009. Kris Hogan, head football coach for the Faith Christian Lions, is receiving more media interview requests than he can accommodate. The campus is buzzing over the coach's upcoming appearance on ESPN and his trip to Tampa, Florida, for the Super Bowl—invited along with his wife, Amy, as special guests of National Football League commissioner Roger Goodell. There, the NFL would arrange more interviews for Hogan on the "Radio Row" filled with sports radio stations from around the country. There's even word circulating that movie producers want to make a film about the football team—all because of one game played last football season, against the Gainesville State School Tornadoes.

Looking back on that game, senior Greg Wright says with a shrug, "We didn't take it to be a big deal." But apparently everyone else did, as accounts of that night had spread all over the Internet. The funny thing is that it never was intended to become a story at all. The final game of the 2008 regular season looked to be meaningless. The Lions had secured their slot in the private-school state playoffs, and the Tornadoes would not even make a good tune-up game. They were winless in eight games and had scored only two touchdowns all year.

The game was supposed to mean nothing.

The game turned out to mean everything.

✦ ✦ ✦

Gainesville State School is a maximum-security correctional facility whose students are teenage prisoners. The football players are among the best students, because they must earn the privilege to play. Every game is a road game for the Tornadoes, and their only fans are school personnel and volunteers, usually twenty or thirty people. With barely a handful of substitutes for most games, the players are used to being outnumbered, outplayed, and outcheered.

Which is what made the game in Grapevine, Texas, so different.

For that game, Faith Christian fans decided to treat the visitors like the home team. To make the Tornadoes *their* team.

Before the game, Faith parents and students formed a 40-yard-long spirit line and held a banner for Tornadoes players to run through when they entered the field. Then about half of the Faith fans and cheerleaders moved over to the visitors' side of the stadium and cheered for Gainesville State players throughout the game. Among those cheering were parents of Faith players, encouraging kids they did not know to tackle their own sons. And the fans did more than cheer for Tornadoes players; they cheered for them by name. That support, an overwhelming surprise, inspired the Tornadoes to their best effort of the season. They lost again, 33–14 this time, but they scored two touchdowns in the second half to double the number of touchdowns they had scored all season.

When the game ended, Gainesville State players high-fived and embraced each other. Little did they know when they had stepped off the bus almost four hours earlier that the game would end like this. That they would feel like this. That people out in "the free world" would root for them. That a high school football game could change their lives.

After the game, the teams met at midfield for prayer with Faith fans standing all around. Mark Williams, the Tornadoes' coach, asked if his quarterback could pray. In a simple manner but with heartfelt depth, the player thanked God for things easily taken for granted, from the sun coming up that morning to the opportunity to play football that night. There was one thing, however, for which he said he did not know how to express thanks, because he never knew that so many people cared for him and his teammates.

At that point, in that circle of several hundred fans, you would have been hard-pressed to find a dry set of eyes. I was in that circle, as a sportswriter for the *Fort Worth Star-Telegram* following up on a tip that something special would take place at the game. The story and photos ran in the Sunday sports section, and the e-mails and phone calls began pouring in to our newspaper and both schools. Our readers began e-mailing the story to friends and family.

When sports columnist Rick Reilly wrote about the game for ESPN.com, the attention exploded. Hogan's assistant, Dana Stone, said she felt like the school's press secretary as Hogan found himself in the unexpected and uncomfortable position of choosing which newspaper, radio, and television interviews he had time to accept. An Australian media outlet requested an interview to be broadcast on more than three hundred radio stations Down Under. A college student also requested an interview: he had been assigned to write a paper on someone he considered a hero, and the coach of the Christian school team from Texas he had read about seemed the perfect candidate.

Reports of the game were passed around the Internet on blogs and message boards. Ministers used the story of the game to compose sermons about compassion and hope. The NFL commissioner's office and movie producers called. Hogan would make appearances on ESPN, *The 700 Club*, and *Good Morning Texas*, among other shows. The story that had never been intended to be known outside the Lions' quaint stadium had literally gone global.

✦ ✦ ✦

In the middle of that publicity—and in the middle of basketball season now—Greg Wright expresses surprise at the ongoing reaction.

"It's kind of what we do," he says, almost apologizing for not understanding the attention. The circumstances, he explains, may have been more dramatic for the Gainesville State game, but the opportunity was one like many others Faith coaches have taught players to look for in using football as a platform for reaching out to and helping others.

I know what Wright means. I had followed the Faith program during the previous season, in 2007, to write a book detailing how the school's coaches teach faith and football hand in hand. I had gotten to know Greg and his teammates well that year, long before anyone even knew that Faith would be playing Gainesville State. And I was impressed with what I'd seen. In fact, I was there because I'd been impressed for years. For the 2007 season the Lions were ranked number one in the state and favored to win the school's first football state championship. Facing the giants? The Lions *were* the giants. Yet despite the expectations from those outside the program, and despite the season-long pursuit of a perfect record and state championship, football remained secondary to a greater purpose.

The question most asked by those who have read or heard of the

Gainesville State game is pretty simple: where did this school get the idea to provide fans for a team of prison-school players? The answer is simple too: their way of life. What took place that night on Faith's campus was not a one-game occurrence or confined to one season. Or even to one sport, or sports in general. It is a lifestyle the coaches teach and model, and football fields are just one place where those lessons play out. And it was time spent inside the Faith football program—even though it had been spent before that big game ever happened—that gave me that answer.

+ + +

I first met Kris Hogan during his second season as Faith's head coach, in the fall of 2004. Under his leadership the Lions had earned the school's first playoff victory the previous week. I attended their next game with friends who knew the coach, and we watched Faith's season end that night with a forty-three-point loss.

Despite the margin of defeat, there was something curiously positive about the team. The Faith players had played all out from first to last whistle. Even more notable was their sportsmanship. Through the last play, Lions players helped their opponents up and patted them on the back or helmet. They handed the football to an official after each play. And following the game, on the field, I observed a group of players and coaches that cared for each other and had set aside that night's disappointment in favor of enjoying their season-long accomplishments. That group seemed to be viewing a picture larger than one game, or even one season.

The next year, 2005, I watched a few more Faith games; the next year, even more. Along the way, I became friends with the coach. We shared similar interests and had two children the same ages. As a sportswriter, I enjoyed talking football with a coach outside of football settings. During those conversations, I could see that coaching football meant much more to him than merely coaching football. Hogan truly cares about his players and has a driving passion for developing teenagers into men of high character.

I have heard many coaches state similar admirable goals, and I also have witnessed how difficult it is to put those goals into practice.

Football can be a game of anger, of physically and mentally dominating an opponent. Of tugs-of-war between coach and players, as the coach pushes the players to physical and mental limits beyond what they realize they can attain. Of burdensome pressure to win games, even—and sometimes especially—at the high school level. Yet here was a coach who hugged his players and told them he loved them no matter what numbers wound up on any scoreboard. In response, his players played like no other team I had watched.

In 2006, the Lions were developing into powerhouse status, yet I continued to notice the same sportsmanship that had sparked my interest at that first game. The Faith Lions won, and they won the right way. By the second round of that year's playoffs, I knew I possessed more than a casual interest in Faith football. I was assigned to write a column for my newspaper from the game between two large public schools, Southlake Carroll and Euless Trinity, both of which were undefeated and had won state championships the previous season. The game drew 46,339 fans to Texas Stadium, home of the Dallas Cowboys. Yet up in the press box, as our Game of the Century played out on the field below, I was receiving e-mail updates from Faith's game.

At three o'clock the next morning, I awoke with an idea. At a much more reasonable hour that day, I pitched that idea to the coach: grant me full access to your program for one season, and I will write a book describing how your program blends faith and football. He embraced the idea, but added one stipulation: the book must be completely open and honest about his program. Anything I observed was fair game. He said if the book was not real in its presentation of how faith and football can work together as teammates, it would not be worth writing. I agreed.

As it turns out, I wrote this book in part to explain how a game like the one played against Gainesville State in 2008 could come about. But before we can get there, we have to go back to the 2007 season—and even further still, to the final game of the 2006 season, the one that took place after I struck my deal with Coach Hogan. Neither of us anticipated how much of an impact that next week's game would have on my season of following Faith football—and faith and football.

CHAPTER 1

Change of Seasons

2006 SEASON: STATE SEMIFINALS

There really was no off-season. The Faith Christian Lions' football season did not begin on the final Friday of August. In reality, it began months before the first scrimmage game two weeks earlier. Before the first two-a-day practices in Texas's midsummer heat. Before even those ten days of after-school practice the previous May.

You could say that the 2007 season, with the Lions a favorite to win the school's first football state championship, actually began December 2, 2006, following Faith's loss in the semifinals of Texas's private-school playoffs. Somewhere between the opposing quarterback's kneeling to expire the clock and the end of the 150-mile trek back home to Grapevine, each player mentally stepped into the next season.

There was no distinct start–finish line between those seasons. No clean break or clear transition point. Not considering the way the 2006 season had ended—with a 27–19 loss to The Regents School of Austin, in a game Faith had led in the second half. And especially not considering *when* it had ended—one weekend before the state championship game, in which the Lions had expected to play.

That loss, in manner and timing, would become a nine-month-long hornet sting. Only the new season could push back the old season's closing scene that still plays out through the players' mental TiVos . . .

Faith Christian has the ball near midfield, the game clock inside its final thirty seconds, and the Lions need a touchdown and two-point conversion to send the game into overtime. It is possible—seemingly anything is possible—with Faith's collection of exciting playmakers. But it is fourth down and a half yard to go for a first down.

One-half of a yard.

Football is funny that way. For almost three hours, two teams cover the expanse of a proving ground measuring 120 yards long by 53 1/3 yards wide. And then both teams' futures—one dream will be extended, one extinguished—are decided by less than a step. Half a yard does not seem like much, but oh, the stories squeezed into that half yard.

+ + +

As a running back growing up, Chance Cochran never thought in terms of half yards. He thought in much bigger numbers. Football had always been easy for him. Laughingly easy. In youth games, he broke free for long run after long run. Opposing teams could not stop him, so his coaches did—taking him out of games, often before the second half, to prevent running up the score and embarrassing opponents. When Cochran reached Faith's varsity, he became the first freshman ever to start for coach Kris Hogan. The first five times Cochran touched the ball, he scored touchdowns. And he scored in five different fashions—a running play, a pass reception, an interception return, a kickoff return, and a punt return. After one score, he came off the field laughing, arms outspread. "I *love* football," he told his coaches, and laughed some more.

But then came the night he experienced every player's nightmare. It was the first scrimmage of his sophomore season, and Cochran was picking up where he had left off as a freshman. He carried the ball left and had one defender to juke for another clear path to the end zone. He planted his left foot to cut back to the right. But the cut never came. His left knee buckled, and he collapsed to the ground. "Like a sniper got him from the bleachers," his coach recalls. Just like that, with one bad step, before it really began, his sophomore season ended.

Problems lingered into this, his junior season. He had hoped to be back at full speed by now, but he was not. Cochran had always had an innate ability to move laterally to create space, and then when the defense ahead of him yielded the slightest opening, the play became a straight-ahead dash to the end zone, and the fastest player—Cochran— won. The knee injury, however, had relegated Cochran from fastest player on the field to also-ran. He was only about 60 percent, at best, in lateral movements. He could see the openings in the defenses, like he always had. But by the time he could make the cut to start his dash to the end zone, too often a defender had beaten him to the spot and slammed shut that opening. Late in the season, the pain in his repaired knee began to increase. His doctor discovered a Baker's cyst—a col- lection of fluid on the back of the knee—that required arthroscopic surgery. Cochran missed the final game of the regular season and the first playoff game.

Now he was back on the field—just not all the way back. This play call on third down and five yards for the first down was for Cochran, a screen play that would allow him to catch a short pass in an isolated part of the field and use his speed to gain the first down and temporarily stop the clock, allowing Faith's offense to reorganize.

Cochran left his running back spot to line up at receiver, on the far left side of the formation. He took a step downfield, then retreated behind the line of scrimmage and back toward the quarterback. It was a "jailbreak screen," with Faith's linemen allowing Regents' defenders to rush the quarterback in jailbreak fashion. Before the defenders could reach the quarterback, Cochran caught a soft pass and turned upfield. The play was working as designed: Cochran had the ball beyond the first wave of attacking defenders with a wall of blockers ahead of him. But one Regents player got a hand on Cochran's right foot. Cochran hit the ground one-half yard short of the first-down marker.

Cochran pounded the ball into the turf. It was more than a half- yard's worth of frustration. This was frustration of a season lost, of a second season greatly limited, and of God-only-knows what will hap- pen in future seasons. Two years ago, everyone who saw Cochran play called him a can't-miss college prospect. He was completely healthy then. A different player. And, he admits, a different person. The hap- piness, the love of playing football, had been replaced by doubt about his ability to recover and uncertainty about his future. He felt it. His coaches and teammates saw it. He no longer came off the field laughing.

A fully healthy Chance Cochran would have eluded that one defender. He would have gained that half yard and more, possibly much more. But that Chance Cochran was not on the field, and Faith did not have its first down.

There was confusion. As the official marked where Cochran was tackled, it appeared from the Faith sideline that Cochran had gained the first down. "Spike the ball! Spike the ball!" coaches instructed quarterback Landon Anderson. Once the sideline markers were set to reflect the first down the coaches believed Cochran had attained, the referee would signal for the clock to restart. Because the Lions had no time-outs remaining, the coaches wanted Anderson to spike the ball into the ground to stop the clock so the Lions could set up the one big play the players felt they had been on the verge of making all day.

But it was not first down. It was fourth down. If Anderson spiked the ball, Faith would lose possession of the ball and the game, and its season, would be over. Senior offensive lineman Brian Gibson turned to the junior quarterback and told him, "It's fourth down! Go for it!" From the sideline, Hogan saw the officials spot the ball short of the first down and shouted for Anderson to run Option Left, a run play around the left side of the offensive line in which Anderson would have the option of keeping the ball if he saw an opening or pitching to Cochran at running back. Option Left had produced big yards all season. Now the Lions needed only a half yard from the play.

Having the ball in Anderson's hands always was an outstanding option. In addition to passing for 1,883 yards on the season, he had rushed for 585 yards, averaging 8.5 yards each time he ran the ball. Half a yard? Easy. Except on this play.

Anderson called for the snap. Faith's linemen had become set in their positions so as to avoid a penalty, but the snap came before they were ready to block. Anderson sprinted left as his linemen scrambled to catch up to the play and block their assigned defenders. He reached the point where Option Left's opening had been all season. But this time, when Faith needed that opening most, a Regents player was there. He brought down Anderson, short of the first down. Half a yard short. It might as well have been the length of the field.

Faith's defensive unit entered the field to stand helplessly as Regents' quarterback executed football's most mistake-proof play, from what is known at all levels of football as the "Victory" formation—the kneel-down. Just like that, void of drama, the comeback and the season were over. Dream denied.

As the final seconds counted down, Anderson looked to the team's seniors. He would have another chance to win that first football champi-onship, but the five seniors would not. "Seeing their high school careers just tick away," Anderson would later recall, "it was like five, four, three, two, one . . . Taylor Hazlewood's never going to step on the field for Faith again. Brian Gibson's never going to step on the field. Austin Huffman's never going to play defensive end, ever again. We're not going to have Johnny Juliano on the practice field. We're not going to have Elijah Hall stuffing those A-gaps anymore. It's really a sobering feeling." Teammate Clayton Messinger, looking back along with Anderson, nodded and added: "It's the kind of feeling like you've let them down."

No one experienced that feeling more than Alex Nerney. He was the defensive back who had allowed a long touchdown pass in the third quarter with his team protecting a 19–14 lead, and another in the fourth quarter that pushed Faith's deficit to its final margin of eight points. As far as he was concerned, his team had lost because of him.

It seemed unfair that football fate would pick on Nerney, too. Less than three months earlier, he had suffered a hip subluxation—a com-plete dislocation of his right hip—during a game. As he lay on the field, told by the team trainer to remain motionless, and with the *pop* still echoing inside his head, he considered for the first time that, only seventeen years old, he might never play football again.

Looking at his six-foot-three, 190-pound frame you wouldn't think it possible, but Nerney had been an offensive lineman in eighth grade. By his sophomore season, dedicated workouts had helped him make the unusual conversion from lineman to skilled-position player—a receiver on offense and a cornerback on defense. His first season at receiver, opposing coaches selected him all-district by unanimous vote. But then something happened. More precisely, a lot began to not happen—those dedicated workouts that had taken him to his peak.

Nerney enjoyed his success. He took it easy a day here, a day there. Gradually, the taking-it-easy days grew closer together. Then consecu-tive. The coaches could see a difference, even if early in his junior season his statistics still ranked him among the area's top receivers. And he was on his way to another long touchdown down the far sideline when the injury occurred. He cried on the field as he waited for the cart that would take him to an ambulance. That night he lay in his hospital bed, asking God, "Why me? Why would You do that to me?" He later recalled, "I was distraught because I felt like everything had worked out and God had just slammed me back to reality. I guess I had been getting too big of a head. God tends to do that."

He expected that his season was over. He hoped to be able to return for his senior year. Doctors, however, told him he had gotten a pass. The bone had a small crack, but no chip. If it had chipped, he would never have played again. In eight weeks, he was told, he would probably be back on the field. Nerney rededicated himself to working out to make sure he would be back for the playoffs. Three weeks after the injury, he was cleared to play.

But now he suffered from a different kind of pain—the pain of believing he had lost the game. So amid the players embracing each other on the field, amid the tears of sorrow, Nerney's embraces and tears packed the most emotion. Next season would be different, he already had determined. He would give it his best again for the whole season.

There were five seniors, however, who would not be around to enjoy the benefits of the old Alex Nerney's return. He embraced each one. "I'm sorry," he said through his tears.

+ + +

Three consecutive season-ending losses for Kris Hogan as a head coach.

Actually, most football coaches would take that. There are only two ways to end the season with a victory. One is by winning the state championship. The other—and this is the case for thousands of teams in high school football—is by winning your final game, but not being good enough in your overall season to qualify for the playoffs.

Hogan's teams make the playoffs. He has been a head coach for eight seasons. Six of the last seven have been playoff seasons. That means six seasons that would end with either a loss or a state championship. Not to say that being eliminated from the playoffs ever becomes easy to accept, but coaches understand that only one team in each classification can have that movie-type ending.

For the rest, there are car rides home like this one. Quiet.

Amy Hogan occupied the passenger seat. Kris and Amy's three children—at ages eight, five, and one—were in the backseat. For fifteen, maybe twenty minutes, the only words were Amy's. "I'm sorry," she said several times. Eventually, Amy began to say more. "Just trying to ease the pain of the situation, that's what she was trying to do," Hogan recalled. "Trying to help me through the situation, comfort me."

They talked about the game, interrupted by consoling cell phone calls from fellow coaches who know the feeling all too well. They read text messages from players thanking Hogan for being their coach, their mentor, their friend. They considered some of the what-ifs of football, they discussed the highlights of another playoff season, and they allowed themselves to imagine aloud—together, as coach and fan, as husband and wife—what could have happened the following week if only they had won this game. Then the ride ended, and suddenly this season-ending loss no longer felt like the others. "It just hit him when we got home," Amy remembered.

Unlike previous years when it was disappointment that dominated Hogan's face, this Saturday night it was sadness. He played with the kids, helped get them ready for bed and for church the next morning, but in the quiet moments, the sadness was there. "He looked like he wanted to cry," Amy said. And at one point, she saw her husband go into their bedroom, sit on his knees, and, alone for the first time since the season had ended, softly cry. Amy had never seen her husband so hurt by a loss.

Before each season, Hogan gives each assistant coach a manual that outlines the football program's goals, rules, expectations, and offensive and defensive schemes. Not once in those fifty-six pages does the head coach who has taken four teams to the state semifinals list "win" as a goal. The front page of the manual asks each coach to consider what kind of Christian he is. What kind of husband and father he is. What kind of son he is. What kind of friend and teammate. But nowhere does it mention winning games.

Yet the creator of that manual, the coach behind that philosophy, shed tears now because his team had not won. This was a state championship–caliber team, he thought, and even after replaying the game in his mind, he could not find one reason why his team was not playing for the state championship. Other than the fact that, somehow, it had lost.

This was Hogan's fourth team to reach the state semifinals. Teams at his previous school possessed better chances to win state and did not. But he had never had a team that he wanted to win state more than this one.

Faith Christian opened its doors in 1999. When Hogan arrived in 2003, the Lions had not won a playoff game. Yet they did so in his second season. Then in 2005 and again in 2006 they reached the semifinals round, one step from playing for the state title. His previous school was accustomed to such success. Sportswriters label those programs "perennial powerhouses." Faith Christian is becoming one. "Here, the success is what's happening right now," Hogan says. "The records are being set right now, and these kids know that."

For that reason, he wanted this team to win it all, even if that's not in the manual. "Winning is important," Hogan says. "I like to win." Winning creates opportunities for what he really wants to do as a coach. Coaching at a Christian school, he sees himself as a minister as well.

"Winning is only a goal," he explains, "in that it increases the platform for ministry. If you're winning, people listen more." Not just his players and assistant coaches. Parents, too. And coaches at other schools, who flock to off-season coaching seminars and conventions to hear the most recent winners—the national champions of colleges, the state champions of high schools—share how they coached players into champions. Hogan wants that platform. He wants to talk about developing champions. And he'll even throw in a little football X's and O's while doing so.

+ + +

It was 3:30 p.m. on a Thursday, and the Faith locker room was quiet. So far, things were as they should have been—until Landon Anderson, Clayton Messinger, and Curtis Roddy came in and sat on the blue footlockers running the length of the room. They should have been out on the field practicing for the championship game. Instead, the uniform hooks lining the wall hung empty. The only remaining signs of the vanished season were the red jerseys stacked neatly on the floor—their next stop was the supply room, where they would spend the long off-season—and those three signs on the wall. The ones stating the players' three pursuits: "Go Undefeated," "Win District," and "State Champs."

Not one of those three was achieved. The first goal fell in the fifth game, with a one-point loss on the final play of the game to a public-school team that would later earn a top-ten ranking in the state and reach the quarterfinals of the playoffs. The district championship possibility was essentially lost when the Lions were defeated by Trinity Christian in their district opener, a game in which quarterback/safety Anderson suffered a sprained ankle on the Lions' first possession. Meeting the third goal, the state championship, would have trumped the other two shortcomings.

The three players recalled their emotions during the final seconds of their ten-win, three-loss season. "Heartbreak," Anderson summed up. "Yeah, heartbreak," Roddy agreed. "Our season, our goals . . . that's our goals. That's our goals over there." He pointed to the three signs. "State champs was our last goal that we had." Messinger remembered the final play, Regents' kneel-down, and standing next to senior Brian Gibson on the defensive line. "It was his last game, and I just wanted it so bad for him. I was just looking at him and . . . it's heartbreak."

Roddy, true to his intense nature, cut straight to the chase. "I wanted to throw up." Roddy's a big Dallas Cowboys fan, but the next day he couldn't even watch their game against the New York Giants. He couldn't do anything associated with football. But then came Monday—back to school. Of course, everyone wanted to talk about the loss, to ask what had gone wrong. And at three o'clock that day, for the first time since the semester began, there was no football practice. No heading home from practice at 6:30 or hanging out with friends on the team for an extra half hour or so. Then on Wednesday, it was Roddy's seventeenth birthday. Before the season, he had let it be known that he planned on celebrating his birthday at football practice. His uncle called to wish a happy birthday and ask how that day's practice had gone—he assumed Faith had won. Although it seemed everything and everyone around him kept him from letting go of this season, Roddy had taken his step into the next one on the ride home from the game. "Dad," he'd said, "I need a gym membership."

There was work to be done. Five days after the semifinals loss, Roddy had turned in four days in the weight room. Today would be the fifth. "Don't take a day off," he said. "Take a workout off, and Trinity Christian just beat us again. Take a workout off, and Regents just beat us again. You don't want to have that regret." That, Messinger agreed, is the attitude he and the rest of the team's seniors-to-be had adopted. "That's what we're trying to get into everyone's head now, that every single moment matters," he said. "No matter if you're in the weight room, if you're out on the field practicing, if you're at home working out, what you're doing right then is preparing you for football."

The images of this year's seniors falling one victory short of playing for their ultimate goal were burned onto the minds of next year's seniors. "It's like, 365 days from now, I'm done with football," said Anderson. "I'm never going to play high school football again. So why waste a workout?"

A wasted workout, in Roddy's eyes, is cheating. Cheating yourself, and cheating your teammates. "We're not going to let anybody goof off," Roddy promised. "This has to be the most important off-season I think the school has ever had."

CHAPTER 2

"Sold Out"

2007 SEASON: FIRST DAY OF PRACTICE

Coach Steve Ford had set his alarm clock for 5:00 a.m. He did not need it. "I woke up, 'It's Christmas Day! Pad up!'"

Pad up. That is among coaches' favorite phrases, because it means it's time to hit the field. On this first Monday morning in August, that meant the first practice of the new season. The first day of two-a-days, the rugged introduction to the season with two practices each day.

Even if Ford had left directly for the field house, he would not have been the first person there. Six seniors—Curtis Roddy, Brent Reeder, Alex Nerney, Weston Clegg, Grant Hockenbrough, and Jeff Kallal—were so ready for practices to start that they had camped out next to the field house the night before.

One minute after 7:00 a.m., the players were in red shorts and gray T-shirts, wearing their white helmets with the red Lion-head logo, and jogging one lap around the practice field to loosen up. Coaches assigned players into three numbered groups and dispatched them to corresponding workout stations.

"Where are the Ones?" one player asked coach Drew Sells. Hogan answered instead, with a point of his finger to the northwest corner of the field where the rest of the first group already was in place. "I hate the first day," Hogan said to Sells. "The learning curve."

Hogan likes a well-run practice. He does not like players standing around or wandering around. "We're burning daylight," he will say when a practice's tempo drops below his desired level. He is a teacher on the field, and a minute wasted is a minute of teaching—and learning—lost.

Fortunately for Hogan, this team may have had the smallest learning curve of any he has coached. With only five seniors graduated from last season's team, and with nine of eleven starters returning on offense and eight on defense, other than for the occasional wandering One, he would not be teaching Football 101 this season. If a season were a ten-chapter textbook, with this team's experience Hogan was starting today at chapter five, at least.

A Web site that covers Texas private-school sports had picked the Lions as the state's number one team in its small-school rankings. Other coaches had told Hogan during the off-season, and he had heard reports of other coaches agreeing, that his would be the team to beat in Division III of TAPPS, the Texas Association of Private and Parochial Schools. The state championship game sat seventeen weeks away—Saturday, December 8. Faith Christian had never played for a state championship in football. This season, that was expected to change.

+ + +

Ten minutes into the season, first round of warm-ups completed, Hogan gathered the fifty-four players in the high school program. They took a knee (they always take a knee when Hogan addresses them) with their helmets on (they always keep their helmets on while on the practice field unless instructed otherwise) and locked their eyes on their coach. "Eyes on Coach," a player would say upon seeing a teammate not looking directly at the coach. Looking directly at who is addressing you is a small thing, and "Discipline in the small things" is an oft-spoken phrase in this program. It's also a belief. Teams that maintain discipline in the small things, Faith's coaches preach, are the teams that win state championships.

Now, for the first time at Faith, nothing less than a state championship would do. Hogan—wearing knee-length tan shorts, red tennis shoes, a white "FAITH FOOTBALL" T-shirt, and a whistle around his neck—made that clear as he addressed his team for the first time.

"First thing is objectives," he began. "For the team, we have one objective, guys. One objective. That's to be the best we can be. We have not reached our potential the last two years. The objective is to be the best we can be at the end of the season, not having lost a game and being the state champion. That's it. That's the objective. For the season."

Whoa, some players thought. *That's a big goal. We haven't even reached a championship game before. Can we really even win a state championship, much less be expected to?*

This was the first time Hogan, not his players, had set a team's objective. This year, with these players, Hogan figured, they could have but one goal, and he set it for them.

He had also decided what reaching that objective would require: his players must be sold out. "Sold Out," he told them, would be this year's theme. Sold out to God, family, school, and state championship. "And that's it," he said. "That's *it*. Got more on your plate than that, you're going to get beat. That's just the bottom line. You're going to have to sell out. Everybody with me?"

"Yes, sir," the players replied in unison.

+ + +

Muscle injuries annoy football coaches about as much as anything. Even the least of muscle injuries has the potential to nag a player for an extended period of time. But the real reason they bother coaches is that muscle injuries are preventable. Breaks, sprains, and twists happen; they're just part of the game. But stretching exercises can prevent muscle pulls and strains, and that's why coaches devote practice time to them.

So when Hogan looked over the players, spread out in seven lines for exercises, and spied a few not properly stretching, he halted the proceedings and called them back into a group. Already having determined that his players would have to do their stretches over from the beginning, Hogan became further irritated when a handful of players walked over to join the group instead of running.

"Number one, don't walk on the field," Hogan told them. "I see people walking out here. Don't ever walk on the field. Number two, if you're going to win the state championship, reach your goal this season, how many things do you have to do right?"

"Everything," the players answered.

"Everything," Hogan repeated. "We just had seniors not stretch right, so we're going to do it again. If you don't do it right, we're gonna do it again. And we'll just go right through our stretches for two, three hours until the next practice if we need to. You're going to do it right."

Hogan told the assistant coaches to spread out and walk through the lines and "coach 'em up on stretching."

"Football in Texas ain't for the weak minded!" Ford yelled. "It takes a special person!"

Then Hogan saw something else he did not like. At the end of each stretch, players are expected to clap in unison before beginning the next stretch. "I just saw two seniors not clap!" Hogan yelled. "You're going to get your butt beat in the semifinals again!"

What does a single hand clap during the first practice have to do with the thirteenth game of the season?

Discipline in the small things.

+ + +

The Texas high school football season begins in August and ends with the playoffs in December. The competition to be the best runs year-round.

In programs such as Faith's, two-a-days are not about getting into shape. Thanks to a summer weight lifting and conditioning program called Lion Power, players report to the first practice already in shape. Yet at the end of this year's first two-hour practice, the conditioning drills coaches were about to put their players through would make the players feel as though they had lounged around all summer.

They're called 360s, after the nearly 360-yard perimeter of a football field. One lap is a 360—although being on the 80-yard practice field technically makes it fall short. Linemen run in one group. Receivers, running backs, and quarterbacks—"flat-bellies," as line coach Ford calls them—run in another.

The players were about to run five 360s, with short, catch-your-breath breaks between each one. They were not told how many they would run, but they were expected to run each as though it would be the last. Maximum effort, in other words. Sold out on each one.

During the third 360, coaches decided the players needed motivation. "We're running for a state championship!" Hogan yelled across the field through cupped hands.

As players completed the run, they bent over to catch their breath. That's a no-no on this practice field. "Stand up!" Ford yelled. "Don't let the other sideline see you're tired! I know there's some pain involved! But don't let them see it!"

On the fourth 360, Ford observed players slowing in their final steps. Ford, who at six-foot-two and with a stocky build carries the most commanding presence among the coaches, pointed to the finish line. Then he walked to the spot about ten yards short of that finish line where he saw players stop being sold out. He knew that three steps, in the overall picture of potentially a fourteen-game season, would mean practically nothing in terms of physical conditioning. But those three steps, mentally, could mean everything in terms of reaching the objective. He chose that spot to represent the state semifinals. "We finished here last year," he said. "This is the semifinals!" This season was about sprinting past the semifinals and through the finish line. With that, the final 360 began. One player was thirty yards into the final lap when he lifted his helmet and vomited. He never stopped running.

The 360s may have been the most difficult for Roddy. The senior had organized "Blood Brothers," a group of players who stayed after Lion Power summer workouts to perform extra conditioning drills. They made T-shirts to show their commitment to working extra hard for an extra-special upcoming season. Roddy was the team's biggest player at 285 pounds, so he had more weight to carry than anyone else, and despite the extra summer conditioning, the fifth 360 appeared to be all he could handle. As he crossed the finish line, he fell. About a half-dozen teammates rallied around him, shouting encouragement. "Get up! Stand up! What are we working for?" Roddy worked his way up to his feet, exhausted.

Hogan told the players to walk to the far sideline to cool down their muscles. They walked together. One voice screamed out from the pack,

"We're not going to have a repeat!" When the players reached the sideline, they turned to start back to meet with the coaches. They jogged, not walked.

Hogan told the players to take their helmets off as they took a knee. "All right, listen closely. This is what it kind of feels like to sell out. Let me tell you something, you're not in a class by yourself. All great programs did what we did today. That's about the minimum amount of running. That's about the *minimum*. There are some programs that did more than us today. They have practice tonight at seven. We'll practice here in a little while, so we're going to save some energy. We'll leave it out here after the other practice. Part of being a champion is going places that nobody else goes. Well, guess what. Everybody comes to practice. How do you go somewhere that nobody else goes? You go to a different level of energy and effort. You go to where it hurts. Because when it hurts, it turns back 80 percent of the people you're ever going to play. They quit. When I say quit, what they do is they trick the coaches. They trick. Coaches know they're going about 80 percent. They just slow down. They go through the motions. They don't push through the pain. If you want to get what nobody else does, which is that state championship—only one team has it—you have to do what they're not willing to do. That's just the bottom line. You have to be sold out. So sold out, there's a little discomfort sometimes. Just a little bit. You know what? In about five minutes, you'll be fine. You'll be fine. It's short-term pain, but long-term gain. You've got to get that mind-set and get sold out. That's just who we are. Coach Ford said get your shoulders back and your chin up. That's who you are. You're Faith. We are Faith. We represent."

After completing his speech, with players still breathing heavily from the 360s, Hogan called on junior Greg Wright to pray. Wright had a broken foot and would not be able to practice for at least three more weeks. As Hogan told him, "You're one of the few people who is breathing correctly."

Wright prayed, then the players huddled with index fingers pointed skyward, for their first huddle breakout of the season. This would be how they would break out of team huddles all season. "Best season, right here!" Josh O'Neal exclaimed. "Best season! 'Sold Out' on three! One, two, three . . ." Then every player together said, "Sold Out!"

The first two-hour practice was complete. The second would begin in ninety minutes.

+ + +

Atwood made his first appearance at the second practice. Atwood is Hogan's six-year-old cowboy hat, and "he" is loved by the players. Each year they hope their coach wears Atwood for the team photo.

Atwood is made with palm leaves, not straw like a typical cowboy hat, so Hogan can reshape the hat himself if a rainstorm hits. One of a team manager's most important jobs is, when Hogan removes the hat, to make sure Atwood is placed in a safe spot on the practice field where he will not be trampled.

Even the players do not know why Hogan named his hat Atwood. The name is one of those fun games Hogan, a habitual prankster, enjoys playing with people. Atwood hats are made by the Atwood Hat Company, and they carry the company's name on the band inside the hat. Real cowboys know that, Hogan says, but even with the large number of his players who drive pickups, listen to country music, and talk about hunting and fishing, Grapevine is all suburban. "There aren't many cowboys in Grapevine," Hogan says, laughing as he thinks about the people through the years who have been impressed with the fact that he owns what appears to be a personalized cowboy hat, with the hat's name branded on the band.

When Hogan is wearing Atwood, you know the sun is out. This year, the Texas weather was giving players a break. An unusually rainy, mild summer had taken the beast out of opening-week temperatures. So when players hit the practice field at 10:30 a.m. for this ninety-minute practice, there was a prevailing sense that things easily could have been worse. It was only 88 degrees.

After fifteen minutes of stretching, nicely executed this time, Hogan gathered the players to expound on his earlier introduction to the Sold Out theme. He listed four jobs his players must perform in order to be sold out, four jobs that the players would hear, according to Hogan, *ad nauseam* throughout the season.

Number 1: Love your teammates. "You have to love each other," Hogan said. "You say, 'Aw, what does that have to do with football?'

Well, just trust me. If you're going to sacrifice, be selfless, get your job down, you've got to love each other." Then he addressed the seniors in particular. "It's your job as seniors to leave a legacy. What are you leaving behind? This guy remembers that Alex Nerney treated him like a jerk his senior year? Oh, that's a nice legacy. How about, 'He coached me up and told me the Faith way—how to win championships. And, by the way, we won a championship that year.' You don't think he's going to do what Alex told him to do for the rest of his career? Heck, yeah. He's going to pass it on. Leaders teach people. They're examples. You have to love each other. Your job is to love your teammates. And us as coaches, our job is to love you. If you do that, the rest will take care of itself."

Number 2: Choose a great attitude. "You've got to choose the right attitude when it's 108 [degrees]. This is pretty mild right now. But when it's three o'clock, four o'clock, end of August, early September, and people are dragging around, you have to choose a good attitude."

Number 3: Play at your highest tempo. "Tempo will win us a state championship this year. You can play so fast that nobody can do anything about it. It's not going to matter if they know [what play] is coming. It doesn't matter."

Number 4: Take care of your responsibility. Before anyone could worry about other people getting their jobs done, Hogan said, each player must first have taken care of his own responsibility. Only then could a player ask a teammate in the film room why he had not fulfilled his responsibility on a particular play. "If eleven people do that, you win every game."

✦ ✦ ✦

Conditioning looms at the end of every practice. When coaches saw the tempo they had hoped to see at the end of practice, they informed the players they would run only two 360s. But there was a catch. The first group, consisting of the fastest players, had to complete their 360s within forty seconds; the second group, in fifty seconds. Ford warned the players that those times would be difficult, and that some would barely meet their requirement.

The first 360 proved Ford right. It was difficult, and there were those who nosed the line just ahead of the countdown's end. For the second circle, two players in the second group slowed in their final steps and failed to beat the clock. "Less than one big step away," Ford informed them as he walked toward the finish line. Near the symbolic semifinals spot, Ford added, "I'm not going to let you finish at the semifinals." There would be an extra 360 for everyone.

The players were not happy, and it showed. One motivated player yelled, "That's selfish! Come on, let's go!" The whistle blew to start the first group's run. Every member of the group beat the clock for a third time. Then the second group, mostly the bigger linemen, began their run. Halfway through their run, senior Grant Hockenbrough, a member of the first group, spotted 285-pound Curtis Roddy bringing up the rear. Hockenbrough ran across the field toward him. "Curtis, you're a captain, and you're in last! Come on, Curtis! Come on, Curtis!"

Ford instructed the first group to encourage the second. The members of the first group formed a tunnel for the final stretch, and they yelled encouragement to each teammate who passed through. Roddy passed two others as he turned the final corner. Ford began counting down the remaining ten seconds. Roddy dropped back to last in the final forty yards. Right at Ford's count of fifty, the senior captain completed a long, last stride across the finish line. A step past the line, he staggered to his right and almost fell. Teammates grabbed him to hold him up, then helped him to the team huddle around Hogan.

Again, the breathing was heavy. "Hey, listen, I know football's not for everybody," the coach said. "That's okay. I would rather you quit than pretend that you're willing to make the commitment to be a state champion. Okay? I really would. I know football's not for everybody. I don't want anybody to quit. But if you don't want to pay the price all the time, if you're thinking, 'Gosh, I'm gonna have to pretend to like this'—listen, quit. Volunteer to do something else. You guys who stay and work your tail off, it will be worth it on that last day in December, when it's cold outside."

Hogan then asked coach Brandon Smeltzer to conclude the practice with prayer. With every player's hands on teammates' shoulders, Smeltzer prayed, "Father, thank You for this day. Thank You for gathering these young men and for the lessons in character that Coach Hogan, Ford, and all of these coaches have given to us. Father, I pray that You will give the energy back to these guys and bring them back healthy tomorrow, and give them encouragement and character. We love You. It's in Jesus' name we pray. Amen."

Day 1 finished, Hogan told the players that he would see them tomorrow. And did. None quit. Football might not be for everybody, but each of these fifty-four players had decided that it was for him. They all wanted to pay the price, and they trusted their coach that it would be worth it on the season's final day in December.

Each player was Sold Out.

CHAPTER 3

"It's about Relationships"

The X's and O's of football drew Kris Hogan into coaching. Their corresponding names and faces keep him coaching.

Have a serious talk with Hogan about football, and there's a good chance that at some point he will say, "It's about relationships." That philosophy is *the* driving force in Faith football. Philosophy has no column in the standings or statistic in Saturday morning box scores. But the belief in this program is that philosophy does show up in the standings and box scores, along with the Faith coaches' aptitude for getting the most out of players in every game, in every situation. Hogan's coaching record at Faith—33–14 through four seasons—indicates that the philosophy is working.

The Faith athletic facility, much like the school's campus itself, sits tucked away, largely unnoticed. There are much larger schools than Faith and brighter stadium lights than Faith's around the Dallas/Fort Worth Metroplex. The school is in a residential neighborhood four blocks east of Grapevine's historic downtown stores running alongside Main Street. The four-way stop signs between downtown and Faith keep the pace slow through the older section of town. Just to the south is Dallas/Fort Worth International Airport, with the world's third-busiest flight schedule. The unending parade of landing planes takes place beyond the football field's east end zone. To the northeast of Faith is the city's newest growth, with the tourist-attracting Grapevine Mills outlet mall and the gigantic, glitzy Gaylord Texan Resort & Convention Center. To the southwest is the so-called Grapevine Funnel, a too-narrow strip of land between the airport and Lake Grapevine where seven major highways conspire to frustrate the more than 190,000 drivers who pass through the Funnel's busiest point each day.

This quiet spot among the suburban bustle has been Faith's home since 2001. The interdenominational school had opened two years earlier in a neighboring city's church, then moved to Grapevine when the Grapevine-Colleyville Independent School District constructed a new middle school and sold the old one to Faith. As a sign of the area's rapid growth, Faith's campus—needing portable buildings to help hold its 615 students in kindergarten through twelfth grade—had served as Grapevine's high school into the late 1960s, when the city's population totaled less than seven thousand. Now Grapevine has almost fifty thousand residents, and the school district it shares with the city of Colleyville has two high schools with more than forty-six hundred students between them. Those two high schools compete in the state's largest classification for public schools. In Texas, unlike many other states, public and private schools compete in separate organizations. Most of the attention in the Metroplex goes to the larger public schools. Yet the recent success of Faith Christian's athletic program has been attracting more headlines in area newspapers.

When Hogan was hired as Faith's head football coach and athletic director at age twenty-nine, the young football program had been through four seasons of growing pains, with one playoff appearance, and Hogan had four seasons of head-coaching experience. He began his career as an assistant coach at a small public school in Boyd, Texas. There, in his second season, he was joined on staff by Ford. The two formed an immediate bond. "Through our season," said Ford, Hogan's senior by ten years, "I knew this kid had a gift. His football intelligence far surpassed anybody I'd ever been around." Ford also observed how well Hogan handled kids and his ability to teach and communicate. "It didn't take long for me to see how special he was."

Ford was at Boyd one year before leaving coaching to start a business. Hogan would spend three seasons at Boyd before becoming, at age twenty-six, head coach at Sacred Heart, a small Catholic school in the German community of Muenster, near the Texas-Oklahoma border. One of Hogan's first calls was to Ford. Would he, Hogan asked, be interested in helping him in Muenster? Ford's business was doing well, but he felt a tugging at his spirit to be working with high school athletes. So he put a friend in charge of his business and helped Hogan on a volunteer basis. The Sacred Heart Tigers went 0–10 that first season—hanging close, in every game but one, until the players would run out of gas in the fourth quarter. Meanwhile, Hogan was making major changes to turn the program around. The payoff came quickly. The next season, Sacred Heart finished 9–3 and reached the second round of the playoffs. In Hogan's third and fourth seasons, the Tigers reached the state semifinals. But, says Ford, who had returned by then to full-time coaching at another Christian school, "I knew Kris wasn't at the right place for him."

Hogan enjoyed the school and community, but felt an internal nudge of his own to see what other opportunities existed. Faith's opening appealed greatly to Hogan. First, he and Amy would be able to live closer to their families. Second, they liked Faith Christian's values, especially now that they had a daughter, Jerilyn, entering kindergarten. Hogan was one of more than forty coaches to apply for the position—several of whom withdrew from consideration when they heard he was in the mix. And once Hogan interviewed with the search committee, its members thought they were wasting their time by talking to other candidates.

What stood out most to the committee was Hogan's *intentionality*—perhaps the one word most commonly used in describing him. He appeared to have anticipated and prepared for every question, from how he would handle playing-time issues with players' parents to how he handles his family time as a parent. He seemed so sure of his answers that when the committee members dismissed Hogan from the room, they had but one question: is he confident or arrogant? To answer that question, members of the committee took Hogan to dinner. They returned with the conclusion that he was—as they were hoping by that point in the search process—confident. The conversation over dinner confirmed that he had prepared extensively for the interview and that because of that he did believe he had arrived at the best answers for each question.

His homework also had convinced Hogan that Faith would be a great place to coach. Hogan saw potential not only to build a good football program, but as athletic director also to put together a solid athletic program. He liked school administrators' commitment to fielding a competitive sports program while keeping athletics within its proper perspective. Athletics was considered an important part of the overall educational experience at Faith, unlike at some other schools Hogan had competed against. Athletics there, he observed, fit nicely into school life. He also noticed that Faith parents, who pay around nine thousand dollars in tuition per year for their children to attend the school, seemed eager to pour their energies into making sports stronger. "They just needed a rudder to guide the ship," Hogan said. "They were ready to be involved. Parental involvement is huge, huge, huge."

Hogan set three goals. First, he wanted to bring unity to the athletic program. He saw passion for individual programs, but not the same passion for all programs. He began presenting a bigger-picture perspective of the overall program instead of separate sports. Second, he wanted to introduce year-round development of athletes through weight lifting and conditioning programs, including the summertime Lion Power workouts. Third, he wanted to incorporate what he considers the school's most important aspect: discipleship. He began training coaches of all sports on discipleship principles so they could implement a uniform system of discipleship as athletes moved from one sport to the next. That seamless transition between sports is significant now with 84 percent of the 256 high school students participating in athletics and 67 percent of all students participating in multiple sports.

Hogan's second year at Faith, he hired Ford to be the baseball coach as well as his offensive and defensive line coach and right-hand man in football. Ford saw what he had noted at Boyd and Sacred Heart: Hogan's ability to coach and command players' respect while also being approachable and having fun with them. He also saw Hogan as a smarter football coach because of his experience and because of growth he had made outside of football.

"He's always been organized, but he's more organized," Ford explained. "He also prioritizes better. He knows more Scripture now by heart, so he can apply that in teaching. All these non-football things make him a better coach. He can come off the cuff with just about anything and teach a message that's impacting. I probably come out of the meetings having learned more than the kids any day. I just soak it up when he teaches."

+ + +

Seeing Hogan at work is to discard the clichéd, cartoonish figures of a typical high school football coach. First, on the practice field, there is Atwood instead of a cap to cover his shaved head, and he's just as likely to wear a Faith volleyball, soccer, or softball T-shirt as a football one. He walks with a lively step around the field, often cupping his hands to shout instructions. And he's rarely in a bad mood. Sure, he will yell when a play breaks down or a player misses an assignment, but he's typically back cracking a joke, or offering a player a piece of life advice, or quoting a Scripture before the next play begins.

Second, for games, Hogan dresses up. He wears a T-shirt and a cowboy hat during pre-game warm-ups, but when the team enters the field for the game, he is in a white, long-sleeved dress shirt, tan dress pants, a tie (red for road games, silver for home), and dark golf shoes. The golf shoes look like dress shoes, but they're actually soft-spiked FootJoys, which he's worn on the sideline ever since the muddy day when he took a step and left a street shoe behind in the muck. In his dress clothes, Hogan stands out. That goes against his disdain for anything that brings attention to himself over his coaches or players, but he dresses up because he'd like to create a good first impression of Faith.

Third, there is Hogan's size. At age thirty-three, he is the same five-foot-ten and 180 pounds as his senior year of high school.

Much has changed inside of Hogan since his high school years, however. Ultracompetitive, Hogan has always hated to lose, whether in organized sports or games with friends. In the past when Hogan played, he would not blatantly cheat, but the rules came with elastic. In neighborhood games, for example, Hogan would not move the football back six inches so the opposing team would not achieve a first down, but there was no limit on what he would do to prevent a team from gaining those six inches. An elbow to the side of the ball carrier's head after he had been tackled? With no referees, Hogan would do that. A drive with the top of his head into an opponent's kidney when a play was over? Hogan would do that, too. And when a ball carrier would run tentatively or not stretch out the ball quite so far on the next play or, even better, fumble, Hogan had his reward: the other team would not gain those six inches needed for the first down.

At age six in a baseball game, Hogan and his unbeaten team were locked in a duel against a pitcher who had held them scoreless. So the next time the pitcher came to bat, Hogan drilled him in the ribs with a fastball. To make sure the opponent knew Hogan's pitch had been on target, Hogan looked at the player when he reached first base and winked. Sore and rattled, the pitcher became hittable for Hogan and his teammates, and they rallied to win the game.

Winning was all Hogan cared about then.

Make no mistake, Hogan still is competitive and wants to win, but winning no longer drives him. His philosophy as a coach is to put his players in position to succeed then let the results take care of themselves. He can accept whatever the results are as long as he and his players give their best effort. He applies the principles of stewardship—a word most often associated with money—to talent and ability. Come up short in effort, he reasons, and you are not being a good steward of the talent God has given you. He considers winning a by-product of doing all the right things as a coach and a player, not the barometer by which he measures himself and his teams. That competitive nature "rears its ugly head" sometimes, he said with a laugh, but for the most part, those days of disproportion are behind him.

"The change now," he explained, "is that I have become better at walking out the principles of Scripture. Consequently, they have become such a dominant force that they are drowning out the need to win, basically, for more important things. It's not that you don't try to do bad things; the Bible teaches that if you walk in the Spirit, you won't *fulfill* the lust of the flesh. So, I've matured as a Christian."

✦ ✦ ✦

Hogan was a standout all-around athlete at Northwest High School, only a twenty-minute drive from Grapevine (unless you get caught in the Grapevine Funnel during rush hour). For the Northwest Texans, Hogan was a quarterback, a guard in basketball able to dunk by the tenth grade, a shortstop and pitcher in baseball, and a sprinter and long jumper in track and field. But when he left high school for East Texas State University—what is now Texas A&M University–Commerce—he thought he was done with sports beyond the recreational level.

His future was in sales and marketing, because that appeared to be his best track to financial security. He held two sales jobs his first two years in college, and he quickly worked to the top of his level at both jobs. He had this hobby at the same time, however, that he could not let go of—watching high school football games. He usually went to games with his father; sometimes he went alone. But every weekend, he was going somewhere—anywhere—to watch games.

He watched two or three games per week. During the playoffs, he would watch up to five games in a weekend. Not only would he watch games near his college or back home, but he also would go through the statewide schedule and pick out the best game he could find. Then he would go see it. He would drive south to the Houston area to watch a game, or even right through the Metroplex to pick up his dad and head west for a game in Abilene or Odessa. "It just didn't matter where," he said. "I just wanted to go to where the best game was, to watch at the highest level."

He would draw X's and O's in class instead of taking notes. He had evaluated all those offenses and defenses firsthand, and he would plot out what each team's coaching staff needed to do to best take advantage of its players' talents. He believed he could be coaching those players and be just as successful.

So he found a place he could coach—as a volunteer for Boys & Girls Clubs. He had signed up late and missed the league draft, so he was assigned a team of fifth and sixth graders. "Your team is poor socio-economically, and they're bad-behavior kids," he was told. "Just remember, it's not about wins and losses." Yet, though his team played against non–Boys & Girls Clubs teams that had been drafted and assembled by enthusiastic fathers, Hogan's team lost only one game.

Hogan had always noticed that in addition to being able to intimidate opponents, whether in organized or pickup games, he also had the ability to get the best effort out of teammates. "I had been coaching people at one level or another in life and in sports since I was a kid," he said. "And the thing that makes a coach is not X's and O's. It's the ability to communicate to somebody at a very deep level, to get their commitment level to something that has a worthwhile cause. When I was younger, the worthwhile cause was making sure that we won."

Now he was doing the same with a group of suddenly overachieving fifth and sixth graders. "I was putting theories into practice right there. It was working like it was magic. And, so, it was obvious what I needed to be doing."

So Hogan left sales and his pursuit of financial security to do what he loved.

+ + +

Richard Dickman is the coach Hogan thought of when he decided to become a coach. Dickman was his coach at Argyle Junior High, and the first coach who ever demonstrated that being a coach was a worthwhile goal. He used sports as a platform to teach kids how to make the right decisions. Dickman, Hogan said, "lived a life, and part of what he did was coaching."

Because of that, no coach came closer to having a greater impact on young Hogan than Dickman. In turn, Hogan seeks to make that kind of impact on his players. Stop by each footlocker in the field house to ask his players what they'd call their coach, and you'll hear "father figure," "role model," "leader," or "mentor."

There is perhaps no player among that group that Hogan has impacted more than Nerney.

Nerney's parents divorced when he was in elementary school, and although his father lived close by, the two spent little quality time together. They would eat an occasional dinner together, but his father did not regularly attend his games or track meets. Nerney's mother remarried after he entered high school, but he and his stepfather clashed, once almost getting into a fistfight before that marriage ended.

One night during football season, when Nerney was sixteen, he showed up unannounced at Hogan's front door. "I picked him to talk to," Nerney said, "because he was all I had. Nobody else could I seriously talk to about what I was going through." The two spent half an hour sitting on the tailgate of Hogan's pickup. Nerney was trying to decide whether he should live with his father, where he would have few rules, or with his mother, where the rules would be much more strict. Hogan told him that, despite the circumstances, he had a responsibility to live with his mother. The coach reminded him of the men who had walked out on him in his life and the disappointment he still felt when he thought about them. If he walked out on his mother now, Hogan told him, he would be more likely to do the same with his future family when times grew tough. "On that night," Nerney said, "Coach Hogan became a replacement for the dad I never had and the man I dreamed of becoming."

Entering this, his senior year, Nerney began to see Hogan as more than a replacement father. He began to consider his coach as his earthly father. He could point to several men—mainly fathers of other football players—who had stepped in to help, but none had become a father figure like Hogan had. And there were times when he would look to his teammates, see their relationships with their fathers, and become jealous. Especially before games when the players would assemble behind the red inflatable tunnel through which they would enter the field. Hogan asks players' dads to stand behind the tunnel and pat all the players on their shoulder pads and backs as they walk past; he wants them to be the last people his players see before taking the field. And each Saturday morning during the season, before the players watch game film and go through a light workout, they first assemble in the school cafeteria, where their dads prepare and serve them a pancake breakfast.

Hogan's striving to create opportunities for fathers to be active in their sons' playing careers is rooted in his own parents' divorce when he was eleven. Just as he was transitioning into his junior high years, he went from having his dad around every day to seeing him only every other weekend. When he would come home from school after being bullied by other boys, his dad was not there to talk to. When he wanted input on which sports he should pursue and why, his dad was not there. Hogan talked about those things with his mom, but he says there are things in a boy's life for which the natural inclination is to talk to his father. "It was a difficult time in my life," Hogan recalled. "Just like for all the others who go through their parents' divorce."

Hogan studied the kids around him and their relationships with their fathers. "I've watched kids who had no father figure, kids who had bad father figures, kids who had average situations, kids who had incredible situations, and I've watched the effect on their lives in terms of confidence, in terms of direction, in terms of decision making, in terms of influence, peer pressure. And I have deduced in my heart that the dad is the greatest influence."

When he sees teenagers like Nerney, who do not have that greatest influence around, "it highlights them in my spirit to look for the gaps that need to be filled in."

Jeff Potts, Faith's high school principal and Hogan's closest friend, has watched relationships develop between Hogan and his players. And Potts has seen Hogan pray and even weep for students throughout the school—not only his players—going through rough times. "He loves those kids," Potts said, "and they love him."

CHAPTER 4

Turning Up the Heat

MT. LEBANON: TEAM RETREAT

So much for the mild summer weather that had made the first week of two-a-day practices almost pleasant. The Texas heat decided to make one grand stand to demonstrate it could still create misery, and it chose to do so during the Lions' five-day retreat featuring three-a-day practices. The weather and the schedule would be grueling, testing the players' commitment. The players expected as much when they hopped aboard the yellow school bus. But they did not anticipate the commitment level they would show by week's end.

This was the program's first weeklong retreat. Inspired partly by the movie *Remember the Titans*, the coaches designed the week to maximize conditioning and to almost force the players to bond with one another. That was why electronic devices such as iPods and handheld video games were forbidden. The week also had a spiritual mission. There would be nightly Bible studies in the Mt. Lebanon Encampment chapel. Hogan also would hold optional afternoon devotions, "old-school prayer time," he called them. And "free time" was built into the hottest parts of the afternoon so that players could have their own quiet time.

There was irony in Mt. Lebanon's location: Cedar Hill, just southwest of Dallas and about a half-hour drive from Grapevine. Cedar Hill also happened to be the home of the Trinity Christian Tigers, the Lions' rival and the only team to defeat them in district play the previous season.

During the first day's afternoon break, a handful of players gathered in the large meeting room inside the barracks to watch game films from the season before. They started with the 58–0 second-round playoff win over Pantego Christian Academy. Next, they watched that 31–7 regular-season loss to Trinity Christian. Hogan walked through the room, noted the Trinity game playing on the wall, and said, "That ought to make you practice harder."

+ + +

"It's hot," running back/linebacker Hockenbrough said. There really was nothing more that needed to be said less than thirty minutes into the ninety-minute evening practice. The first 100-degree day of the year had been recorded the day before. Monday was the second. Trees boxed in the makeshift practice field, blocking out what little breeze could be seen at the treetops.

Two linemen—"the fatties," as line coach Ford affectionately calls his big boys—wrung out their T-shirts underneath their shoulder pads, and it looked as if the linemen had poured water down their practice jerseys and were shedding the excess water. "Nope," one said. "That's all sweat."

Earlier, Hogan had proclaimed the weather bearable in the limited shade on one side of the field. But by now, even he had changed his tune. "Okay, it just got sweltering," he said out of earshot from his players. By midpoint of the session, players had become noticeably slower to rise from the ground. "We're breathing hard," Hogan said. "We've got to shake it off. It's hot and muggy everywhere in Texas. Get an advantage!" Other teams had the same conditions—not all would be working so hard under them.

These words recalled Hogan's closing remarks to the first practice the previous week. *Part of being a champion is going places that nobody else goes. . . . You go to where it hurts. . . . You have to be sold out.*

There was a price to be paid, and Hogan reminded the players of that when their first day of work at Mt. Lebanon was complete. "I know you guys want a special season. I can feel it. It's a little bit different from last season. I can really feel you want a special season. It depends on how much you want it. You've got to pay the price. Trust me. You know what it feels like to be at that point and not do what you feel like you should. You've got to pay the price. If you want something special, you've got to pay the price."

+ + +

Following the post-practice, fourth meal of the day, the team walked across the campground to the chapel for Bible study. The players arranged chairs in a semicircle at the front, where Hogan was opening his Bible to Philippians 3:12-14.

"Not that I have already obtained it or have already become perfect," he read, "but I press on so that I may lay hold of that for which also I was laid hold of by Christ Jesus. Brethren, I do not regard myself as having laid hold of it yet; but one thing I do: forgetting what lies behind and reaching forward to what lies ahead, I press on toward the goal for the prize of the upward call of God in Christ Jesus."

Not surprisingly, the theme of tonight's devotional was "Sold Out"— "For the season," Hogan said, "and, more important, for God." He called Paul "probably the most influential Christian of all time." "Why?" Hogan asked, before answering his own question: "He was sold out."

+ + +

There are better ways to be awakened—and certainly better times— than by coach Andy Postema walking into the juniors' and seniors' dorm room at 6:15 a.m. Tuesday singing, "Mamas, don't let your babies grow up to be cowboys." The players were lucky. The coaches had awakened to the same voice and lyrics a full hour earlier.

That gave the coaches time to discover that the coffeemaker in their room produced less-than-desirable coffee, and that the coffee from the camp cafeteria was even worse. So Hogan headed into town to pick up coffee for the coaches at McDonald's. The players did not realize how fortunate they were that by the time they hit the practice field, their coaches had found suitable coffee.

It allowed Hogan to issue one of his favorite declarations—"It's a great day!"—as the players performed their stretches. Across the field, Ford asked the players, "Don't you love it when the coaches are in a good mood?"

An hour into practice, the coaches' coffee and good moods were gone. Special teams practice was not going well. When the coaches noted a lack of hustle on punt coverage, the command was given to start up-downs. Up-downs are the coaches' preferred attention-getters. Players jog in place, then when a coach blows his whistle, the players fall flat to the ground and spring quickly to their feet to jog in place until the next whistle. For their punt coverage transgressions, the players did eighteen up-downs, not including three that coaches did not count because at least one player's chest had not properly hit the ground.

Ford's mood took another downturn when a junior varsity player copped an attitude, even crossing his arms defiantly at Ford's order to run the length of the 300-yard field and back to give the player time to evaluate his attitude.

That moment cost Hogan breakfast. He skipped the meal to remain with the player on the field and see if the two of them could work through the problem. Initially, Sells stayed with Hogan but soon left to join the team in the cafeteria. Sells described for Ford what he had witnessed, and then added that he had never seen a player disrespect a coach like the player had disrespected Hogan. "He used to be a sweet kid," Sells concluded, "but now something is wrong in his heart. It's a spiritual thing."

Back in the coaches' room before the second morning practice, Hogan provided few details of the interaction, but he did agree with Sells's assessment of the problem as spiritual.

"It was the most restraint I've ever used as a coach," Hogan said. At one point, he had tried to call the player's father on his cell phone to come get his son, but the father had not answered. The player insisted he did not want to quit, even as he performed front rolls—continuously rolling forward, head over heels—down the length of the field.

At some point during the front rolls, Hogan stopped being a coach and became a spiritual mentor. The freshman stopped rolling and started crying. The two talked, solving little but taking an important first step.

When the second practice had ended, and after the team had

endured another round of conditioning followed by some extra work because a few players had left a mess on the breakfast tables, the player who had disrupted the first practice approached Ford. The player said nothing, but extended his right hand. Ford shook his hand, patted him on the shoulder pads, and embraced him.

+ + +

Tuesday's final practice ended with varsity and junior varsity players on separate ends of the field for conditioning. On the JV side, a group of smaller players were running together. From that group, a voice yelled encouragement to one of the last finishers of a group: "Have the right attitude!"

That was Number 2 on Hogan's list of four priorities. Not only did the words catch his attention some one hundred yards away, but Hogan also noticed from which group of players the voice had come.

"You never know," he said, "if that is a future associate pastor of a ten thousand–member church who's saying, 'Have the right attitude.' If I judge my program on how he is as a linebacker, I'm doing it wrong." Hogan added that he gets convicted when he strays from that perspective. Sometimes he feels that conviction about once a month. Last year, he said, he went two or three months without feeling convicted about his perspective. "It hurts when I get that conviction."

+ + +

Wednesday morning meant another 6:15 wake-up song from Postema. This time, it was Buck Owens's "Act Naturally." The coaches already had their McDonald's cups in hand, and thanks to coffee-induced good moods, they were telling stories and laughing. Meanwhile, sleepy-eyed players dragged themselves around retrieving their now-smelly practice gear from where they'd left it to dry overnight on the back porch.

The early-morning special teams practice went better, and Hogan used part of the time to emphasize the importance of special teams. He reminded the players of that Regents loss, when Faith had scored a touchdown to take momentum, but Regents had blocked the extra-point attempt and its players had celebrated as they ran back to their sideline. "They had just given up a touchdown," he said, "but here they were all pumped up because they blocked the kick."

+ + +

In the coaches' Wednesday between-practices meeting, Hogan announced it was time to change the atmosphere. He told them to "get hard and mad," especially regarding technique. Use up-downs as much as needed, he said. If one player did not clap with the rest during stretching, it would be three up-downs for everyone.

"In practice," he said, "let's turn into tyrants. We've been too nice." Hogan wanted a noticeable change in the coaches, and he wanted that to drive the players together. "You do that with pain and irritation," he said. "Let's wear 'em out."

It took about a minute into the next practice for the first sign of change among the coaches. Hogan was back in the dorm talking to the coach of Windthorst High School via cell phone about the teams' upcoming scrimmage on Saturday. Ford, the disciplinarian of the coaching staff, told the players at the start of stretching to "turn the screws." "We're halfway there," he said. "Windthorst is the number one team in the state versus the number one [private school] team in the state."

Soon Ford had to start the first three up-downs of the day. "Get your feet moving!" he yelled. "I've got a couple of guys not stretching! Stretch, dadgummit! I'm gonna get it out of you guys! You don't have state-championship focus! You guys can hate me—I don't care! I'm here to make you better!" Then before stretching was completed, one player did not clap. Three more up-downs for everyone.

A little later, with the players grouped by positions, Ford explained his approach, minus all the exclamation points. "You guys think I'm in a bad mood?" he asked his linemen. "I'm not. I see something special about to happen, and I'm not going to let you disappoint yourselves."

The sounds of whistles for up-downs filled the air throughout the first part of practice. If the coaches needed any outside help driving the players together, the weather offered its assistance. During breaks players talked about the heat, and it was not yet 11 a.m. Weather comments were followed by a teammate nodding in agreement then offering a word of encouragement.

By the time the first-team offense was running plays at full speed against the scout-team defense, there was a noticeable boost to the practice. Hogan led the way, more intense and more vocal than he had been through the first week and a half of the season's practices.

After the offense ran ten consecutive plays perfectly, Hogan called for a water break. As the coaches huddled, they were pleased with how the team had responded to the stepped-up intensity. Hogan told the coaches that the Regents loss, which came at the end of a week of inexplicably flat practices, was his fault. "We can make every practice this intense if we choose to."

Five offensive plays later—each executed to the coaches' approval—the day's second practice ended. "This was the best offensive practice we've had," Hogan told his players. "It's all in the details." He referenced 1 Timothy 4:15: "Take pains with these things; be absorbed in them, so that your progress will be evident to all." "Be wholly absorbed," Hogan said. "That's how you win. That's how you should live."

Then the team circled, each player raising his index finger, for the customary breakout. But this time there was something different. The opening "One, two, three" had been replaced: "We are Faith!" Anderson said. "Sold Out!" he and his teammates shouted together.

Hogan turned toward his players in surprise. "I love it!"

✦ ✦ ✦

A steady breeze was a welcome guest at Thursday's morning practices, the last full day at camp. Heat-related newspaper stories pop up during August in Texas because of the start of high school football practices, and there was one in that day's edition of the *Fort Worth Star-Telegram* that had made its way into the coaches' room. The headline told the story: "A hot topic: playing it safe."

The article detailed how different coaches in the area deal with heat. One pulls his team off the field when the thermometer hits 102 degrees. One cuts off a practice when he believes the heat is making practice counterproductive. Another—one who coaches in Faith's district—does not put his team through two-a-days on consecutive days.

Faith coaches read the story with interest on this fourth consecutive day of three-a-days—and the first when the mercury would not climb to the 100 mark. They explained how they safely put their team through such practices while others choose not to, about the issue of deciding whether a player simply needs to tough it out or to take a break.

"We make data-driven decisions," Hogan explained, "and the data doesn't say anything about tough or non-tough. . . . That's an opinion: tough or not tough. You may think he's tough or he's not tough, but data-driven decisions say water every fifteen minutes and plenty of it, with the availability of it in between, and that takes care of it."

That is why Faith practice schedules include short breaks every fifteen minutes, why players can ask for water at any point during a practice, and why players are constantly reminded to hydrate during and after practices.

"We're going by science," Hogan summarized, "not someone's opinion."

+ + +

Hogan drove the coaches' golf cart up to the dorm and spotted a junior varsity player outside talking on his cell phone.

"Who you talking to?" Hogan asked.

"My mother," the player answered.

"Make sure," Hogan told him, "you tell her you love her."

"Yes, sir."

+ + +

By Thursday night, the tension of the practices had broken. The next day's schedule would be light, with only the early-morning practice, and that would merely be a walk-through in which players, not in full practice gear, would literally walk through their assignments for Saturday's Windthorst scrimmage. So Thursday night was established as the big finish to the week, in terms of both football training and spiritual training.

That night's practice was billed as Family Night, with parents encouraged to attend. Their presence lent extra spirit to the final practice in full pads. And it didn't hurt that two minutes into the practice, rain began to fall. The players cheered. The shower stopped after only four minutes, but after a week full of steaming sunshine, four minutes of rain provided genuine relief.

When practice began to wind down, a half hour earlier than the other evening practices, about ninety parents, brothers, and sisters were stretched along the practice field. Ford noted aloud the extra motivation the families had brought to the practice. There was an extra snap in the air as the offense and defense displayed their plays at full speed.

The players weren't the only ones whose families had showed up. During one break, six-year-old Deuce Hogan ran up to his father. His dad picked him up, gave him a hug, then carried him around for a minute or so. During a later break, Hogan would be holding his two-year-old son, Zeke, while addressing the team, his twin commitments of family and football on display as well.

CHAPTER 5

Committed

COMMITMENT NIGHT

Hogan's camp schedule saved the best for last: Commitment Night. Throughout the week, he had told his players to prepare for this night. First, there were skits. Each class would present one, and Hogan had issued but one requirement: they must be funny. They were. Especially the seniors' skit—but they had a huge advantage in that they were the only class allowed to make fun of coaches. Being a senior has its perks.

Of course, the serious part of Commitment Night, and the part Hogan most anticipated, came at the end. That was when coaches, seniors, and juniors would stand one by one at the front of the chapel, in front of the coaching staff and team, and read the commitments each had resolved he would keep throughout the season. It was a night of emotion not to be expected from a typical high school football team. But this team was—to use the word that kept cropping up the first two weeks of practices—special. On the field and off.

Hogan made the first commitment at 9:50 p.m., and the commitments would continue for an hour and a half, through six coaches and twenty-six players and student managers. In between, there were tears, embraces, moments of unexpected vulnerability, and lots of Number 1 in action—"Love your teammates."

The tone was set early when Hogan shared his two commitments: "I'm not going to let you fail in practice" (a commitment he said he borrowed from Ford) and "I will always meet with God before you see me every day." As Ford walked to the lectern to take Hogan's place, the two embraced and said, "I love you," loudly enough for all to hear.

"If I have to choose to be away from my family," began Ford, a father of three, "it's going to be with you guys." He stopped and looked at the freshman who had publicly disrespected him earlier in the week. Ford called the player by name. "I love you."

Faces across the hushed chapel began showing tears. There was no doubting that what would follow the rest of the night would be about much more than football.

The players knew little about coach Axel Rivera, next to step behind the lectern. He was a new coach, and a part-time one at that, on the job for about eight days. Working for the postal service was his career. Working with high school football players was his passion. He committed to giving 110 percent in practice. Then his voice cracked. He gathered himself and told the players how much Family Night had meant to him, to see the number of parents who had come to support their sons, to see sons sitting with parents and discussing the week's happenings over a pizza dinner. "It's painful to not have parents in your life," Rivera said, looking directly at players. "It did me good to see the parents tonight, because I didn't have that at your age."

Rivera left the stand to meet an embrace from Anderson. The previous season as the starting quarterback, Anderson had assumed a leader's role. This year, as a senior, there was no way he would not be the first player to speak on Commitment Night. But before he spoke, he began to cry. He looked to his right, to where most of the coaches were seated, and straight at Ford. "I love you," he said. Ford nodded. Then Anderson locked his eyes on Hogan. "You are my role model," he said through a weakening voice. "I want to be a coach like you, and I want to be a dad like you."

Both Ford and Hogan swallowed deeply. It was not their turn to speak, and it is doubtful they could have at that moment anyway. Across the chapel, Roddy had given up on holding back any tears. College coaches were looking at Roddy to join their offensive line because he could block any charging defender on Faith's schedule. But tonight, he could not block his emotions.

Anderson then looked to the other side of the room. "Coach Sells," he said, "you're like a big brother to me. I love you, too."

One by one, players took their turns at the lectern. Some made football commitments, some made spiritual commitments. Some made both.

There was Alex Nerney, committing to be a good teammate. "Last year, I wasn't a teammate. I want to be the best teammate I can." It was the love for his football brothers that drove his commitment. "My dad doesn't understand why I play football. He just doesn't get it. I told him it's because you guys are my family."

There was Weston Clegg, committing to doing whatever he could to make sure there would be no repeat of last season's bitter ending. "I never want to see the clock at zeros and the other team taking a knee with the ball. It's *not* going to happen this year. It's *not*. Whatever it takes."

There was Jeff Kallal, crying as he stepped behind the lectern. He grasped the stand with both hands and looked to the floor. He held that pose for a full minute. Finally, he looked up at the room. "I love you guys." He had to look back to the floor. Again, he looked up. Every eye was on him as he talked about his parents' divorce his sophomore year. And then he said, "I never told anyone this." After the divorce, his mother suffered through a sickness. No one at school knew Kallal's troubles, yet everyone on the team had brought him strength. "Every day when I saw you guys, it put a smile on my face. Faith has changed my life."

There was Brent Reeder, saying he had missed out on opportunities to develop deeper relationships with teammates the past two years. But in his final year at Faith, he would make the most of those relationships.

There was Tanner Gesek, talking about how easy it is to give less than your best—even to quit—when doing something only for yourself. Having this roomful of teammates would push him to always give his best. "I'm committing to mental toughness, and I love you guys."

Then, a little more than halfway through the parade of players, there was Dexter. Good ol' Dexter. Dexter Cheneweth was a five-foot-ten, 180-pound lineman on the junior varsity. The only junior on the junior varsity; the rest of those players were freshmen and sophomores. Dexter was new to both Faith and football. His parents had moved in more than a year ago from California, where Dexter had been homeschooled. He wanted to attend a school for social reasons, so his parents enrolled him at Faith. And he wanted to play football so that, for the first time, he could experience what it is like to be part of a team. So Dexter's parents talked to Sells before the first practices. They told Sells that Dexter had never played organized sports, that they did not care whether he played on the varsity or junior varsity, or even how much he played. Football at Faith, like many of even the large public schools in the area, is a no-cut sport. Dexter's parents just wanted him to be a part of this team. Sells told Dexter that he probably did not understand how difficult football would be, even discouraging him from playing. But Dexter wanted to be on the team.

Other than his attitude, Dexter's biggest contribution to Faith football may have been his sense of humor. After almost an hour of high emotions, Dexter delivered a comedic time-out. He made everyone laugh when he said that before coming out for football, the closest he had come to making contact with anything was when he tried to hit a golf ball. He illustrated his words with an awkward golf swing that suggested even his golf game did not feature much contact. He told the players that he fully realized that every time the team ran conditioning drills, he would be the last to finish. But, he promised, he would finish. Every time. That was his commitment to his teammates—to always finish, regardless of where he finished. "I don't care if it kills me," he concluded. "It's worth it."

A few moments later, Josh O'Neal spoke of Dexter and looked directly at the self-acknowledged last-place finisher. "I respect you," O'Neal said, and reminded everyone of the team's theme. "Dexter is the most sold-out person I have ever seen."

Garrett Cox did not even mention football. He committed to putting God back on top of his priorities list. Hogan wiped tears as Ford reached to pat the coach on the back.

After the final junior had stated his commitment, the head coach returned to the front of the chapel. Hogan is not an outwardly emotional guy. He is even-keeled, and he wants his teams to play that way. He does not want them emotionless, but he wants them to avoid emotional highs and lows that can drain their energy. But this night had been far more emotional than he had expected. He would later admit to being "blown away" by the players' transparency. "Teenagers just don't do that," he said. "They risk being made fun of by their peers."

On this night, however, those fears had been shoved aside because, it seemed, his players could trust their brothers. And after a week of tough practices in which the coaches had sought to drive the players together, after a week of leaving families behind to forge a football family, with the team's first on-field test less than thirty-six hours away, he saw something special in his team.

For all those reasons, Hogan had to pause before he could speak. Emotions gathered, he read John 15:13: "Greater love has no one than this, that one lay down his life for his friends."

Back at the dorm later that night—it might even have been early the next morning—Hogan reflected on Commitment Night, then said, "We've already had a winning season."

CHAPTER 6

An Appropriate Response

PRESEASON SCRIMMAGES

After twenty-two practices over a twelve-day period, players and coaches were eager to find out how they stacked up against another team. The Windthorst Trojans would provide a great first test in the first of the Lions' two scrimmage games.

Windthorst typically fields one of the top teams in Class A, the smallest classification of the University Interscholastic League, the governing body of Texas's almost thirteen-hundred public high schools. The Trojans' only loss among their previous year's fifteen games was the state finals, and this year some preseason rankings had pegged Windthorst as the top team in its classification entering this season.

The Lions boarded the bus at 6:30 a.m. Saturday for the hour-and-a-half trip northwest. Once the bus, with Ford at the wheel, turned west off U.S. Highway 287 and onto Farm-to-Market Road 174 for the final forty or so miles, the suburban lifestyle of Grapevine was nowhere to be found.

For coaches Ford, Hogan, and Sells—country boys at heart—the drive through the North Texas farmland was like going home. For the players, the occasional and unmistakable dairy farm odor drifting through the bus windows meant a chance to poke fun at Sells, who at twenty-two years old seemed to the players like having a big brother on the coaching staff. Each time the players' noses caught wind of a farm, they would repeat, in unison, "Se-llllls" in their best city-boys' mooing voices.

Windthorst is a one-blinking-red-light, German-Catholic community of less than five hundred. To the southwest of the blinking red light stands St. Mary's Catholic Church, set on the highest point in town. In the shadow of the church's steeple, behind the church, sits the home of the Trojans. Rolling farmland is visible from the home side of the small stadium. Dairy farms, the Catholic church, and the blue and white Trojans—that's Windthorst. About two hundred fans were on hand as the teams took the field. Even Windthorst's cheerleaders and mascot were in full uniform for the scrimmage.

"My goodness," Hogan said upon seeing the Trojans trot out onto the field. "I thought *we* were big." But Windthorst teams typically are big too, known for players strengthened and toughened by the 365/24/7 schedule of working on family dairy farms. This Windthorst team was typical.

It would be at least the fifth game, and possibly later than that, Faith players figured, before they would go up against a team as good as Windthorst. Although the scrimmage would not appear on the team's record, as far as the players were concerned, the games were starting today. "This is our last chance," Hockenbrough, a senior, told teammates moments before the scrimmage began. "Let's make every minute of it."

No official score was kept, but Windthorst's offense scored one touchdown, and Faith scored three. Or perhaps two. On one Faith touchdown—a 45-yard run by Anderson—the officials threw a penalty flag against Faith for holding. But according to the scrimmage format, the penalty was not enforced and Anderson's run counted. Whether or not his touchdown counted depended on which team's fans you asked. Regardless of the unofficial tally, Faith players left the field knowing they had come out ahead against a big, strong, hard-hitting opponent.

On the trip home, as players enjoyed the concession stand's German sausages on buns, Anderson and Nerney talked about how good a team Windthorst had yet again, and how pleased they were to have played so well. "Good first showing," Nerney said.

Now, finally, two-a-day practices were behind them. So was the

weeklong camp of three-a-days. Anderson and Nerney were tired—
more mentally than physically, they said. School would start next
Tuesday, and that meant only single practices each day leading up to
their second and final scrimmage. The difficult part was behind. With
a day off Monday, the routine for the rest of the season was but three
days away.

"Now it's just football," Nerney said.

+ + +

The next scrimmage opponent, the Rice Bulldogs, came from a larger
school than Windthorst and is a member of UIL's Class 2A. But Rice
had nowhere near the tradition and players' skill level of Windthorst.
The Bulldogs had provided little resistance in last season's scrimmage
and finished the regular season 2–8. This year's team did not appear
to be much better, and even after two flat practices, the Lions rolled
through their Thursday night scrimmage.

The scrimmage format was confusing for fans to follow: a series of
plays that alternated between the first, second, and junior varsity teams,
concluding with the varsities playing a "live quarter"—or twelve minutes of game conditions, minus kickoffs and punt returns. With both
varsity units and the junior varsities factored in through the sets of plays,
the goal-line situations, and the live quarter, Faith scored twelve touchdowns to Rice's one. An unofficial stab at keeping statistics showed that
for the varsity segments, Faith had outgained Rice 527 yards to 147.

But the memory that Faith players and fans would take back to
Grapevine that night occurred less than midway through the scrimmage.

With the Lions' second-team offense on the field, backup quarterback Pierce Shivers took a helmet to his left wrist while being sacked on
a botched pass play. With third-string quarterback Peter Ashton already
taking snaps in the JV portion, Anderson returned to the field with the
second unit. Anderson took the first play around right end for about an
8-yard gain, then was hit by a Rice player out-of-bounds. The official
tossed his flag high in the air for the obvious late-hit penalty. Before the
flag had fallen to the ground, Anderson had hopped back to his feet and
jumped into the guilty party's face to ask, "What the crap was that?"

The next voice heard was Hogan's, shouting for Anderson to leave the sideline and spend the rest of the scrimmage in the locker room. "We *represent* first and play football second," Hogan told him as he pointed to the dressing room. The crowd was stunned. The player delivering the obvious late hit would remain in the game. The player who had been hit would not.

Coach Smeltzer followed Anderson to the locker room. As Anderson changed out of his uniform, Smeltzer reminded him of his leadership role, the influence he carries, and how he needs to learn not to abuse that influence.

Anderson is the type of talkative leader a coach wants on the field, especially at quarterback. That talkativeness, though, also gets Anderson into trouble. "I'm a pretty passionate player," he explained a few days removed from the incident. "I do some stupid stuff, and my mouth gets me in trouble sometimes. My mouth is definitely my strength and my weakness."

It was difficult for him when hit late not to follow his natural instinct of wanting to, as he said, "get back up and start swinging. That's just the player that I am, on fire. I'm getting back up, looking at an intense situation, and I'm all ready to jump in. I'm looking to antagonize the player, to get into his head. I have to pull my reins a little bit, my mental reins, and pull myself back and, you know, push some of that passion back down. I've learned a lot since being a freshman. You can ask anybody: I was the cockiest, loudest, most annoying kid ever. Oh my gosh. I was awful. I just learned to grow up."

Part of that growing up came through the realization that, for Hogan, football at Faith is about more than football. In the coaches' pre-game prayers, Hogan often prays that Faith's coaches, players, and fans will be a witness to someone from the other side of the contest.

"I am a Christian," Anderson said. "I represent Christ, I represent my family, and I represent the Faith Lions on the field. It's not about me. It's not about me going out there and me fighting that kid. It's not about me going into that fight. It's not about me getting up and making sure he knows that I said something. That doesn't matter."

Anderson told himself these things when he was off the field to help him combat his natural instincts on the field. Hogan calls it having a planned response. Think now about what you will do then, he teaches his players. Anderson thought about those things, but it was still a struggle. Especially knowing that most teams he would face would not play by Hogan's lofty standards.

"But that's what makes us different," Anderson said. "And that's what makes us have the target on our back. That's what makes us Faith."

+ + +

On the field, Shivers returned to quarterback but ran only two plays before it was obvious his wrist was too injured for him to continue playing.

Hogan leaned his head forward and rubbed his temples with his fingers, then rolled his neck around—his telltale sign of stress. He had just watched his senior leader lose his temper on the field, then watched trainer Augustus "Auggie" Gomez examine the backup's wrist and say that he was done for the night too. That meant Ashton, a freshman, would play the rest of the scrimmage at quarterback. A bad week threatened to become a total nightmare. But instead, Ashton led the Lions to six of their twelve touchdowns. Faith's offense continued to churn out yardage against an outmatched team.

After the scrimmage, Hogan gathered his team near midfield. He apologized for the level of competition. "I wish they would have been better. You evaluate this by personal responsibility, not necessarily if the play worked. I have a feeling some plays worked because *they* weren't too hot. Make sure we don't get trapped in that, okay? The next one is for real." At that, the players responded with an excited mixture of "Yes, sir!" "Yeah!" and "Woo-hoo!"

"Can't wait," Hogan continued. "The next one is for real. It's going to be fun. We're going to talk about this on film. We're not going to talk about this tonight."

But Hogan was not through addressing the team. There still was the matter of what had happened to their senior quarterback. Everyone saw the Rice player's late hit. Even Rice's coach had apologized to Hogan after the scrimmage. Then the coach added that he was surprised that Hogan had removed his own player, the victim of that hit, from the game. Those who have followed Faith since Hogan arrived were not surprised. Two years earlier, they witnessed Hogan remove a defensive back late in a close district contest at home because, after breaking up a pass play, the player had waved an incomplete signal over the receiver. Hogan marched onto the field and told the referee, who had motioned for a 15-yard unsportsmanlike conduct penalty against Faith, that he was out there "to make your job easier." Hogan went up to the player and pointed him to the locker room for the rest of an important game.

That player was a sophomore named Landon Anderson.

Hogan had explained his decision then by saying that his players would not get away with humiliating opponents. "That kid's mother might have been in the stands, and we're not going to mock him in front of her. She doesn't need to see that happen to her son."

Hogan had removed a player from a game under such circumstances three times at his previous school. This scrimmage was the second time he had done so at Faith. When Anderson's backup left the game, and when Hogan had to insert a freshman for who knows what would happen while his team was needing to get ready for next week's season opener against the Santo Wildcats, the thought of bringing Anderson back onto the field never entered Hogan's mind.

"Not at all," he said, "because that's predetermined for me." Hogan said it would not matter if he would have to put a player at quarterback who had never played the position. He said he would not hesitate to pull a player from the state semifinals, and his players know that. "That's why I've only done it five times."

Hogan used the incident to remind his players after the game of the standards he expected them to meet on the field, regardless of circumstances. "We need to control how we respond. We had a reaction over there, not a response," he said as he pointed to the sideline. "Think in advance how you'll deal with stuff. Somebody hits you late, well, okay, think about how to respond now so that if Santo does it—and people are going to do that stuff—when you're down on the ground getting punched, think out a response. Something funny, like, 'Ow, my sister hits harder than that' in a small voice. That's fine. I totally understand that. But to go, 'Hey!' and do all this stuff and hit and get kicked out? Who's always the guy who gets the penalty?"

"The second guy," his players answered.

"The second guy," Hogan continued. "It'd be a lot better just to take a punch in the gut and say, 'Aw, God bless you'—and after the game, look at them like, I'm so sorry it's forty-nine to zero."

The players laughed.

"Understand," Hogan concluded, "what class is."

+ + +

With the team addressed, there remained one more conversation for Hogan to have on the matter. On the bus ride home, he cleared a spot next to him on the front row and called Anderson forward.

Hogan did not want to wait until the next day, or even until they arrived back at the field house, to talk with Anderson.

"He needs to know where I stand immediately," Hogan explained. "It's like an employee working for you. They want feedback all the time. 'Tell me, how am I doing? Am I doing good, bad, ugly, whatever?' He needed to know where *he* stands—and where he stood is a clean slate."

The two shared a private conversation. Throughout, Hogan had his arm around Anderson's shoulders. When the talk concluded, after the coach had told his senior leader that he had a clean slate again, he then told his player, "I love you." And the player who someday wants to be a coach just like Hogan, and a father just like him, reached over to embrace him and said, "I love you, too."

CHAPTER 7

No Chance

GAME 1: SANTO WILDCATS

"Who are we?!" a disgusted Kallal yelled. "What are we playing for?"

"This is where we're sold out for the team!" came one voice from the JV side of the drills.

Subpar practices from the previous week filtered over into the first week of the regular season, and as if coaches had not been given enough to complain about heading into the season opener, some players had been caught cheating during Tuesday's conditioning drills—starting ahead of the start line or walking the first two or three steps.

After a series of sprints, Hogan called his players in. "Only because it's six o'clock are we stopping," he told them. "We should run about seven, eight more of those, according to the way we practiced." He told the players that in the future they could either work hard during practice or stop practice early and run for thirty minutes. "One of the two. You choose from now on." With that, he asked a player to dismiss practice in prayer. "Nobody's gonna give you a state championship," Sells said as the players broke the huddle. "You've got to earn it."

Sells, the offensive coordinator, pulled Nerney aside and told him the players needed to get motivated. Nerney shrugged. He had tried to push his teammates, he said, and now he did not know what to do. "Well, you'd better figure it out," Sells said.

Coach Postema pondered the string of poor practices as he made his way toward the field house. He wondered if the culprit might be the preseason expectations of winning the state championship. *That is a long way down the road*, he reasoned. Maybe the players would be better served by focusing more on the process of winning a state championship—the weekly progress they would need to make to achieve their goal.

Seniors Nerney, Reeder, Messinger, Clegg, Hockenbrough, and Daniel Ackerman remained on the practice field, removing their shoulder pads to sit or lie on the grass and discuss the state of the team. Whatever the players needed to do to come together more, they decided, should come from the players, not the coaches.

"This is the last thing we're going to do together as a team," Clegg said. "We'll have other sports, but this is the last thing we'll do as a unit."

"This is the last time we'll play for Coach Hogan," Hockenbrough added.

"Even if we're not going to do it for ourselves, let's do it for Coach Hogan," Clegg said. "Think of everything he's done for us."

"This has to be frustrating for him," said Nerney. "He knew we had a team last year that should have won state and didn't."

In the field house, the coaches' office door was, in a rare occurrence, closed. Inside, the coaches were doing some hand-wringing of their own, with Hogan blaming himself for recent practices. "Coach, I dropped the ball," interrupted Ford, who had been the first coach to commit to not allowing the players to fail in practice. "You can take the heat if you want—and I would, too, if I were in your position—but I dropped the ball."

The coaches decided that beginning the next day, perfect plays would be the goal and feedback immediate. Hogan reminded them how during three-a-days at camp, up-downs had served as highly effective immediate feedback. With a plan in place, Hogan headed toward the field house door forty-five minutes after practice had ended. On his way out, he amended his trademark expression. "It was a *horrible* day!" he exclaimed, then hopped into his pickup and drove off.

+ + +

Not since the first practice had coaches and players both been so eager to hit the practice field as they were on Wednesday. The coaches anticipated that the players would seek to prove they were focused and ready for the season. The players' chatter as they dressed for practice indicated they would.

But before sending the players to the field, Hogan stood in front of the whiteboard and talked. First, discipline matters needed discussion. The school operates on a same-day notification; teachers are asked to report any misdoings by athletes to coaches the same day they occur. Punishment would be immediate and, thus, Hogan believes, more effective. The same goes for violating the school dress code. If a player's shirt is untucked or he did not shave, the minimum is 100 updowns. "Someone did 300 up-downs last year for something," Hogan reminded, "but 100 is the starting point."

Now, Hogan said, he wanted to discuss spiritual issues. "Be sold out to your spiritual growth," he said. Being a Christian is not just a Sunday occurrence, he told them. Being a Christian is an all-the-time commitment—at school, on the football field, everywhere you go. Hogan recited John 13:35: "By this all men will know that you are My disciples"—he paused to emphasize the next part—"if you have love for one another." And then, drawing from 1 John 3:14-15, Hogan told them, "Anyone who does not love remains in death."

"What does that have to do with football?" Hogan asked. He answered by relating a play from Tuesday's practice. Anderson had completed a pass to Nerney, a short route to the sideline. Meanwhile, Reeder had run deep downfield, but he circled back and came all the way back upfield to block for Nerney. In a practice. "You play harder for the people you love," Hogan said. "That's the most powerful thing on the planet. Love is the most powerful motivator. You want an advantage over other [teams]? You love everybody in this room." In other words, being motivated by genuine love would be the true advantage.

Hogan dispatched the players to the practice field to fix those nagging football problems. But on their way, they were met by junior high players jogging back to the field house. Lightning had been spotted.

The varsity players wanted to practice anyway, some continuing to walk toward the field. Coaches had to order them back inside.

A few minutes later, with an edge of clouds over the school, players were cleared to return to the field. Only four minutes after that, with stretches barely underway, the lightning meter on Hogan's waist sounded. Lightning had been detected within one mile. "Back inside!" the coaches shouted. "Awww!" the players responded. "This is a very important practice too," Hogan said as everyone retreated indoors.

In the coaches' office, Hogan looked over the practice schedule then up to the clock. Wednesday practices end at 5 p.m., an hour earlier than Monday and Tuesday practices, so that the players and coaches can attend church. Wednesday is also the last contact practice for the week and Hogan's deadline for having everything in place for the next game. Hogan reviewed in his mind what absolutely had to be worked on once the weather cleared enough to return to the field. His planning was interrupted by another beep from the lightning meter. "Gosh!" he exclaimed.

There still had not been a single raindrop when coaches stepped out underneath the overhang at the front door to the field house. Hogan had never had a practice wiped out in his coaching career. A few had been interrupted by weather, but none completely lost. The lightning detector had gone quiet, so Hogan told the players to start stretching inside the locker room. The detector was not far from giving an all clear, then, another beep. Roddy stuck his head out of the field house and looked up at skies that showed no threat of bad weather. "This really stinks," he said and turned back inside. Then, Hogan told the team there would be no practice. "This is really gonna hurt us," he said. "This is gonna affect us." After a quick quiz over Santo's tendencies from the weekly scouting report, the players were dismissed ten minutes early. Everything the coaches were looking for from today's practice, and everything the players had been eager to display—none of those things took place because of the temperamental Texas weather. And it didn't even rain.

+ + +

Thursdays are special. On-field work is limited to special teams needing a final tune-up. Other than that, the last team gathering before game day is set aside as "Open Floor Thursday."

Open Floors are part inspirational, part confessional, and part soul baring. At times, they are part entertaining. Coaches and players gather in the locker room to share quotes, exchange thoughts on the week's practices and game, and discuss and resolve any issues that need to be cleared up before the coming game. Invariably, a few jokes make their way into the proceedings, but as Hogan reminded the players as they convened their first Open Floor of the season, "This is a time to make us better and talk about what's been going on."

Anderson was the first to speak, apologizing for his outburst during last week's scrimmage. "I didn't have a predetermined response," he said, assuring he already had one ready for next time.

"The more you can predetermine in life, the better," Hogan followed. He brought up last year's Homecoming game against Union Hill, the Lions' first loss of the season. Faith had a big lead at halftime but lost on the final play. Hogan reminded the players they had not prepared themselves mentally to play with a big lead, then had not prepared themselves for how to respond when a team cuts away at such a lead. "What if we go down 14–0 to Reicher?" Hogan asked, looking ten games ahead to the final week of the regular season, envisioning a potential scenario that could decide the district championship. "If you depend on circumstances to create the good things in you—it doesn't work that way."

Gesek shared tips he had read from a sports psychologist on dealing with nervousness. Roddy talked about proper nourishment, beginning the night before a game. Then he shared a quote from Vince Lombardi. "Vincent. *Saint* Vincent," Hogan corrected, with respect for the legendary coach. Ford talked about visualizing success. Jordan Dunnington shared a quote from Muhammad Ali: "Don't quit. Suffer now and live the rest of your life as a champion."

"'Suffer now and spend your life as a champion,'" Hogan repeated. "That's good." Nerney, harkening back to his commitment from camp, apologized for getting frustrated at teammates during Tuesday's baffling practice. "Sometimes I forget who you guys are," he said. "You guys are my brothers, my teammates. . . . I really got reminded of this quote: 'Trust men and they'll be true to you; treat them greatly and they'll show you greatness.' I'm sorry for not treating you guys greatly. I really want to put you guys in the forefront of everything that I do. I'm sorry about that, guys." This game, Nerney said, he would be playing for all of them.

Hogan nodded. "That's good." Moments like that are the reason he started Open Floor Thursdays. Players kept adding their thoughts to the discussion, and as the forty-five-minute session progressed, it became evident that although the players had seemed headed in different directions on the practice field during the week, they sat in a horseshoe around the locker room unified on the eve of their season opener.

"Have you noticed how much of this stuff centered around *team*?" Hogan asked, as he began to move the session toward its conclusion. "Guys, your life is only—let me start by saying this: the more selfish you are, the less satisfying life is. Your life is only enriched when you live it for a purpose bigger than yourself. That's why we talk about playing for each other. What if you tried to motivate yourself by saying, 'How many catches can I get? How many yards?' You know. That's why there's something unique to a team atmosphere. Your purpose is bigger than yourself if you're living for something bigger than yourself. You perform at a higher level. You perform your best in team sports. I want you to think about who you are. Just think about who you are for a second as a group. What is your identity? . . . Why do we say 'Sold Out'? Why do we say 'We are Faith'? Why do we put 'Faith Football' on these red shorts that you're wearing? Because that's who you are. That's who you are."

Hogan told his players how they were connected to a 10–0 team from two years earlier, and to teams that had reached the state semifinals back-to-back years. "Once you know your identity, you'll do anything. That's why the strongest unit in any country is the family. That's where I belong. These people share my blood. I can slap my brother or sister in the head all I want to, but if you do, now we have an issue. Every society in history—you just look this up—every society in history who loses the family folds. Every one of them. Not one has ever survived the demise of the family. That's why it's a big deal that people get divorced in this country. Because as soon as we're up to 60, 65, 75 percent [divorce rate], someone's going to come over here and take our stuff. We're going to instantly drop. We will not be a superpower anymore. Any country that's still around is all about that tight-knit group who love each other. *That* breeds greatness. And if that's what we have here, [greatness is] what we'll have."

+ + +

It wasn't that Chance Cochran himself looked out of place standing in the middle of the locker room on Friday night, saying he wanted to say a few words before the Lions took the field. What did not fit the scene was Cochran wearing jeans and a T-shirt. This was supposed to be the season that everything came together for him on Faith's football field. Instead, it had all unraveled.

His left knee was healthy, and it had been so since track season in the spring, when he finished second at the state meet in the 400 meters and ran on two medal-winning relay teams for the state-champion Lions. He felt like things were beginning to make sense personally, too—partly because, athletically, he felt back to normal. He had experienced a year of what he called "being seriously depressed," struggling with the knee injury and personal issues. Perhaps the football and personal problems had even blurred into one. Hogan had worked through a Bible study with Cochran. "Once a week we'd have lunch and deal with what was going on in my life, besides football," Cochran recalled. "That helped me a lot. It was a good thing."

Then three weeks before the end of his junior year, Hogan took him aside after athletics period and told him he had bad news. A teacher had reported being told that Cochran had had sex with his girlfriend from another school. Principal Jeff Potts joined the two in Hogan's office. Cochran was asked if what the teacher had heard was true. He said yes. Cochran was asked if the girl, who had broken up with him a week earlier, asked to be with him again, would he? Cochran said he would. Looking back, Cochran said perhaps he tried too much to handle the conversation "like a man." Perhaps if he hadn't, things would have turned out differently. School officials determined Cochran would not be able to attend Faith his senior year.

So Cochran stood in the center of the locker room now not a Faith Lion but a Grapevine Mustang. Cochran had enrolled at Grapevine High School, the Class 5A public school on the opposite side of town. In some ways, that had completed a football circle for Cochran. Those days of youth football when he was breaking long touchdown run after long touchdown run—his teammates then had once again become his teammates for his senior season as a Mustang. But there had been a long gap between then and now. Those guys felt more like acquaintances now, and he certainly was not as close to them as his friends at Faith. That is why he had walked into CiCi's Pizza the previous Monday night, wearing his Grapevine Mustangs T-shirt, and sat among the dozen or so Faith players there to kick off their weekly buffet-devouring ritual.

Plus, Cochran now played for a completely new coaching staff that would determine where and how much he would play. A senior season is the worst to be changing schools. Hogan had called the Grapevine coach to put in a good word, but Cochran still joined the Mustangs as an unknown running back on a team with two established running backs sharing duties in a one-running-back offense. At first, Grapevine coaches told Cochran they would look at him on defense, at safety. Then as a cornerback. Most recently, they had told him he would have a chance to play receiver on offense. Now, about the only certainty in football for Cochran was that his repaired left knee felt great.

And his girlfriend? Having sex, Cochran said, ruined their two-year relationship. His mother had cautioned him about sex before marriage. "Now I know why my mom was so big on not having sex. Now I know why, because you can't escape that bond." They had made a physical bond for which neither was ready. As he put it, they both "were not mature enough to take on such a big thing as sex. It naturally just caused problems—worry of pregnancy, jealousy—and it turned a Christian relationship into a lustful one. To this day, [we] both have feelings for each other, which honestly, I wish I did not have."

The players in the locker room knew that story as Cochran told them, "I want to see y'all do something special this year." There was no doubt among the players that if Cochran were wearing a red jersey instead of that T-shirt, they would indeed do something special this year. The coaches entered the locker room just as Cochran concluded, through a wavering voice, "I miss playing next to people I love."

Cochran turned to his left to meet an embrace from Clegg. Then one from Sells, followed by another from Ford, and as he made his way out of the locker room, he walked into coach Matt Russell's open arms. They held a long embrace as Cochran cried. Cochran walked out of the front door of the field house, eyes red from tears. His former teammates exited the same door a few minutes later to head single file to the field. As Clegg reached up to slap the "Tradition Never Graduates" sign hanging above the walkway to the door, on his right forearm, in black ink, was the number 7—Cochran's old jersey number.

+ + +

The Santo Wildcats were not anticipated to present much of a challenge. Faith had defeated the Wildcats 45–6 the previous season, and Santo had gone on to finish the season 1–9 and change head coaches. The new coach, Randy Thornton, was young and energetic, and Hogan liked what he had heard about the values the coach wanted to instill in his program. But enacting those changes had resulted in a drop-off in the number of players, with only fourteen dressed out for the first game.

As if the Lions did not already sense a big advantage, they received confirmation of it when the teams' captains met at midfield of Faith's home field, The Jungle, for the pre-game coin toss. "We're in for it, aren't we?" one of Santo's captains asked as he shook Anderson's hand. "Yeah," Anderson replied.

The captain's fears were realized. Faith stopped the Wildcats on their first possession. On the Lions' first offensive play—Option Left, of all plays—Hockenbrough raced thirty-six yards for a touchdown. Anderson ran to the sideline, jumping up and down and hollering. To the side of the home bleachers, Cochran turned for the parking lot. His best friend had just scored, and he could not be on the field celebrating with him. Nor could he stay.

Faith's Spread offense, though, was just getting started. On the next possession, Hockenbrough ran twenty-three yards for a first down. Anderson scored on a 10-yard run on the next play. On the second play of the Lions' second possession, Anderson broke free for a 71-yard touchdown run. Hockenbrough scored again on Faith's next possession. Eight minutes into the season, the Lions had possessed the ball four times and scored four touchdowns on a total of only eight plays.

The scoreboard read 62–8 when the teams met at midfield to shake hands. "You have a great team," Thornton told Hogan. Hogan offered encouragement to the first-year coach, then followed up on their pregame conversation by asking if the coach still wanted the teams to pray together. "Let's do it," the coach said.

As players from both teams took a knee on the Lion head painted at midfield, Santo white and Faith red jerseys intermingled and players' hands on one another's shoulder pads, Hogan addressed the Santo players. "Keep believing in each other. Don't quit. Sometimes you have tough seasons; we've all been there. It'll get better. Stick together. You have good coaches. Let's pray."

After Hogan's prayer, the teams stood to go their separate ways. One Santo player stopped a Faith player, shook his hand, and asked that the Faith player remember playing against him "when you win state."

CHAPTER 8

Take Nothing for Granted

GAME 2: PERRIN-WHITT PIRATES
Jordan Dunnington reported to practice Monday the owner of a prayer answered. The junior had started at left cornerback in the season opener and intercepted a pass on the last play of the first quarter. As the second running back, alternating with starter Hockenbrough, he had one carry for nine yards in the second quarter before yielding the backfield to guys deeper on the depth chart.

Now, officially, he was back after spending his sophomore year, coaches joked, as "the fastest team manager in Texas."

Up until this school year, Dunnington had been homeschooled. He had played for Faith his eighth-grade year and on the junior varsity as a freshman. But TAPPS and the school changed their policies regarding homeschooled students' eligibility to participate in extracurricular activities, and he could no longer play unless he enrolled at Faith. That was not financially possible, because his father's computer consulting company had suffered through a two-year drought without a contract, nearly depleting the family's savings and resources.

Dunnington didn't want to leave the program. He had grown spiritually through Faith football. He had made friends who were truly accepting, caring, and encouraging. He loved the school's atmosphere,

65

too, and wanted to remain as much a part of the campus as possible. So he volunteered to be a manager, filling water bottles, setting up the footballs and equipment before practice, and—perhaps his most important job—making sure Atwood was properly cared for when Hogan removed his hat. Although the work was not exciting, it was the only way he could be around the coaches and players and the only way he could contribute to the team. Every practice, he wanted to be padded up, hitting and sweating and being in there with the team instead of out there for the team. Friday nights were really tough.

After the first game his sophomore year, Dunnington's father, Darryl, left a message on Jordan's cell phone saying he knew how difficult it would be staying on the sideline, but that Jordan would make it through the season. Those words of encouragement—hearing his dad say he understood—meant so much to Dunnington that he did not delete the message and still listens to it when he goes through his saved messages. "It's just a constant reminder of what God's brought me through."

Still, the season was difficult. "It's a whole different perspective when you're a manager sitting on the sideline and you're this close to the game," he recalled. "But it's like the sideline—you can't go past it, so it keeps you off." From that sideline, Dunnington would visualize himself as a player on the field. There were times, though, when he could cross that line and step onto the field. After Faith kickoffs, he would retrieve the kicking tee. Sometimes, he would run off the field a little slower than he had run on so that he could look back to the coaches and players on the sideline. He would look up into the stands, at the red-clad fans cheering their team. He would absorb the scene as he retreated toward his spot on the other side of that sideline, and he would think, *It would be so cool to be out here.*

So he would pray. *Please take the hurt away. Please just take the pain away.* Despite the prayers, despite his father's phone message, despite his belief and hope that he would adjust to his new role, every game hurt a little more. The fifth game of that season, it became more than he could take. That was the Homecoming loss to Union Hill. He saw the players' disbelief on the field. He saw their pain in the privacy of the locker room. How much he had wanted to be on the field with them that night. It wasn't that he thought his presence would have made a difference in the outcome. But if he were in uniform, at least he would be with them. He would be hurting as one of them. "That's how much I love Faith, that's how much I love this school, that's how much I love this team. To see them hurting hurt me."

Finally it hurt so much that Dunnington decided to quit. Not being the team manager; he would never quit on his commitment. But away from the field house, where the coaches and players did not see him, he would quit two things.

First, he would quit working out. He had been working out at home, anticipating some miracle that would give him a chance to return to the field that season. If he did come back, he had determined, he would do so stronger and more ready to play than when he had left. Instead, as the time frame for that miracle decreased, he lost his drive to keep working. He had cut back on his workouts because he could not see any way he would play again. Now, he would quit working out at all.

Second, he would quit trusting God. When he returned home after the Union Hill game, "I was just really mad at God. I didn't want to talk to Him. You can't ignore God, but you can still kind of tune Him out. That's what I was doing."

Dunnington had learned a valuable lesson in trusting God during his freshman year. His father's company had been without a contract, and the family was struggling through financial pressures. He kept praying that his family would hold up through the tough times and that his dad would land a contract. At one point, he felt God telling him that by May 1, everything would be resolved. "I didn't say anything at first, and then He kept telling me that over and over. And then He said, 'All right, go tell your family.' I'm like, 'My family's going to think I'm crazy.' And so I go and tell them at the dinner table." Days were ripped off the calendar, and by April 30, his dad still did not have a contract. Jordan's mood sank. He did not understand. Hadn't God said it would be fixed?

At four o'clock that afternoon, his father received a phone call regarding a promising contract. The contract would not be offered that day, however, and probably not until the following week. He pondered what to say to Jordan. He did not want his son's faith shaken. At 5:15, Darryl Dunnington's office phone rang again. Meanwhile, back at home, Jordan suddenly stood up from his algebra lesson. "Daddy got the contract," he declared. Not long afterward, his dad called. They discovered that at the same time Jordan was standing at the kitchen table, his father was being offered that contract. "That," he said, "boosted my faith in Him so much, to know that He could do something that big."

But where was *that* God during *this* season? Surely, enabling a sixteen-year-old to play high school football was not as difficult as fixing a family's finances.

His decision to quit lasted all the way through the weekend. "It's just crazy," he recalled, "because when you give up and surrender, God just works in your life so big."

Before the next practice on Monday, Hogan told him he wanted him to pad up as a scout-team running back, helping prepare the defense for games. Dunnington had been praying all season that he could at least practice with the team. "All of a sudden, I'm over here trying to ignore God, and He answers one of my prayers by letting me practice. It was just kind of like an affirmation of, 'All right, you may not understand, but I still have a plan for you. No matter what. If you're going to play little baby and get mad at Me and turn your back on Me, I'm bigger than that and I'm showing you I'm bigger than that.' It was mind-blowing and humbling at the same time." The workouts and the trusting resumed immediately.

Wearing a sweaty-smelling mesh practice jersey was not the same as a fresh, shiny game jersey. But even if he could not help the team on the field during games, he at least could help them on the practice field. It was better, although not what he most wanted.

As the season progressed, Dunnington later realized, God used the sideline view to show him ways in which he had taken football for granted. His eighth-grade year, he had always given his best effort. His freshman year, he had not. He still worked hard, but not his hardest. "Sometimes I felt like working real hard, and I'd work real hard and get all inspired. But other times, I felt my way into action. Coach Hogan always says you act your way into feeling, but I felt my way into actions." He sensed God telling him that even if he were playing football that sophomore season, he would not have been ready to contribute like he'd wanted.

Piece by piece, he began trusting God again. He kept working out, too. Then the final game of the season, against Regents, he again watched the players suffer a painful loss. Things had slowly begun coming together

Take Nothing for Granted

in his mind, but Dunnington still struggled with why he had been kept off the field, and losing in the semifinals angered him again. "To see a team with so many people that you respect and that you love and that you got to know, to see them giving their all and for them to come up short—that hurts because you want to be out there experiencing that with them."

Darryl Dunnington was waiting for his son to come home that night. He had observed Jordan before and after every game, seeing how much he missed playing football. "I knew he was hurting inside because an entire season had passed without him participating," his father recalled. "Time he would never get back. Memories of running and tackling that were never made. It was painful for me, knowing how much Jordan loved the game but could not participate. Since I had begun coaching him at age six, he had always played. Every season."

The father placed a hand on his son's shoulder. "You're playing next year," he said. "We're going to make it work."

So this year, on Commitment Night back at Mt. Lebanon, Dunnington had taken his turn at the podium. He is soft-spoken, yes-sir/no-sir respectful. He plans his words carefully—he wants to be a writer—and speaks articulately. He stood before his teammates and gathered his thoughts. He was unemotional, yet purposeful in speech. He told the guys they know how passionate he is about football. Teammates nodded. Dunnington may be five-foot-seven and 155 pounds, but ask any player who has encountered him on the field, and he will tell you Dunnington is one of the team's two or three hardest hitters. He then told them something they did not know, about how he went home angry after the Union Hill loss. "Angry at myself and angry at God," he told them. "I asked God why He let this happen. He told me I wasn't ready." Dunnington committed that night to always be ready. To not take anything for granted.

So with the Santo game behind and Perrin-Whitt next on the schedule, Dunnington stood between the home bleachers and field house before Monday's practice and talked about that first game back. He had slept horribly the night before the game. He was too excited to sleep. He had started playing on this field at age six in pee-wee leagues. Ten years and one painful season later, he was back. He pointed over his shoulder. "I love that field," he said.

Now more than ever.

69

+ + +

Hogan broke out a new slogan during Monday's scouting report: "Work your ground." He took that from Proverbs 28:19, which begins, "He who works his land will have abundant food."[1] The concept, he said, would work in all areas of life, from farming to spiritual matters. "In football," Hogan told them, "work *your* ground and don't worry about what others do. What I want is for Brent [Reeder] to harvest the full abundance of his talent. I want that for everyone. You know what will happen if that happens."

On Wednesday, the coaches broke out new T-shirts: gray with a red "12.08.07" on the front for the date of the state championship game. "What's that date for?" a player asked Ford. As often happens around Faith coaches, the serious question drew a comical answer. "That's my birthday," Ford said. "I'm tired of you all forgetting."

At the end of practice, Hogan reminded the team that despite the score of the first game, there had been too much inconsistency. At times, the Lions looked like a championship team. At others—well, not so good. "We can't have lulls like that," he said, standing in front of the team in his new T-shirt, "and reach the goals and the date we've set." Then before the closing prayer, Hogan instructed his players, "Get your tails to church. That's why we let you out early."

+ + +

Fourth period each day is boys' athletic period. Mondays and Wednesdays are devoted to weight lifting, Tuesdays and Thursdays are for sport-specific time. During Thursday's period, Hogan sent the players onto the field without coaches. He instructed them to sit around the Lion head at midfield and create different situations the team could face during the season and then decide how they would respond to each one.

For half an hour, the players imagined scenarios positive and negative. A big halftime lead on Union Hill. A close game in the fourth quarter against Trinity Christian. A twenty-point lead on Reicher. Trailing Reicher by thirty at halftime and Anderson gets hurt.

That afternoon, Hogan started Open Floor Thursday by referring to the midfield discussion. He had given the players that assignment because he wanted them to learn how to think. To prove the importance of thinking, he reminded them of the previous season's loss to Union Hill, when Faith's eighteen-point lead late in the third quarter had turned into a loss. The players had not been prepared mentally for how to play with that kind of lead, he said. With the game seemingly in hand, the players let up. They were not prepared for Union Hill's comeback. The reason for that loss went deeper than not playing right. They lost because they did not think right. "Something affected your actions; and we know, as a man thinks, that's who he is, that's what he does. That's who he is," Hogan said, referring to Proverbs 23:7.[2] "So what I'm telling you is, if you know how to think, you'll be a lot closer to reaching your goals. I want you guys to figure it out."

"You said injury," Hogan continued, responding to the scenarios his players had envisioned. "What happens if somebody's knee goes out? Well, what are we going to do? Are we going to panic? Are we going to guess? No. We've already determined in advance that we're going to say, 'Hey, everybody's got to work your ground more, just got to pick up the slack. Let's go. Keep working.' It's just this mind-set. Mind-set *works*—not only for you, but for everybody you play."

Hogan then displayed an article from the *Mineral Wells Index* on that week's opponent, the Perrin-Whitt Pirates. The writer called the Lions a "private-school powerhouse." The Perrin-Whitt coach said his team had nothing to lose against Faith. "It's going to be a tough game," Hogan read from the coach's quote, "but we're in a win-win situation. We just want to keep the game close and have a chance to win."

"Do you see how they think of you?" Hogan asked his players. "You may not know that, but that's how a lot of people think of us. Now here's my thought to you. We could look at this and say, 'Yeah, right, we're going to kill you,' and take them lightly. My hope is that you would say, 'I am so glad.' Because I could tell you right now, reading that, that is a fearful coach knowing he could easily get routed Friday night. He knows that's a possibility. My hope is that you will recognize and say, 'Oh, people see us this way? Maybe this is the way we are. Maybe we should win every game.' And then I would like to beat them as bad or worse than Santo because guess who else reads this stuff? Everybody we play. I want Trinity saying, 'You know what, we recruited all these studs last year, but this is probably Faith's year. We've got to do this, that, and the other.'" Hogan concluded, "You don't always have to be perfect. But if they think you are, that's good enough."

Anderson again was the first player to speak, renewing his commitment from the week before to have planned responses instead of reactions. "I want you guys to hold me accountable," Anderson said. "You can bet I'll hold you accountable," Hogan responded. "Thank you very much, Coach," Anderson said with a laugh. "You bet," the coach said.

Dunnington was last to speak. He had not been running the ball with confidence because he had not been finding the open lanes coaches could see when he would break through the line of scrimmage. This week, though, he would run with confidence. He concluded with the words of Paul: "For God has not given us a spirit of fear and timidity, but of power, love, and self-discipline."[3]

+ + +

Players were "walking the field" in street clothes two hours before kickoff, most wearing earbuds and listening to music. Some tossed footballs back and forth. Anderson threw soft passes for a few minutes then began running plays barefoot. Every play was run going toward the near end zone. Roddy and Messinger picked separate open spots on the field to begin firing off an imaginary line of scrimmage and to go through the blocking schemes of various plays—working their ground. Reeder retreated alone up into the stands to look out over the field. Each player had his own ritual, his own way of preparing.

Back in the locker room, Dunnington went through his own pregame routine. He did not walk the field. Instead, he stretched indoors, got his ankles taped, and lay across his footlocker listening to rap music. His mother encourages him to listen to a variety of music. On Friday evenings, though, rap pumps him up to play. Before this game, as was his routine, he turned off the music and prayed. He remembered the sacrifices his parents made to get him into Faith, and he remembered Hogan's support. He wanted to play for them, he told God. Then he thanked Him for the opportunity He had given him to play football again. "This is for Your glory," he prayed. "This is for what You have done for me."

+ + +

If the Perrin-Whitt coach had feared a blowout, he was right. Faith's defense held the Pirates without a first down on their first possession, forcing a punt. The big play Perrin-Whitt's coach said his team could not allow soon followed, with Anderson connecting with receiver Brock Jameson for a 42-yard pass into Perrin-Whitt territory. From there, Dunnington took a pitch from Anderson and raced untouched around the left side for a 23-yard touchdown run on his first carry. He would score again early in the second quarter to give the Lions a 28–0 advantage, then again late in the quarter as Faith took a 42–0 lead into halftime.

"This game ain't over," Ford told the players during the break. "Yes, it's probably over as far as a 'W' goes. I'll give you that. But it ain't over as far as improving as a program." Hogan challenged the defense to finish the game with a shutout. "We ain't gonna take a step back again," Ford added, reminding how the Lions had looked sloppy when making substitutions during the season opener. "We're not going to let you fail." The players stood to leave the locker room. On their way out, Messinger gave his defensive teammates a reminder: "Cedar Hill's going to read the paper. Don't let them see a six. Show 'em a zero." The Lions did show 'em a zero, winning 63–0.

Hogan assembled his players at the Lion head and asked a first-grade student from among the fans gathered around to pray. "Dear Lord, thank you for this wonderful day," the boy began. "Thank you for letting our team win." Ford chuckled, Hogan smiled. "Please help everyone else to have a safe trip home tonight. Please help all the players to get rest from this game. And please help all the other players to not feel bad and go home safely. In Jesus' name, amen."

Back in the coaches' office, the coaches munched on leftover hamburgers, sausages, and hot dogs from the concession stand while looking over the game's statistics. They had gained 566 yards while holding Perrin-Whitt to 49. Hockenbrough had gone over 100 yards rushing for the second time, with 165. And in addition to his three touchdowns, Dunnington had rushed for 103 yards on only seven carries. He had upheld his commitment to run with confidence.

CHAPTER 9

"Don't Cheat Yourself"

GAME 3: RIO VISTA EAGLES
After the bell sounded to end the school day, the players gathered in
a classroom for the Monday scouting session. Hogan cleaned the dry-
erase board as scouting reports—packets that included everything the
players would need to know about the Rio Vista Eagles—were passed
around until every varsity player had one. Curious junior varsity players
looked over varsity players' shoulders for a peek at what would be in
store for this week.

Hogan turned and called the players' attention to the bottom of
the cover page. Beneath the players' four jobs for the season, which are
listed on the cover of every week's scouting report, were these words:

> **Whatever a man sows, this he shall also reap.**
> **–GOD (Galatians 6:7)**
> **Keep working . . .**

Referring to a radio program he'd recently heard on the subject of rela-
tivism, Hogan told his players that it is incorrect to believe that values
differ according to circumstances. Instead, he said, "It's all black-and-
white," just as the verse on the scouting report says. "You will reap

in this football season what you sow." Part of players' working their ground meant weeding out distractions. Then Hogan turned to the week's opponent: unbeaten Rio Vista, with victories by sixteen and thirty-two points.

"They are significantly better than Perrin-Whitt," he said. "Thank goodness." Hogan, as defensive coordinator, announced he would do something out of the ordinary on defense this week by making personnel changes. Other than that, however, Hogan called the game plan simple.

Then he had a word about that day's conditions. The practice field had been soaked all day by rain, but he instructed players to ignore the conditions. "We could easily play a game in this. We're not going to stop running the Spread because it rains."

He offered one final piece of advice before dismissing the players to the field, making the players aware of the work of school facilities director Andy Beene. "Make sure you hug Mr. Beene, because he arranged to kill all of the fire ants before the season."

+ + +

They are called fire ants for good reason, as anyone who has experienced their sting can attest. After a rain in Texas, rainbows sometimes appear—but fire ants always appear, and they are always in a bad mood after evacuating their flooded homes. Thanks to Mr. Beene, the practice field was fire ant free.

Almost four inches of rain had fallen by midafternoon, leaving behind a messy practice field. Shorts were soaked as soon as players hit the ground in their opening drills, and players offered weather-related remarks—"My shoes weigh so much," said one—as they rolled through the mud and sprang into position for the next drill.

One player not complaining was Greg Wright, the junior linebacker practicing for the first time after recovering from a broken foot. Wright did not merely go through the drills; he attacked them. Since the first day of practice, he had dragged his booted right foot around the practice field, doing whatever he could to both help the team and make himself feel as though he had participated in something—anything—during practice. Before and after practices, he often visited the coaches' office, a near no-players' land. That office, with a table in the middle and a long dry-erase board along one wall, is where high-level strategy discussions take place. The room also is known as "The Popsicle Capital of the World" for the coaches' propensity to cool off from practices with a flavored treat. Because of his injury and his middle linebacker position—the defense's quarterback—Wright had received access to the room for post-practice breakdowns and, yes, an occasional Popsicle.

Monday's mud and slop were not going to slow Wright's first-day-of-practice enthusiasm. Hogan, whose typical cheery mood was brightened further by seeing Wright finally in shoulder pads and helmet, walked over to him early in the practice and told him, "Not a fire ant one."

Then Hogan moved over to where quarterbacks, running backs, and receivers were rhythmically running through offensive plays. He discovered his players were having wet footballs dried off before each play. To him, that was failing to take advantage of an opportunity to practice in poor conditions they could possibly face in a game. "Why are we keeping the balls so dry?" Hogan inquired. "I'm trying to create bad situations."

+ + +

The players had created a bad situation for themselves. One player had left shoes on his footlocker, a definite infraction of the coaches' strict locker-room rules. One player had forgotten his blue practice jersey, so he was wearing shoulder pads without a jersey and making clacking noises as he ran around the field. And who knows how many players had not worn their girdles and pads that protect thighs, hips, and tail-bones. The players bore the consequences: an unspecified number of up-downs. Not a particularly kind welcome back to practice for Wright. "Yeah," he said, rolling his eyes. "First day."

One by one, the players counted off each of the up-downs aloud. The count crossed into double digits. "You've got to be disciplined in the little things," Ford yelled. Whistle, down to the ground, back up. "You've got to think of your teammates. You get a thigh bruise, you hurt the team." Another whistle. "I know why you didn't wear thigh pads: You're selfish. It's not comfortable." Another whistle.

One accidental helmet to an unprotected thigh in practice could cause a painful thigh bruise that could keep a player out of action for a week or two. Choosing not to wear thigh pads, Ford told the players, was not thinking about their teammates.

The count continued climbing, and the huffing and puffing grew louder across the field. "If winning a championship was easy," Ford barked, "everybody would win one!"

"You guys remember your commitment!" Kallal screamed, then dropped his 230 pounds flat to the ground and immediately jumped back up to complete another up-down. "Are you really sold out?" Coach Rivera yelled from the middle of the pack of players.

Finally, the whistle stopped after the seventy-fifth up-down. There were eight others that did not count because someone had not properly hit his chest flat on the ground. There would be twenty-five more for the offenders who had made their teammates suffer because of their actions, Hogan announced. But first would be the regular conditioning session, a set of 360s directly on the heels of the tiring up-downs.

Completing the first 360, Dexter Cheneweth fell across the finish line into a group of teammates. "Remember, you said you'd rather die," a voice from the group reminded him of his Commitment Night statement. Teammates helped him to his feet. "I always finish!" Dexter yelled.

The second trip around the field would be a 400—a regular 360 plus the length of the field. Ford and Hogan watched as the group started out on its next run. Ford told Hogan that the players must understand that in life, mistakes come with a price. "Eternal consequences are far worse than up-downs," said Ford, and Hogan nodded.

After the second run, the players walked back to the start line for a final 400. Legs and arms were caked in mud. Shorts were soaked, clinging to thighs and butts. Through the red face masks, mud was visible on players' faces. Small blades of grass were plastered to bare stomachs and lower backs. "I know it hurts, boys," Nerney told his teammates. "How bad do you want it?"

Ford, still upset over the players' lack of individual responsibility that day, pointed to the cover of his scouting report. "Number 4," he said to Hogan. *Take care of your responsibility.* It's there every week as a reminder.

"You may not like my friendly 'reminders' to live in integrity," Hogan told the players as they caught their breath for the next run. "But I can tell you right now, I'm your biggest ally. Yeah, I'm making you run, but it's because you've chosen to violate the rules designed to help you win."

The final 400 was, not surprisingly, the slowest. The last player headed up the final straightaway was Dexter. All his teammates had finished their run and were back at the other end of the field. Except for two JV players who had stopped to help Dexter. With his arms around their shoulders, and as he had promised he would on Commitment Night and again less than five minutes earlier, Dexter finished. He finished last, but Dexter always finishes.

After the closing prayer, Hogan instructed those who were not wearing the proper equipment—and the coaches would trust the players instead of checking them—to stay and do twenty-five more up-downs. Twenty-nine players started the extra up-downs.

To Hogan, punishing players is never easy, and certainly not fun. It requires thinking beyond the moment to a long-range plan. "I cannot figure out why coaches feel any need to be accepted as a friend," he said. "Clearly a relationship with players is an important part of the grand scheme, but when a decision concerning the proper functioning of the program needs to be made, I'm not real interested in taking an opinion poll of the players. My duty is to facilitate and cultivate lifelong behaviors that lead to success in every area of life, and if that means being unpopular for a period of time with a few teenage boys, so be it. Sometimes a kid's narrow perspective cannot fully appreciate why a coach brings sharp consequences to an unwanted action, and I'm okay with that. I'm only *interested* in a kid thinking I'm an all-right guy, but I am *committed* to making sure they are held accountable to the integrity of the program."

Just the day before, Hogan had received an e-mail that affirmed that approach. The mother of senior softball player Tori Guinan had forwarded Hogan the first draft of her daughter's English paper. The assignment: describe a defining moment in her life.

Guinan recounted how Hogan, as the school's athletic director, had walked into the athletics class one January day her freshman year and told the softball players that they would be running during the period instead of practicing softball, that they would not need their gloves and cleats until after-school practices. All Faith athletes know about Hogan's emphasis on their year-round development through weight lifting and conditioning programs, but after a month of conditioning drills, Guinan felt Hogan did not respect softball and the softball players. The Lady Lions won the state championship that season—despite Hogan's intrusion, she reasoned. For Guinan, bitterness toward Hogan overshadowed the team's success. But surely, because of that championship, he would leave the softball program alone the next season.

Instead, the conditioning program continued. Guinan noticed her increased speed, strength, and stamina, but still she refused to give Hogan credit. Toward the end of her sophomore season, she was invited to join a top-level select team during the summer, one filled with players from much larger, more-recognized public schools. About one-third of the way through conditioning drills at the first practice, players began dropping out. At the end of the drills, the new player from the small private school was the only one still running. For the first time, Guinan allowed herself to credit Hogan. She had thought that the only way to improve at softball was through hitting, throwing, and fielding. Now she was able to say that Hogan knew better.

In her final paragraph, Guinan wrote, "As I reflect on my four years of athletics under Coach Hogan's leadership, I think about a lot of sweat and tears. Nothing came easily or quickly. When my attitude improved, it became easier to follow the program and achieve the success he desired for me. I know that I had to have the moment of revelation before I could fully understand Coach Hogan's passion for my overall success in life, not just on a playing field."[1]

+ + +

Hogan likes to set aside five minutes of practice time for "non-football exhortations," a time to teach life lessons. The end of Tuesday's two-and-a-half-hour practice was one of those times. Faith's annual Student Leadership University retreat would be next week. Athletic schedules are built around SLU, and that meant an off-week after the Rio Vista game. With the retreat nearing, Hogan talked to his players about always having a clear direction.

"What is your main goal in math class? What did you make last year? What's your goal this year?" he asked. "If you don't have a goal, you're operating sub-championship in math class. Now let me tell you something: Those people who are the least mature and achieve the least in society are people who compartmentalize. They make their life into compartments. When they go to church, they act this way. But when they're with this idiot over here who tries to get them to drink beer, they'll drink beer because they're a weak idiot. They've compartmentalized. 'Oh, I'll be a sissy over here. Or I'll be cool with this group. And then I'm going to blow off math and I'm going to be an all-state linebacker.' That stuff doesn't work. If you've ever done it, then you know you'll always feel some twinge of guilt. You'll feel emptiness, you'll feel irritable, you'll feel restless in the summertime. Nothing to do, you're going to feel restless. If you're not giving your best in every area of your life, you'll never be fulfilled. Never. And not just football. If you don't do your best in all of your classes, you're going to be restless. It's a law of God. If you give all you have, you don't have regrets. That's just the way it is.

"Think about the time when you studied up harder than you ever had, you got with your buddies, you studied, you made a commitment, you felt good going into class, you knew you did good afterward. You didn't have to worry about it after school. You just took off and messed around. You've been there, right? And you've also been there when you haven't studied. And your guts turned over when you thought you might be ineligible. We've all been there. Here's what I'm going to tell you: if you compartmentalize, you're going to cheat yourself. You say, 'Well, I'll make it up later.'" He then told of a former student who had missed out on a $160,000 scholarship by .83 of a point on his grade average. "We're talking about he screwed off as a freshman in Algebra I and it cost him, maybe forever. You just can't compartmentalize.

"Don't be a wimp. If you're a Christian, act like one. Don't be weak and have a female teacher that you let some other guy in class [disrespect]. Don't do that stuff. Be the guy God created you to be. Control your surroundings." Hogan offered a hypothetical example of having a teammate who practices well but acts disrespectful toward a lunchroom worker. In that case, a mature teammate should be strong, put football aside, and stand up for the lunchroom worker. "It doesn't matter if you're at practice. Listen, it's still an immature boy who . . . [is] disrespectful to a lady who works in the lunchroom, still just an immature little jerk. What's more important, a good practice or treating somebody's mom right? You see what I'm saying? We don't think of it that way, though. You don't think of that stuff.

"Just don't cheat yourself, that's all I'm saying. Don't cheat your parents, God, or yourself. If you leave it all on the line, you do your best, there are no regrets. Everybody with me here? Don't compartmentalize. You'll cheat yourself. Trust me."

+ + +

Junior Josh O'Neal has a future as a motivational speaker. When he raises his hand to speak during Open Floor Thursday, there is a discernible anticipation of what he will say. This week, he wanted to point out the efforts of two teammates—Grant Hockenbrough and Greg Wright. Hockenbrough had been sick during the week and looked like he felt terrible during one practice. Except for when it was time to run a play. "As soon as someone said 'Set,' it was *snap*, he was into it. He just threw everything else out the window, and he was ready to go on that play." O'Neal also noticed Wright giving extra effort in the weight room. There was a point when Wright, working his way back into shape after finally being cleared to practice, had tired and was about to put a lighter weight on the bar. But a teammate encouraged him to lift the heavier weight. "And he did. You could tell he didn't think he could get it, but somebody just said, 'You can do it. You can do it. You can do it.' And Greg jumped up there and he did.

"Guys," O'Neal continued, "that's how I know we're going to be a championship team. That's how I know this is our year. Because I see guys like Grant. Being a champion, I think, is about being tired and beat up. People think you can't do it. But you persevere anyway, and you get it done. Guys, this is our year. I think it's going to happen this year because of guys like Grant and Greg, who are dedicated so much that even when they're tired, even when they feel bad, they take the extra step and get it done. I think if we follow their example, we'll win a state championship. And if everyone just lets everything go when we're on the field and we can focus on what we have to do, the task at hand, we'll get it done. No matter what happens, no matter what anyone says, we just do our job. We'll never stop winning if we keep that mind-set."

O'Neal then brought a hush to the room. "There's no one else I'd rather put the legacy of Faith football, in the hands of anyone else, but Grant. If I was going to trust anyone to work hard and get it done, it would be Grant. I would say if we're going to win, attitude like Grant, attitude like Greg, that's going to get it done. Look at them if you need anyone to look at for an example of being sold out—it's Greg and Grant."

Those words—"the legacy of Faith football"—hung in the air as the locker room remained silent. Legacy. That is a heavy word, and it had just been dropped upon the shoulders of perhaps the most respected teammate in that locker room.

Ford broke the silence to follow up on O'Neal's words, quoting former professional basketball star Jerry West: "You can't get much done in life if you only work on the days when you feel good."

"And that applies to everything in life. He sets a great example," said Ford, pointing to Hockenbrough. "Grant didn't feel good, but dadgum, he worked hard on that day, too. He sets a great example. And I know that's going to carry on with Grant out in life—as a dad, as a leader in the community, and in society. There's going to be days he doesn't feel good, but he is going to go represent, he's going to lead, he's going to be a great father, a great business leader, or whatever it is, because he's establishing his habits right now. He's overcoming those little pains and fighting through them because he's got a commitment to you guys. That's what's going to do it for him. He's going to commit in the future to his family, his wife, his kids, his business, whatever it is."

+ + +

"That looks great right there," Hogan said as Wright, with the red "12" on his all-white uniform, jogged onto the Rio Vista field. "I've been waiting for that. That's 200 pounds of smart."

As fans from both schools assembled in the stands, there was a sense of expectation that had lacked at the first two games. With about three hundred students in grades nine through twelve, Rio Vista was the largest school Faith would face this season. And if the previous night's junior varsity game—a 14–6 Faith victory—was any indication, Rio Vista would bring a physical style of play into this game.

Behind the corners of the end zones, four vertical flags emblazoned with the Eagles' name and logo on them snapped in the late-evening breeze. Hogan pointed out the surroundings to his players, all on one knee, in one line along the goal line, fifteen minutes before kickoff. "I'm just telling you, you'd better take this bunch serious," Hogan warned. "They're 2–0, and they are after you."

He spoke in his factual tone, with none of the stereotypical drama he dislikes, but there was vivid determination and confidence in his voice as he began to conclude his pre-game words. "That's just where we are. Now, there's nothing wrong with being in this position. Let me tell you what you need to do: You've got to create doubt—now. Right when the game starts, no matter if we're kick or kick return, go in there and grab their heart. . . . First five minutes, rip it out and say, 'Nope. You read about us, you know about us, it's true, and you're done.' And let's do it in the first quarter. Everybody with me?" "Yes, sir!" the players answered. "All right," their coach said. "Let's go."

+ + +

As the players had hoped, Faith kicked off to start the game. Even though the fast start to the season had everyone talking about Faith's offense, it was the defense that players preferred to send onto the field to deliver a game's first statement.

But on the first play from scrimmage, Rio Vista ripped off a 27-yard run to the Faith 40 yard line. The Lions were called for offside on the play, and that penalty was declined and the long gain stood. On the next play, Nerney sacked the quarterback from his left defensive end spot, but Faith again was called offside. The Lions had already been called for two penalties and had allowed a long run. But the defense held the Eagles without a gain on the next three plays, and a punt gave Faith its first possession at its own 12.

Eight plays later, Anderson was in the end zone with a 28-yard touchdown run, and Messinger's point-after-touchdown kick gave the Lions a 7–0 lead. Clegg, starting at defensive back as part of Hogan's personnel changes, intercepted a pass on Rio Vista's next possession and, with Faith's offense back on the field, Anderson again ran for a score.

In a game between two unbeaten teams, Faith's lead reached 21–0 before the first quarter ended and had ballooned to 35–0 by halftime. Despite the lead, Faith's coaches were not satisfied. "They won the last five minutes of the half," Ford told the other coaches. "Maybe more than that." And that was a time when the Lions could have closed the deal. Instead, the coaches agreed, Rio Vista's players would feel like they could play with Faith and would come out fired up to start the second half. Though Hogan agreed that there were too many mistakes, citing "seven or eight things to fix," he was pleased with the team's tempo and effort, and he did not want to jump on the players for those mistakes. "They're going full speed. Let's do some psychology here. But it's your duty," he told the coaches, "to fix the small things."

The players, meanwhile, were confident. In fact, the biggest problem they anticipated for the second half would be with the players who had selected fettuccine Alfredo at the Italian restaurant on the way to the game. Dunnington needed to throw up, so he was sticking his finger in his throat hoping that would help. Clegg felt weighed down by a heaviness in his stomach, saying he could almost feel inside him both breadsticks he had eaten.

Most of the players were sitting or lying on the sidewalk outside their steamy locker room as the coaches walked toward the players for the halftime talk. "We've got to shut the door on them in the first five minutes of the second half," Messinger told his teammates as the coaches arrived.

As he said he would, Hogan mentioned the mistakes but did not dwell on them. He emphasized job Number 4—personal responsibility—and paying attention to the small things. "Listen, we don't want to let off. We want to go smother them. We gave them a little bit of life. Let's just go smother them. But it's details. Details."

In the couple of minutes before it was time to return to the field, Ford told a parent about Hogan's pre-game speech, "I was ready to put the pads on and play."

The second half started much better for Faith than the first. On the first play from scrimmage, Anderson raced sixty-one yards for his fifth touchdown of the night. He would add a sixth rushing touchdown to go with the touchdown pass he threw in the first half and finished with 225 yards rushing and 124 passing. The Lions' 440 yards of offense were seventy-eight more than the Eagles had allowed in their first two games combined. Final score: Faith 56, Rio Vista 7.

The Lions boarded the bus for the sixty-mile trip home with a 3–0 record and, for the first time, a sense of just how good they were.

CHAPTER 10

Character = Motivation

GAME 4: MILLSAP BULLDOGS

The players expected an old-fashioned chewing-out. Sure, they were up 21–0 on Millsap at halftime, but the players' mood as they entered the cramped visitors' locker room seemed more like they were trailing by three touchdowns.

"All right, it's done!" Messinger yelled. "Let's go! We've got to go out and play a better half." Added O'Neal: "No more of that! We've got to have a better half. We're not playing our game. We've got to play our game. Our game is tempo. Enough of that!"

Indicators throughout the week had warned of a potential subpar performance. First, the players were coming back from a week away from football. At the SLU retreat, football players went through fifteen-minute conditioning sessions each day. Other than that, there was no football. Then there was this week's opponent. Millsap had a 2–2 record. The players had studied the poster board in the locker room that tracks opponents' results. Faith and Millsap had three common opponents. The Bulldogs had defeated Santo and Perrin-Whitt, but not by near the impressive scores as Faith had. Millsap had lost 39–7 to Rio Vista, and Faith had dominated Rio Vista before the off-week.

The Monday scouting report session on Millsap had lasted only ten minutes, and the players seemed more interested in whether the coaches might say anything about Trinity Christian. Hogan, Ford, and Sells had taken advantage of the Friday night off to watch the Tigers play in Dallas. Trinity Christian had lost 28–27 for its first loss, but the coaches left impressed. The teams' district opener against each other in less than three weeks looked to be as close of a matchup as expected.

It also had been difficult not to look ahead to next week's game at Union Hill. Finally, the Lions would have a chance to make up for one of last season's three losses. Getting their minds back to this week's game, the players wondered aloud whether Millsap would be looking ahead too. This was the Bulldogs' last non-district game. They would be off the next week before starting their district schedule. The players speculated that Millsap coaches might look at their unfavorable matchup with Faith and decide to keep the game plan simple in order to not show anything out of the ordinary for district opponents that would scout this game on film.

Then there were Tuesday's problems. The players had not been going full speed early in practice, earning forty-five attention-getting up-downs. The up-downs did little to help the players' energy level for the rest of practice. Hogan huddled his players before the conditioning drills that would conclude practice.

"The man who tells you the truth is not your enemy. Right?" Hogan asked. "Yes, sir," the players responded. "The person who tells you the truth is not your enemy," Hogan repeated. "They have your best interest in mind. So let me tell you the truth. Were you happy with today's practice? Let me tell you why we had this practice. I need you to listen. This is why we had this practice. It's seeping back in. Let me tell you what your problem has been. Primarily this senior class. You think you're better than you are. That's the truth. You think you're better than you are. That's why we had a bad practice. I love you guys, but you think you're better than you really are."

Hogan alluded to teams these seniors had been a part of that failed to live up to expectations. He did not specifically mention the track team that had fallen one point shy of a state championship, the soccer team expected to win state that had lost in the early rounds of the playoffs, the previous football season's loss to Regents. He didn't have to mention those teams. The seniors remembered the feeling of coming up short in each instance.

"You're good. You're just not as good as you think you are. It kills me because sometimes the work ethic and the work level and the self-motivation—I'm thinking, all right, they've got it. But then we have a day like today. I just don't know how to explain that. Wouldn't you agree to some extent that's bit us in the butt a few times? I'm not slamming you guys. You know I'm your biggest ally, your biggest fan, and hope you succeed. The guy who tells you the truth is not your enemy. I want you to think about that."

Then there were Thursday's problems. Thursday was picture day, and the picture taking did not go as scheduled. Falling behind schedule irritated Hogan. So with picture day running long, there would be no time for Open Floor. "This Open Floor Thursday will be the fastest in history," Hogan had told the players. "We just need to play instead of talk this week."

+ + +

All those problems snowballed into Friday night. There was something missing about the team as players hopped off the bus at Millsap's stadium. They went straight to walking the field. The atmosphere was near dead. Millsap was playing its last season in this old stadium behind the elementary and middle schools off a farm-to-market road. There was no activity around the stadium as the players toured the place. Not even Millsap's team had arrived from the high school. A steady breeze blew from the south end zone to the north, but without the aroma of a concession stand grill firing up or the small talk of cheerleaders hanging paper banners, there was nothing for the wind to carry that indicated a game soon would take place.

Finally, the Bulldogs arrived on a yellow school bus escorted by the Millsap Fire Department. Fans began to make their way into the stadium, but it was obvious heading up toward game time that the crowd would be thin. Even Faith's small seating section looked as though it would not fill. Perhaps it was the thought of fighting Metroplex traffic to get to the rural town fifty miles west of Fort Worth. Perhaps the fans had done their score research, too, and decided this game would offer little to watch. Whatever the reason, there was no buzz present as the stadium lights began taking over for the setting sun.

Even as the players knelt on the goal line and listened to Hogan's final pre-game instructions before heading to the locker room, other than that the cornerbacks should guard against Millsap's receivers' slant and fade routes, the most important piece of information concerned wearing tail pads. Players loathe tail pads. They are uncomfortable, especially when players run. During the previous game at Rio Vista, when officials warned that anyone not wearing tail pads would be removed from the game, players scurried to put their pads in or find something soft enough to roll up in the shape of a tail pad so it would at least look as though they were wearing one.

"If you come to a game again and you don't have a butt pad in, you ain't playing," Hogan warned. "I don't care if it's Curtis or Landon or anybody else around here. You ain't playing unless you're properly equipped. That's it, that's the end of the discussion. If you legitimately forgot a tail pad, that's one thing. But if you show up out here and prance out here without a tail pad, forget it. You wear your stinking pads, because I have to tell the official whether or not we're properly equipped, and I ain't going to lie to him. So wear your junk."

As had happened in the first three games, the Lions forced a quick punt on their opponents' first possession. Nerney returned the punt fifty-six yards to put the offense in great field position at the Millsap 30. It took only three plays for Hockenbrough to score the game's first points on a touchdown run. After another quick defensive series, the Lions again drove into Millsap territory. This time, the drive stalled on a fourth-down pass completion that came up short of the first-down marker. A Bulldogs fumble set Faith up only sixteen yards from the end zone, and the Lions punched the ball in on Anderson's 1-yard run to take a 14–0 lead late in the first quarter.

Millsap picked up its initial first down of the game on its fourth possession, before an interception by Dunnington in Faith territory ended the Bulldogs' drive. The Lions drove efficiently down the field, with consecutive completions of nine, nineteen, ten, and thirty-eight yards before Anderson scored again on a 12-yard run. The final nine minutes and thirty-five seconds of the first half passed by scoreless.

The Lions had scored three touchdowns, but everything seemed so businesslike. So ho-hum. So different from the first three games, when they had scored at least five touchdowns in the first half each time. That was why the players were upset as they entered the locker room at half-time, and why they braced themselves for an upset coach when Hogan came in to address the team. They did not get one.

Hogan figured that to go in and jump the players verbally would be a waste of time. If his players aren't motivated during a game, he reasons, they can't be motivated by a halftime speech. A quote from former Dallas Cowboys coach Tom Landry guides Hogan. If players have character, Landry once said, that is all the motivation they need. If a coach invests enough in his players, Hogan believes, if he coaches them enough and teaches them about life, the players will understand where they are. If a coach can help a team gain that perspective, Hogan says, he can walk into an upset locker room at halftime and "communicate like adults."

"Listen," Hogan began. "Let me give you a real quick overview, and then the O-line is going to be with Coach Ford. Where do you want them, Coach? Outside, over there, where do you want them? Okay, O-line, you're going outside." Instead of starting with the lack of emotion, the drives that had stalled because of uninspired play, or even a told-you-so about what bad practices during the week can lead to on Friday night, the coach wanted to designate a place for the offensive linemen to meet. There was more surprise than dread on the players' faces when Hogan finally got around to his real quick overview.

"Now everybody listen, listen," Hogan said matter-of-factly. "Here's what happened in the first half. We made about five or six plays where we dug our own grave. Somebody didn't execute. That's all there is to it. We missed a block, bad throw, bad catch, whatever. Didn't finish a run, whatever. Didn't pick up a block. Five or six plays, we did it, and that seems like a lot for us percentage-wise." Second, he said, the chain gang—the men from Millsap working the first-down markers on the sideline—were slow to mark first downs, and that dragged the tempo on the possessions when Faith went into its "NASCAR," or hurry-up, offense. "Number three, there's this *lullllll* out there. We're playing at their pace and doing some goofy stuff, like losing contain, and then they get a 10-yard run. All of that makes it feel like a subpar half, doesn't it? It just does. That's good, because that's our expectation level.

"Most people like 21 to 0 at halftime, but it ought to be about 35. Now listen. We're going to overcome that. Here's what we're going to do. We're going to overcome that and come out and score twenty-one in the third quarter, zap this sucker where it needs to be. Don't get down on yourselves. I can kind of see this whole thing put together making us feel this way. At the same time, we can control more than what we did. We're a good team, and we've got to play to our expectations. We don't want to get in that trap like last year and not live up to where we are. So we're going to get it together and we're going to kick their tail in the second half."

Hogan then sent the offensive line off to meet with Ford for a few second-half adjustments. That was it. No yelling, no questioning, no scolding.

"Halftime rah-rah stuff is overrated," Hogan told Ford as they walked alone to the field for the second half. "You've got to communicate."

+ + +

Hogan was wrong about one thing: The Lions did not come out and score three touchdowns in the third quarter. He was off by two plays. They scored their third touchdown of the half on the second play of the fourth quarter when the freshman Ashton again dazzled the Faith faithful with a 65-yard punt return. The next time Faith had the ball, Ashton quarterbacked a touchdown drive, carrying the ball once for thirty yards and again for a 36-yard touchdown that put the score at its final margin of 48–0.

"Let's go home," Hogan told his players after the game. "We're a long way from home, so let's get out of here." After the team prayed, the Lions rose to break out with "We are Faith . . . Sold Out!" "You guys remember Union Hill last year?" Hogan asked. "Yes, sir," the players responded. Nothing more was said, or needed to be said.

CHAPTER 11

Is Revenge Biblical?

GAME 5: UNION HILL BULLDOGS

"Notice the bottom," Hogan said as the players received their Monday scouting report, this one for Union Hill. There, Hogan reminded the players that their 42–38 loss to Union Hill the year before was the only home game Faith had lost in the past two seasons.

One player groaned. "Why would you do that?" asked another. The players had not forgotten, and they didn't want to be reminded.

"Last year, this week began our downward spiral," Hogan said. The 2006 Lions had been undefeated through their first four games. The second-half meltdown against Union Hill was followed by a 31–7 loss at Trinity Christian to start district play, and that team never again played to its potential.

"The line at the bottom—your personal responsibility—is tanta-mount."

Making up for last season's loss was motivation enough. Hogan chose to add more. "I'm starting to feel like it's us against the world. I think the public schools have all traded films. They're trying to knock us off. I guarantee it."

The Union Hill coach, he said, had not wanted to make the usual game-film trade early on the previous Saturday morning. With the schools situated a three-hour drive apart, Union Hill's coach said he preferred to exchange information over the phone. Hogan agreed. Then he changed his mind because he did not trust what the Bulldogs coach had told him. That, Hogan told the players, angered the opposing coach.

"And he took it out on me," Sells interrupted.

That comment piqued the players' curiosity. If the school's teachers could have witnessed the players edging forward in their seats, they would have started inserting Story Time with Coach Hogan into their lesson plans.

"I told Coach Sells," Hogan said, "'Instead of meeting them, why don't you just drive out there?' Because he really wanted the tape because he thought they were going to lie and run a different defense. So he drove out to East Texas alone. He got out there, and I'm not joking, they really did gang up on him when he got there. Their coaches said, 'Oh, we can't cuss now, because Christians are here.' I mean, they were ripping him."

"Wow!" one player exclaimed as the group started to laugh.

"I almost got into a fight," Sells joked.

Hogan, now in full storytelling mode, extended the joke. "I'll show you a Christian," he said, making a punching motion.

"I was there fifteen, twenty minutes," Sells continued. "The whole time, in a nice, funny way to them, they took shots at us. The whole team. Especially, you know, me." More laughter.

"I went to shake their hands. 'You don't believe me? Why are you here? You drove a long way for nothing.'"

"They did mess with him for a good fifteen, twenty minutes," Hogan said. "Totally unprofessional. You can pick on some people, but not Coach Sells."

The players laughed at the Hogan and Sells comedy routine. But in their minds, they bookmarked the story. The players were not told about the e-mails, and by the end of the week, that probably was a good thing.

After securing the Bulldogs' game films and heading back toward the Metroplex, Sells called Hogan to relate his experience. That sent Hogan and high school principal Jeff Potts into action. The best friends never miss an opportunity for a good prank. Especially when the greenhorn offensive coordinator is at the receiving end. So in the principal's office, Potts created an e-mail account with "BulldogCoach" in the address, and Hogan helped him compose an e-mail that read as though it had been written by a coach.

When Sells arrived from East Texas, the e-mail awaited him. It picked up the themes from that morning's film exchange. Why make that trip? Didn't he trust the Union Hill coach? The issue could be resolved that coming Friday night when the teams met, the e-mail suggested.

Sells asked who was pranking him. "I don't even know how to create an e-mail account," said Hogan, which was probably true. Ford, who had been tipped off by Hogan, played along perfectly, asking Sells whether he was going to let the opposing coach treat him like that. The more Hogan denied sending the e-mail, and the more Ford agitated Sells, the more Sells began to consider that, just possibly, the e-mail had come from the Union Hill coach.

It was all veteran pranksters Hogan and Ford could do to keep a straight face. The joke, however, would almost backfire Friday night.

+ + +

Barely twenty-three years old, Sells is a tweener: he's between the players' and other coaches' ages. He is, without a doubt, the most picked-on person in the program.

When a coach drops a legendary name from football history, he is apt to interrupt himself to ask, "You probably haven't heard of him, have you, Sells?" The players love to tease the coach by mooing his last name when the bus passes any country scenery or encounters any farm odors. Sells accepts the banter with an easy smile on his boyish, round face.

The respect, however, comes just as quickly; coaches and players alike say Sells has earned it. That does not keep Hogan from occasionally reminding Sells that twenty-three-year-olds are not supposed to be calling the plays for one of the state's best private-school offenses.

Coaching had not been a goal for Sells. He expected at this age to still be playing baseball. He received a baseball/academic scholarship to West Texas A&M University, but left school after only one season. He wanted to be near his mother, who was dealing with family issues, and he did not like West Texas. Sells says now that he believes God was pulling his heart away from baseball. He returned to the Fort Worth area, enrolled in a community college, and worked full-time at an outdoors retail store. One Friday night, he decided to attend a football game of his alma mater, Harvest Christian Academy. Harvest was playing Faith. On a halftime trip to the concession stand, he bumped into Faith assistant coach Brandon Smeltzer, whom he'd met a few years before.

Smeltzer had been a guest speaker at a high school church lock-in Sells attended in fall 2001. When Sells's mother decided to move from their hometown to one near Harvest, Sells remembered Smeltzer was coaching there at the time and wanted to attend that school. He transferred to Harvest in the spring of his junior year. In baseball, he became an all-state pitcher; in football, all-district quarterback and all-state linebacker. He was good enough on defense to be selected starter in a postseason all-star game. Oddly enough, one of the assistant coaches on that all-star team was Hogan, although the two do not recall meeting that week.

So when Sells and Smeltzer met up at halftime of that Harvest-Faith game, Smeltzer asked how things were going. Sells told him he was back home. Smeltzer, by now coaching at Faith, suggested Sells coach baseball and invited him to Faith's next game so he could introduce him to Ford, the baseball coach. What Sells had not told Smeltzer was that the outdoors retailer he worked for was opening a new store in Arizona, and he was considering pursuing a manager's position there.

Sells met Hogan and Ford at the next game, which Faith won to move into position to claim the school's first district championship. That meeting led to an interview with Ford and, over pizza in the coaches' office, Ford offered Sells a job as an assistant baseball coach. Well, sort of a job. It was a volunteer position. That was in the spring of 2006. Sells enjoyed his first experience at coaching so much that when Hogan asked Sells one day what he thought about coaching football, Sells said he could give that a try too.

Sells quickly impressed Hogan. He is what Hogan calls a "what-next guy," as in, "What next needs to be done?" "I have a list in my office on my computer, and it's a file of things that needed to be done that he did with nobody asking him," Hogan said. "He just did it. He wanted to be here. He said, 'I love sports, I love kids, I love to coach. I'll do whatever.

I'll serve at any level—junior high, JV, batboy, whatever.' But then he started doing things that nobody else wanted to do—staying late, locking up, mopping, sweeping, fixing things—doing things nobody else wanted to do, at a higher level than other people on this campus."

Hogan asked Faith president Ed Smith if a vacant full-time position could be moved to the athletic department as an assistant to the athletic director. Hogan contended that if the school would make a commitment to Sells before he completed his degree, he already would be at the school, and remain there, at the time when most schools would be ready to hire him.

"I had to have him," Hogan said. "He was a what-next type guy, and he did it at a high level. Those kind of people don't come along very often. I've coached with a lot of coaches. A lot of them. None of them that I would have hired at this stage of the game. He's just far ahead of the game."

Still, not even Hogan expected Sells to be offensive coordinator this season, especially with this being one of those special teams and seasons that don't come along often enough for head coaches. Hogan thought Sells would be a receivers' coach with freedom to offer much input to the offense. But when Hogan decided to tweak Faith's offense during the off-season—keeping the Spread formation, but changing its function—Sells not only grasped the changes but contributed greatly to the planning. Hogan decided to make Sells offensive coordinator. He was doing everything else earlier than he should have, so why not call plays a season earlier?

Sells's football knowledge and his work ethic helped him quickly gain the respect of the players. Hockenbrough admitted he was unsure about Sells's becoming offensive coordinator at such a young age for such an important season. "I thought it was going to be weird with him first coming in. I was like, 'How are we going to listen to this guy?'" But the players saw how hard he worked and how well he knew the offense. Any remaining doubts, Hockenbrough said, were erased at Mt. Lebanon. At one practice when Hogan wanted defensive players to see how aggressively he wanted them to attack, Sells donned shoulder pads and a helmet. Running back Cox took a handoff and before he could take two steps, Sells had blitzed from his linebacker position and met Cox with a head-on hit that had players rewinding and rewinding the film back at the dorm, laughing each time they watched the collision. "After that," Hockenbrough said, "we were all just like, 'Okay, Sells is the man.'"

On the sideline during games, Hogan stayed connected with Sells atop the press box, through headsets. He entered the season expecting Sells to call about 80 percent of the plays. Through the first four games, Hogan had yet to override one of Sells's play calls.

+ + +

Thoughts of payback for the previous season's loss had grown even more by Tuesday's practice. Previously during starting defense, players had been breaking out of their huddle with middle linebacker Wright saying, "Tempo! Ready?" and the players responding with, "Break!" But for this day, Wright had changed his part to "Revenge, revenge! Ready?"

After a few such huddle breaks, the defenders began playfully discussing between plays whether revenge is biblically acceptable. Perhaps, one suggested, they should say "Righteous anger."

"Revenge?" Hogan asked the first time he heard the players. "Is that biblical? The Bible says, 'Never pay back evil with evil. Respect what is right in the sight of all men. Vengeance is mine, I will repay, says the Lord.'"[1]

+ + +

About ten minutes into Open Floor Thursday, the discussion turned to Sells. "When we talked on Monday," Hockenbrough said, "I don't think anything's made me as mad this season than when I heard that their coaches were trashing Sells. That really hurt my feelings to hear that. We have a coach that's dedicated enough to drive all the way out to Gilmer to get a tape for us to watch and to scout, and to just sit there and trash him—I want to go out there tomorrow, and I want to play for everyone in this room, but a big part of that for me this week is playing for Sells."

"You said Open Floor is to encourage someone," Nerney said as he looked at Hogan. "I just want to encourage Coach Sells." Nerney then looked past Hogan to Sells. "You're a winner, Coach, and we all see it.

We all see how dedicated you are to each one of us. Just hearing them make fun of you, like Grant said, it made us all pretty mad."

Clegg continued the theme. "I think we all, as we walked out of that classroom, we all had the same look on our face. We were like, 'That did not just happen to Coach Sells.' It offended us. I remember talking to people just on the way back from the classroom to here. Coaches are a part of this team too. They're a part of us, too. They're all a part of the same body. It ticked me off, and I know it made everyone else mad. That's part of my drive tomorrow night, too. Honestly, it made me mad. You guys are just as much a part of the family—you are the head of the family."

"We're allowed to pick on you," O'Neal interjected. "They're not." The locker room erupted in laughter and voices of agreement.

Hockenbrough changed the topic to playing with class. He had liked the team's demeanor during the Millsap victory. "Let's do it like we did last week. We were real respectful last week. We helped them up when they were down." That is something Hockenbrough felt had been missing in previous weeks. Although no unsportsmanlike conduct penalties had been called or anything out of the ordinary had been visible from the stands during the early games, the players felt bad about some of the in-game talk between teams. The Millsap game, by comparison, had been much better. "We came out of that game winning," Hockenbrough continued, "and they know we deserved to win that game, and they didn't complain about it after we were done. I think we should win like that again. Honestly, I think everybody felt way better about that."

Nerney pointed out that after Faith players had started offering a hand to help Millsap players off the ground, their opponents had begun to do the same.

"After the game's over," Clegg said, "you can tell there's a different vibe. I remember Rio Vista. I left feeling like, 'Man, what is the paper going to say about us being thugs or about us being this or that?' There were a few times when we lost our cool. I'm not saying. . . . They were awful. I counted like four late hits on one play on a return one time, as I was looking out the side [of] my ear hole or whatever. I left the field feeling real uncomfortable about it." Things were different, however, against Millsap. "They were all joking around with us and stuff, and it felt a lot better. It felt like we gave Faith a good name."

Ford entered the discussion. He said the Millsap chain crew, which worked along the Faith sideline, had been complimentary of the players. Some Millsap players had told Coach Rivera after the game that Faith had been the most respectful group they had played in a long time. After the game, as the players showered and boarded the bus, a few coaches from both teams had gotten together and discussed the game. The Millsap coaches had some specific questions about Faith's offense, and the coaches agreed to exchange information via e-mail. Then Ford told the players of something he had observed from a distance before the game.

Two girls from Millsap had been trying to lift a large ice bucket near the concession stand. "I looked back and told Coach Hogan, 'I wish a couple of our guys would grab that for them,' twenty or thirty yards away from [the team]. I looked back and Tommy Rost and Weston had grabbed it for those girls." Senior Steven Little added that he had overheard the girls telling a Millsap fan that their own team would not have done that for them.

"That's what we need to do this week. Same thing," Ford said. "Kick their tails, be motivated. Kick their tails a little bit worse than we did Millsap. But represent. Be a great witness and let them, after this, be calling Sells and be asking him, 'Hey, man, would you guys be willing to send us some information? Your kids represented, your coaches represented.' If you have an opportunity to help someone there, help out."

The session had reached the half-hour mark when Hogan said he wanted to close. Earlier, he had walked across the locker room and placed a Lion-head helmet decal on the top center of the whiteboard. Now, he instructed the players to look at that decal and think about what the players mean when they say, "We are Faith." Who do they think Faith represents? Players began listing former players. Through the early part of the season, the players had talked about playing for each other. Now, Hogan wanted to give them a larger group of people to play for. "What about the parent [of a fourth grader] who lost their spouse two years ago? Told me if they could do anything in the world, their kid would be a varsity athlete at Faith. That's what their kid's goal is. I said, 'How old?' They said, 'Fourth grade.' You think that Lion means something to that guy? What about Bruce Wilson Sr., who nine years ago was praying and God told him to start a Christian school in Grapevine? Think about that." Then Hogan mentioned the Cub Club, Faith elementary school students for whom the players would be signing autographs in a few minutes. "Guys, that Lion right there is everybody in everything that has to do with Faith. That's why we put it on the helmet. Think about that. Think about an army that has a flag or something. *This is who we are, we put it right here for you to see.* That's who you are. And every time you put your helmet on, it's glowing who you are.

"That Lion represents a lot of people. A lot of people. I think when the day comes that we do anything for what that represents. What about the orphans that will now walk into eternity and now go into heaven because Faith kids were over there [on missions trips]? That's part of what that Lion represents. What about the shut-in lady who's eighty years old, who we brought her bread three years ago? She came to the Thanksgiving feast and didn't have any groceries and happened to tell someone that. So somebody from Faith, a couple of teachers, went and spent four hundred dollars, went into her house, put all the food into her house and truly when they got there, there was nothing in the house except for sugar, salt, and old spaghetti. Think about that. That represents Faith. That's the spirit of Faith. See, when the goal is clear, the price gets easy. When I think and meditate how a perfect man, Jesus Christ, who never wanted to do any harm to anybody, getting punched in the face, thorns stabbed in His head, hit with rods and [snaps his fingers] could have done that and killed everybody, and instead took it on the chin and head and everywhere else. Had His facial hair ripped out, stabbed in the side, broken ribs, beaten beyond recognition, so that His eyes were loose in their sockets—it ain't hard for me to say, 'No, I don't want a beer' to the all-star [team] coach who tries to get me to go out and have a beer with him.

"See, I'm motivated when I think about what Christ went through and what He did for me. Surely I can live for Him. I'm motivated. Any price is easy when I consider that goal. Does that make sense? When your goal is clear, you understand what that right there stands for. You'll be ready to go to battle in such a way that Reicher, Cedar Hill, Austin Regents, or anybody else in your classification has no shot to beat you. Because of how clear you know what that means, and what you're willing to pay for it. Does that make sense? That's how you derive passion. What does Faith mean to you? What does that Lion represent? Well, it represents people who have gone, people who are coming, and everybody in this room who's dressed like me. And every family who's ever touched Faith. It represents the mission of Jesus Christ. When you get that in your head, you won't need anybody to give you a speech or a pep talk. You'll knock down the door walking out to every football game. All right, let's pray."

After Hogan's prayer, Sells walked over to Clegg at his locker and gave him a hug. "I love you," Sells said. "I love you," Clegg responded as he tightened the embrace.

+ + +

The bus pulled into the Billy Bass Stadium parking lot—three hours before game time—early enough for Hogan to see sprinklers watering the field.

"Hey, you're watering the field!" he said as he bounced off the bus and greeted the Union Hill coach. The coach chuckled. Hadn't rained in forever in East Texas, he told Hogan, so they were trying to soften the hard-as-concrete field. Hogan knew what really was happening was that the coach of a big, powerful, run-it-straight-ahead team was looking for any advantage he could muster against the faster Lions. A few minutes later, the watering stopped, and Faith players began walking the field that was nowhere near hard as concrete. Roddy was wearing his red "Blood Brothers" T-shirt he had distributed to teammates during their voluntary summer workouts. "NEVER AGAIN," it said on the back. Beneath that, the first line read, "OCTOBER 6, 2006—38–42."

A couple of coaches took up a spot along the chain-link fence outside the locker room. There, a man who introduced himself as the "Booster Club President/P.A. Announcer/Griller" was firing up the grill to prepare turkey legs for the concession stand. East Texas friendly, he struck up a conversation with the coaches. Union Hill, the man said, had eighty-nine students. Although the school is known around the state as "Gilmer Union Hill" because its mailing address is from nearby Gilmer, the campus is actually closest to the community of Bettie. You won't find Bettie on many maps. In fact, the man said, for that year's Homecoming game, a pilot of a small plane had been enlisted to execute a pre-game flyover. But the pilot had trouble finding the stadium, and not until the stadium lights became visible midway through the first quarter was he able to buzz the field.

Although the school was small, its players were not. As the Bulldogs took the field for warm-ups, the sight of four players sent Faith coaches looking for the Union Hill roster. They matched their jersey numbers to their weights: 375, 349, 280, 375. They didn't even look up two of the players, weighing 241 and 245, who looked small alongside the others. After Roddy, Faith's next heaviest players were Kallal (230), Rost (230), and Ackerman (220). And to think that back home, opposing coaches had talked about Faith's big linemen.

+ + +

The players lined up along the goal line as the team captains met at midfield for the coin toss. Faith won the toss and deferred its option to kick or receive until the second half. Union Hill chose to take the ball first.

"They beat us on our Homecoming last year!" Anderson yelled as he sprinted from the coin toss toward his teammates. "All night! All night!" The players then entered their inflatable tunnel. Inside, as the smoke began to pour out from the machine, the reminders of last year's game continued. "We've got one loss at home in two years!" "Get everything back right now! Take everything back!"

Union Hill, however, took the opening kickoff and also something none of Faith's first four opponents had: a lead. After four consecutive run plays, a mix-up in the Faith secondary left the tight end wide open. A short pass turned into a 50-yard touchdown. The Bulldogs added a two-point conversion and led 8–0 three minutes into the game.

That score proved to be a mere speed bump for the Lions. Faith coaches, looking ahead to next week's district opener against Trinity Christian, had added four fake extra-point attempts to their playbook this week. Trinity Christian's speed and the Lions' struggles in blocking for extra-point kicks concerned the coaches. With next week's matchup projected to be such an even one that one missed or blocked kick could determine the winner, Faith coaches were hoping that Trinity Christian coaches would be more concerned about defending the fakes than with attempting to block kicks. The Lions had exhausted their supply of fakes only two minutes into the second quarter. All four failed miserably, in almost comical fashion. But with the Lions taking early control of the game, even their coaches could chuckle at the fakes.

While the coaches were looking ahead a week, the players continued to look back a year and, for extra motivation, to the events of the past week. Faith took a 38–8 lead with 5:48 remaining in the second quarter. "We're not quitting until we get to 70," Anderson said on the sideline. "Do it for Sells," Nathan Alcantara added.

The score remained unchanged through the rest of the half. The coaches' halftime talk was predictable. The score was 38–8 . . . but Faith had led Union Hill 38–20 at one point last year. "You've got to finish the game," Hogan told the players. "Kill the will," Ford added. "They're talking right now about last year." "The first five minutes of that third quarter is most important," Messinger told his teammates. "Show them it's over."

Union Hill recovered an onside kick to start the second half and drove forty-three yards for a touchdown that made the score 38–16. Then, for the first time, Union Hill's defense forced the Lions to send their punt team onto the field. Surely not again this year? But Faith shut down any possibility of another Union Hill comeback by recovering a fumble on that punt. On the first play after the turnover, Anderson fired a 25-yard touchdown strike to Reeder for a 45–16 lead. Another Bulldogs fumble led to another Lions touchdown and a thirty-seven-point lead. "We're making them like it," Clegg told Reeder on the sideline.

With a little more than a minute left in the third quarter, the referee signaled to the clock operator to keep the clock running. The score had gotten out of hand. Tempers almost got out of hand too. Midway through the fourth quarter, Union Hill's quarterback broke free for a 46-yard touchdown run. Behind the play, a Bulldogs lineman began shoving Faith's John Elder. Elder turned and walked away. But the opposing player took a run toward Elder, and mild-mannered Ackerman stepped in front of the charging player, who grabbed Ackerman's face mask and pushed until his helmet came off. Ackerman did not retaliate. This all happened in front of the referee, who threw his penalty flag into the air and ejected the Union Hill player. Hogan gathered his players before the following kickoff. "Number 60 got ejected for being an idiot," he told them. "Don't do that kind of junk to them. Play hard. The scoreboard will be burned into their minds." In other words, let the scoreboard do the talking—and at 60–24, the scoreboard was saying plenty.

And that's when the prank e-mails almost backfired on Hogan. Sells, who had left his coaches' booth in the press box to join the team on the sideline, called only running plays on Faith's final possession. But even with backups in the game, the Lions drove to Union Hill's 10. With the clock running, Faith would have time for one more play. Thinking of the teasing he had absorbed during the film exchange and the e-mails that had followed, which he had become even more convinced actually were from the Union Hill coach, Sells muttered, "I want to score a touchdown." So he called a running play for Ashton. After the play went in, Hogan asked for the play call. Sells told him. "That sucker will score!" Hogan said with alarm, as he started running down the sideline to get an official's attention and call time-out. Time-out called, he instructed Ashton to take a knee for the final play, and the score remained 60–24.

It was the first time all season Hogan had changed a play called by his rookie offensive coordinator.

CHAPTER 12

No Doubt

GAME 6: TRINITY CHRISTIAN–CEDAR HILL TIGERS
Weston Clegg walked up to the newspaper article taped to the locker room whiteboard. "TC–Cedar Hill remains unbeaten," the headline read. It was the story from the previous season's game in which Trinity Christian had defeated the Lions 31–7. Clegg grabbed a black marker and wrote above the article, "We'll see." He underlined his words and returned to his locker, music playing through his iPod as he sat to resume his pre-game routine of mentally preparing for another game. Except this was not just another game. This was the district opener against the rival Tigers. It was *the* game the Lions had been waiting for.

+ + +

"First of all," Hogan began his Monday scouting report, "we're going to beat Cedar Hill if you do what we tell you to do. We're going to kick their stinking tail. We've watched them on film. I know everything about them." The players perked up at that proclamation.

Hogan is a confident man. When he makes a decision, rest assured that he has researched, analyzed, and considered every possibility. He had researched, analyzed, and considered every possibility concerning the Trinity Christian game, and he had decided that the first thing his players needed was to see him this confident. He and the coaches would not tolerate any appearance of doubt this week, and he set that tone before the first time his players hit the practice field.

Hogan pointed his capped marker toward the whiteboard. While the players filed into the room, still in their school dress shirts and slacks, Hogan had been busily drawing the X's and O's of his plan for stopping Trinity Christian's offense, led by number 20, running back Dominique Rambo. Rambo, Hogan told the players, had accounted for 82 percent of Trinity Christian's offense. Rambo had played in four of the Tigers' five non-district games and had rushed for more than seven hundred yards with eight touchdowns. Twice, he had darted through and around opponents for more than two hundred yards. The night when Hogan, Ford, and Sells watched in person as Trinity Christian had suffered its only defeat, Rambo had rushed for 293 yards. "The real deal," Faith coaches had called him. Yet Hogan pointed to his defensive game plan and confidently stated, "I promise you guys, they are not going to run the football on us." Again, the players' postures reflected their coach's confidence.

That confidence carried over to the practice field, where the pass offense had what Anderson called its best practice session since preseason two-a-days. Then at five o'clock, with an hour of practice remaining, the confidence carried over into the gymnasium when the lightning meter sent the team indoors. "Hey, take this serious," Ford said as practice resumed indoors. An apt admonition, with Wright in sandals and Messinger and Nerney "attacking" Trinity Christian's offensive formations on a basketball court while wearing brightly colored Crocs to protect the floor. At least above their footwear, the players were serious.

"There is a much better vibe this year," Clegg said from the bleachers as he watched the defense. "Last year, I went into the game thinking it's going to be a close game. This year, the vibe is much more positive."

The tone had been set.

+ + +

But Tuesday, the week's first practice in full pads, did not go well. The offense performed so poorly that Hogan called for an extra set of sixteen plays. The first extra play was a pass from Anderson to Nerney. The pass fell incomplete. Hogan took Anderson with him to meet briefly with Nerney away from the rest of the offense. Talk completed, Hogan returned to his customary place behind the offense.

The offense looked better through the final round of plays, but when the last play did not meet Hogan's liking, he told his players, "We're not going to end on a screwup." It took two more plays to satisfy the coach. When the practice switched from offense to defense, the defense, too, failed to satisfy Hogan. "More intense now, isn't it?" Alcantara noted.

About the only thing the coaches praised during the defensive portion of practice was the performance of Tanner Gesek. Gesek was playing the role of Rambo for the week, simulating Trinity Christian's star running back. "Tanner may be faster than Rambo," coach Postema said to Ford. "It'd be a good race," Ford replied.

The coaches had struggled to find a position for the junior on a senior-filled team with roles mostly defined before even the first practice. At first they had placed Gesek at receiver but hadn't been sure he had the catching ability for that position. He also had worked at defensive back, where his speed could be an asset in coverage skills. Indeed, he had displayed flashes of what the coaches had expected at that position, but his inexperience also showed. Cornerbacks in Faith's defense are asked to cover opposing players one-on-one, with no help, and one mistake in coverage could yield a touchdown.

Gesek had made it into the offensive backfield late in the Union Hill blowout, even though he had not practiced at running back. He didn't know the plays from that position, so teammates pointed him in the right direction. He received three carries that game, rushing for sixteen yards and Faith's eighth and final touchdown.

He had called home afterward to tell his father he had scored. "I thought it was really cool," Gesek said. Then he watched the game film with the rest of the team the next morning and noticed he had scored on a 1-yard run. "That was nothing," he said with a laugh.

What he was doing at scout-team running back this week, though, was far from nothing. Although he thought coaches had made him Rambo's stand-in only because he was fast, he still embraced the role of helping the defense prepare for likely the best running back they would see all season. But it was not the contribution Gesek had hoped to make. He wanted to offer more.

Gesek's father, John, played nine seasons in the National Football League. An offensive lineman, he won Super Bowl rings with the Dallas Cowboys in the 1992 and 1993 seasons. Gesek grew up around sons of other NFL players. He had watched some battle the pressures of living up to their fathers' football accomplishments. "I know a lot of people," he said, "who were really pressured from their dads to live up to their legacy and walk in their steps." But it was different for Gesek. "My dad—I don't know, I never really felt that pressure. I always felt pressure to be in a sport, but I never felt pressure to be the best. I just knew my parents expected me to be in a sport, to be physically active, and to be healthy. Basically, that's the only pressure I got from them about it."

Gesek's parents insist that he and his three younger sisters participate in sports so that they can be well-rounded physically, spiritually, and mentally. The sport is their choosing. Tanner played various sports growing up—soccer, basketball, baseball. His father saw a kid with athletic potential at an early age. For one, he was fast. Superfast, actually. And sports came easily to him.

It was at that point that the parental expectations—the shadow of a father's legacy that Gesek had observed other teenagers struggle through—could have started to become a son's burden. Instead, John Gesek points to one realization about his son that has guided him as a sports dad. "I think a long time ago, and this is when he was young, I realized that he wasn't the same person as I was," John Gesek said. "He wasn't just a mini-me."

Although he saw an above-average athlete, the father also saw a kid who took to music at an early age, who loved to read and to write. Cerebral, yes. Aggressive, no. So when Tanner was young, his father reached a conclusion that was difficult at first to accept as a former NFL player: football would not be his son's sport too. He actually encouraged his son to play sports other than football.

Tanner played football at Faith in seventh, eighth, and ninth grades, saying he "just kind of bounced around." He was more interested in music, becoming accomplished enough as a pianist to play at weddings and teach lessons. He learned to play three other instruments and started a band with friends. "We were terrible," he said. But he enjoyed music and hanging out with his friends most. "Sports, for some reason, never was a huge part of things."

He quit football after his ninth-grade season. "I was kind of demoralized, just kind of sick of football." To stay in sports and to be physically active, he joined a lacrosse club outside of school. Throughout Gesek's sophomore year, Sells kept talking to him about rejoining the program. Gesek's speed and natural ability sure were appealing to coaches who built a program around speedy players. Gesek kept resisting. He enjoyed lacrosse, and he was excelling. Lacrosse proved a good fit because of his speed and because, other than stick-checking, it does not require an aggressive personality. And, also to its advantage, lacrosse was not football.

Hogan overheard some of Sells's conversations with Gesek. He, too, talked to Tanner about playing football. Hogan could see a kid who he thought was being trained right by his father. He could see that his father had not burdened Tanner with the pressure of excelling in his own sport. But still, when Gesek said he did not want to play football, Hogan could sense behind the claims a concern about not living up to what he perceived to be his dad's expectations if he did play. "It seemed like in the back of every answer," Hogan recalled, "was, 'I want to, but what if it doesn't work out?'"

Over the summer, though, Gesek began to consider playing football again. He really had enjoyed being around the guys in the locker room. Plus, he had hit a bit of a growth spurt. His father was six-foot-five, his mother five-two—and Gesek had always been closer to his mother's height. But now he was five-ten and 165 pounds. Although not hulking by any stretch, at least he would no longer be one of the smallest players. In the final two weeks leading up to practice, he decided to give football one more shot. From the first day of practice, his speed and athletic ability stood out. At times, so did the rust from his year away from football.

The coaches had yet to find the right position for him. As a result, his playing time was limited to going in with special teams and late during blowouts. His father would watch his son standing on the sideline. John Gesek knew what his son was thinking: that he was letting his team—his friends—down by not contributing more. "It just kills me to see him standing there. As a father, I've had to deal with that part of it. It's not so much that I had these expectations of him. It's just that I know how disappointed he was, and that hurts me more than anything else." Worst of all, John Gesek added, "there's nothing I can do to make it better."

Now, five games into the season, Tanner Gesek was making his biggest contribution to this point. In practice, of all places. Simulating an opposing player, of all things.

"It really didn't click at first because I was still involved in *me* and, like, 'Dang, this hurts a little bit,'" Gesek said of being the opposing running back. "But then when I got past, 'Okay, I'm getting hit, it's no big deal'—when I got past that, then it was like, 'Now I need to be working hard enough, I need to be accurately simulating what the other team's running back is going to be doing. If I'm not, I'm just running for me. That's cool, maybe I'll get a little better. But it's not going to help the defense, and that's why I'm here.'"

+ + +

"I just want to say something," O'Neal said in his customary introductory manner during Open Floor Thursday. He called out Gesek's name. "He's really stepped up from the beginning of the season. I know he was in a little bit and he didn't play that big of a role. In practice, even though he doesn't start on offense, he plays that scout-team offense, and he plays it like it's game speed. And he gives us the reps we need. I know he's helped me a lot this week. I think I'm going to be ready because he's done a good job at running back. The reads are going to be similar in the game because he's giving his all. Even though he knows he's not going to be playing that much, he's giving it all, all week. I've seen that all week. And even all season. Even when he's not in the game, he's practicing full speed like it is the game. I just want to recognize him for doing that."

Hogan smiled at a scout-team player giving his best effort for the team and a starter recognizing and commending those contributions. The day before, Hogan had stopped Gesek as he drove out of the field house parking lot and thanked him for his efforts. Hogan didn't believe Trinity Christian's players had seen any simulations of Faith's starters in their practices near the level of what they would see Friday night.

He had watched his defensive ends have to hustle to pursue Gesek on Rambo's outside runs and knew his team had gained an advantage over its opponent, largely because of the efforts of unheralded players such as Gesek. "That's a good point," Hogan said to O'Neal. "You can't overlook that. That's a good point."

+ + +

At 5:15 p.m., more than two hours before game time, players were making their usual pre-game strolls on their home field. Unlike previous games, however, there was no talking. The only sounds came from feet shuffling on the grass and thrown balls hitting hands. The Lions had not played a team of Trinity Christian's ability this season, and their pre-game concentration level reflected that.

Reeder sat alone near the top of the home stands, looking over the field. Down on the field, Anderson was barefoot, throwing 25-yard passes to Jameson. Clegg was squatting on the Lion head at midfield, hands cupped around his forehead, eyes staring straight through the thick grass, "Your Hand in Mine" playing over and over on his iPod; the three-and-a-half minute instrumental from the movie *Friday Night Lights* was all he listened to before games. Nerney and Wright walked over to the seats, where they sat apart from each other, not acknowledging each other's presence, each deep in his own pre-game focus. Messinger pounded the grass with his feet, blocking imaginary defenders. Hockenbrough strolled around the field, hands tucked into his tan shorts pockets, toothpick dangling from his lips.

The only words were Hogan's as he surveyed the scene. Red plastic cups spelled out "FAITH LIONS" on the chain-link fence facing the nearby street. Eight white Lions flags, with the team's red helmet logo, flapped in the wind atop the home stands. There was a definite big-game feel. "This is a great venue, isn't it?" Hogan asked, already knowing the answer.

As game time neared, a visitor entered the locker room carrying a television camera. A local high school football highlights show had selected this game as the Metroplex's Game of the Week for private schools. The camera's light came on as Hogan walked into the locker room to address his team.

"Are we ready to go?"

"Yes, sir," the players replied.

"I'll tell you what. You know what our theme is this season. It's 'Sold Out.' Here's what I want you to do. For four quarters—for four quarters—I want you to sell out at one speed. That's the key to tonight's game: one speed. If you run a 4.6, that's what you've got to play at. Remember we talked about unit speed? Overwhelming people? That's what it's about tonight." He pointed to the Lion head on the dry-erase board. "You sell out for everybody this represents, at one speed. You don't need a pep talk from me tonight; you just need me to turn you loose." The cameraman smiled, knowing he had just recorded a great sound bite for the next morning's show.

Anderson paced the sidewalk as teammates finished putting on their cleats outside the field house, with packs of fans passing by toward the stands. "Forty-eight minutes of Sold Out!" Anderson yelled. "I'm playing for you guys—Sold Out."

Much quieter, with helmet strapped on, Shivers said, "We've waited 364 days to prove ourselves."

With that, the single-file line marched around the corner of the field house, past the concession stand, through the smoke of the aromatic "Faith Burgers" cooking on the grills, and to the field. This was the game they had been waiting for, and they were confident this would be the night they would prove themselves.

+ + +

Faith's defense was immediately tested, with Rambo and the Trinity Christian offense receiving the ball first. The Tigers' first series, as expected, featured Rambo. On first down from their 28, Rambo ran off right tackle for four yards. The next play, he went through the left side of the line for three yards. On third and three, for the first time, the Tiger coaches attempted to spring Rambo free outside with a toss play. Nerney, having seen similar speed from Gesek all week in practice, prevented Rambo from reaching the corner, stopping Trinity Christian for no gain.

The Tigers punted to the Lions' 20. On the Lions' first offensive play, Anderson dropped the snap, picked the ball up off the grass, and was met by two hard-charging Tigers defenders for an 8-yard loss. Just like that, the Lions faced second and long from their own 12.

Sells sent in a running play. Anderson faked a handoff and darted through a big opening in the middle of the field, then broke left toward the Lions' sideline. He picked up a big block from Jameson, the receiver blocking downfield, broke two tackles along the sideline, received another block from Reeder, another receiver downfield, and eased into the Tigers' end zone. Clegg, the third of Faith's four receivers, had pursued the play all eighty-eight yards, looking for someone to block.

"When I saw the other receivers downfield blocking for Landon," Clegg said later, "I knew there was no way we would lose this game."

Both teams scored touchdowns on their next possessions. Rambo ran on three consecutive plays for twenty-eight yards to set up a 44-yard touchdown pass that tied the score at 7 less than five minutes into the first quarter. The Lions answered with a methodical twelve-play, 71-yard drive, with Anderson throwing a 14-yard touchdown pass to Jameson that made the score 14–7 Faith.

Again, Trinity Christian's offense came right back. Rambo carried the ball on seven of eight plays, capped by his 21-yard scoring run to tie the score at 14 with 8:28 left until halftime.

After Faith had a field-goal attempt blocked and Trinity Christian punted, Faith gained possession at its own 45. The Lions' third touchdown came quickly. Dunnington carried eighteen yards, with a 15-yard face mask penalty against the Tigers tacked on. Anderson kept for nine yards and Dunnington then raced into the middle of the end zone from twelve yards out for a 21–14 lead with 4:17 remaining in the half.

A defensive stop gave Faith one more possession in the half, starting at its own 30 yard line with 1:44 showing on the clock. There was no way Hogan was not going to press the accelerator as his offense took the field. Mixing runs and passes, the Lions reached the Trinity Christian 4 with twenty-two seconds left. Following a time-out, Reeder made a sliding catch in the right corner of the end zone. The Lions had covered seventy yards in eighty-six seconds to lead 28–14 at halftime.

Hogan addressed his squad in the locker room. There are four quarters in a game, he reminded them. Trinity Christian is good, a physical team, so his players could not let up. And once more, he referred to the previous season's game against Union Hill. "I almost feel like we were trained last year for this. That Union Hill thing, I'll never forget that, and I know you won't either. It's four quarters."

When Hogan finished, Anderson stood up. "Right now," he said to his teammates as he looked around the locker room, "is when Blood Brothers takes over." To Anderson, those voluntary summer workouts also were training for this moment. "All that extra work, it takes over right now."

A Faith fumble to start the second half, though, set up a Trinity Christian touchdown pass that made the score 28–21. The Lions absorbed the body blow and came out swinging. They needed but six plays—all running plays with big Trinity penalties for unsportsmanlike conduct and a face mask added in—to march fifty-five yards to the Tigers' end zone and push their lead back to fourteen points.

Faith's lead grew to 42–21 on an Anderson 14-yard run on the first play of the fourth quarter. That would be the final score, and as the final seconds ticked away, students ran onto the field to celebrate. Players hugged and high-fived each other as though it were a playoff game. In many ways for the Faith Lions, considering the loss they had suffered to this team the previous season, this was a playoff game.

After the teams had lined up and congratulated one another, Hogan gathered his players on the Lion head at midfield. "How do you guys feel today?" The players responded with whoops and hollers. "Hey," Hogan continued, "you guys played a great game—a great game. I want to point out something about this game, and I don't want you to forget it. This game should indicate to you that you are in total control of your future. Not a bad bounce, not a set of officials, not a [bad] weather game. You control what happens to you. I told you you'd be in position to win, and you executed, and that's why you won. We took care of personal responsibility. You'll see on the film, time after time after time after time, one guy intent on his job. And you do that eleven times and you kick people's tail, doesn't matter who they are. That's just the way it is. And that's the way it is with this group. You control your destiny. Don't forget that."

Later on the coaches looked over the game's final stats. Faith had rushed for an incredible 416 yards; Anderson alone had accounted for 228. The coaches never anticipated accumulating those kinds of totals against Trinity's defense. On the other side, Faith's defense had basically shut down the mighty Rambo. He had rushed for 101 yards—the coaches regretted that it couldn't have been less than one hundred—but he had needed twenty-four carries to do so, for barely four yards per carry. Throw in the negative three yards Rambo had on three receptions, and Rambo had finished the game with ninety-eight total yards. It didn't seem possible, but the coaches' smiles had just grown wider.

+ + +

When the Saturday morning film session wrapped up, players stood from their seats on their footlockers and started to head home for the rest of the weekend. Tommy Rost walked up to the whiteboard. The story from last year's loss to the Tigers remained in place. Rost read the headline: "TC–Cedar Hill remains unbeaten." He grabbed the black marker and drew a line through "TC–Cedar Hill." In its place, he penned "FCS."

This season, it was Faith Christian that remained unbeaten.

CHAPTER 13

Measures of Respect

GAME 7: PANTEGO CHRISTIAN PANTHERS

The opposing coaches shook hands at midfield forty-five minutes before kickoff. "You're the class of Division III," Pantego Christian Academy coach Steve Hohulin told Hogan. "Thank you," Hogan replied. Hohulin handed the Faith program a series of other compliments during their chat. The programs share a common respect for each other, particularly in regard to that often elusive quality of class. Some programs succeed at being competitive, some at displaying class. Hogan does not understand why more schools are not successful at both, as Pantego is. In his first season at Faith, he saw in Hohulin a coach who recognized that life is bigger than football. "While he's competitive, his kids play with class," Hogan said. "They're clearly instructed before competition on how to act. Clearly. And I know that you have to be intentional for that."

Hogan had told his players to expect Pantego's best effort. Actually, he told his players that about every opponent this season; the state's top-ranked team might as well sew big, fat targets on its uniforms, because every game was a potential season maker for an upset-minded opponent. But there was a different reason for Hogan's warning this week.

The Panthers had played in four state championship games under

Hohulin, winning the title in 1997, and there was a time when Faith coaches looked at a game against Pantego as a measuring stick.

In 2004, Hogan's second season at Faith, the teams met in Week 8. The Panthers were not only leading the district race, they were also undefeated. The Lions, 4–4 overall, had split their two district games. Pantego defeated Faith 52–29. Hogan still remembers that Pantego's players had conducted themselves as well as they had played and that Hohulin had offered encouraging words to Faith, saying the coaches were building their program the right way.

Faith quickly rose to Pantego's competitive level. The following season, the Lions were undefeated heading into the teams' meeting, eight games into the season. Pantego led Faith 12–7 at halftime. It was the first time Faith had trailed at halftime all season. But the Lions scored thirty-six points in the second half and won 43–18. That was the season Faith advanced to the state semifinals for the first time.

In 2006, at The Jungle, it was the Lions who led at halftime, 25–7. Pantego came back with thirteen fourth-quarter points before Faith held on for a 25–20 win. Faith and Pantego met again four weeks later in the second round of the playoffs. The result was stunning—a 58–0 Faith victory.

Faith players had heard from friends at Pantego that after that loss, Panthers players created a "58 Reasons" motto as motivation for their off-season work. Lions players expected Pantego's best effort. They also eagerly anticipated a good, clean, hard-fought game. After the players had reviewed the Trinity Christian game film Saturday morning, they exchanged stories of the profanity their opponents had used and some of the names they had been called during the game. Faith players knew that would not occur with this week's opponent, and that is why many described Pantego as their favorite opponent. "I've got a lot of respect for Pantego," Clegg said.

Pantego's is a proud program, and proud programs are eager to make up for their losses. To find an example, the Lions had to look back no further than their previous week's win. Clegg made that comparison during Open Floor Thursday, reminding his teammates how much they had wanted to defeat Trinity Christian after last year's 31–7 loss. "Last time we were on the field with Pantego, we beat them 58–0," Clegg said. "How do you think they feel? So, they're putting so much energy into this game almost like we put into Cedar Hill. I think it goes in the same category as we're going to get everybody's best game, stuff like that. But they are mad. We embarrassed them last year. We made them look like they shouldn't have been in the postseason. Just keep that same mentality that they are going to be so fired up like we were for Cedar Hill."

Hogan admitted to being uneasy during pre-game warm-ups. The Panthers were young, much less experienced than Faith. Their quarterback, Nathan Hohulin, was a sophomore. Pantego had gone 4–1 in non-district play but suffered a 53–14 loss the previous week to Reicher Catholic to start district play. During Monday's scouting report, Hogan had told his players that they held a decisive speed advantage over Pantego. But what he had not told his players, or even his assistant coaches, at any point during the week was that Pantego's offensive scheme matched up well with his defense. "My concern," Hogan said, "is that they can get five or six yards a pop and keep our offense off the field."

That made a fast start—the "get off" Hogan emphasizes—even more important. Lions players talked in Open Floor about how, if they could get off to a 14–0 lead, perhaps 21–0, early, doubt would take over in their opponents' minds. After the physical and emotional Trinity Christian game, the Lions sure could use a game that was in hand by the fourth quarter. So could Hogan's pre-game nerves.

A half hour before kickoff, there was no doubt that the host team was spirited. The thirty-nine players in black jerseys, pants, and helmets, loudly spelled out "P-A-N-T-H-E-R-S" during jumping-jack exercises. Faith players took notice.

Anderson completed a pass during offensive drills. "You can't stop that no matter how hard you yell," Anderson said only loud enough for his teammates to hear. "We don't need that," Hockenbrough said as he looked toward the opposite end of the field. But Hogan thought the Lions needed something. They did not look crisp. Hogan stopped warm-ups and called his team to him. A gut feeling told him to tell his players about his conversation with the Pantego coach.

"He said, 'I'd love to tell your kids congratulations on where they've come from, because we used to think you guys—we ignored you in preseason,'" Hogan related. "'Now you're the class of Division III, in my opinion.' And, he said, 'You're like real Christians.'"

Hohulin had gone on to say that Faith's quarterback, Anderson, had been sending Pantego's quarterback—his own son— uplifting messages via Facebook. "He said, 'I can't tell you what that says about your program.'" Then Hogan shared something else Hohulin had told him, something Hogan thought his players especially needed to hear now: "'Our kids will play so hard tonight, it will shock all of our coaches.' He said, 'They want to beat you guys so bad.' He said they have been locked in this week. He was giving me a compliment, but he was also reaffirming. I told you. I told you. They're going to be ready.'"

+ + +

It is a double blessing for a coach to receive motivation for his team and affirmation for his program in the same conversation. To Hogan, the affirmation meant more. Despite the impressive record his teams have accumulated, Hogan does not judge programs by wins and losses. "I just don't reckon success with the final score. I mean, you can only ask a team to reach their potential. You can't ask them to beat everybody."

Pick a school, any school, even Faith, out of the Saturday morning sports section, and there will be parents at that school who do not share that belief. But Hogan says he doesn't care. "I have dealt with human beings for a long time at one level or another, and I recognize that people are going to have certain perceptions that are inaccurate, and they're always going to be there. So I can choose to knock my head against a wall, continue lobbying for something that maybe doesn't even need to be lobbied for, or I can do what I know is right. I just choose the third one because I don't have enough time or energy to battle the other stuff."

Those battles, he is convinced, make it difficult for coaches who want to win the right way.

"I would say about half the coaches have a difficult time keeping it in perspective," he said. "And of the ones that say they want to keep it in perspective, you still probably have about 30 percent of them that don't. The thing is, it depends—and this sounds terrible, but it's reality—it depends on whether they've just won or lost."

And that, he believes, is completely attributable to external pressures. He knows it is difficult, because the large majority of coaches' jobs depend on the outcome of games. Coaching is their livelihood. In Texas at the state's larger public schools, coaching can be a high-paying livelihood. In 2006, an *Austin American-Statesman* survey found that head football coaches in the state's two largest classifications had an average salary of $73,804, which was about $31,000 more than the average teacher's salary at those same schools. The newspaper reported that twenty-seven coaches had higher salaries than their school's principal. Five coaches in Texas earned more than $100,000 per year.

Coaching, Hogan summarized, "is serious business." He has been offered chances to coach at schools where football is serious business and the pay is higher than at Faith; in some cases, much higher. But Hogan considers Faith the place where God wants him at this point in his life. Football is ministry for Hogan. He does not judge his program by wins and losses, and neither, he said, does his boss. Faith football, by Hogan's design, exists to fulfill the school's mission statement: "To develop and graduate authentic Christian leaders."

That is a sign of Hogan's maturation, both as a Christian and as a coach. Hogan says that after he became a Christian at age eleven, he still carried a skewed perspective on winning and losing. It wasn't until his second year as a head coach that he understood proper perspective.

His first team at Sacred Heart lost all ten of its games. But whereas he had expected to go 0–10 that season, he saw the potential to win games in the next. So his first season was one of instilling his philosophy in the program—and weeding out players who weren't giving maximum effort, players he didn't think could help him win the next season. "That was more important than winning and losing that year, because I was building for the future. But my not caring about 0–10 was still driven by winning."

The looking-ahead work of that winless first season paid off quickly. Midway through his second season there, Sacred Heart was better than expected. But during a morning devotional in Hogan's office, with his head down on his wooden desk, "God brought to my attention that I made the right decision but for the wrong reason. And the decision [should have been] not to tolerate all those people because they weren't giving their God-given best effort. They weren't honoring His creative power in them. They were squandering, being poor stewards of their ability. And if I would have gotten rid of them because of their effort, it would have been more honoring to Him. It was the right decision, but it would have been honoring to Him if I had gotten rid of them for the right reason, not because of winning. And then He kind of showed me over the course of a few weeks that the by-product is winning. But first-things-first is effort with what you've been given."

The transformation began that morning. Still, Hogan said, he continues to mature as a Christian and a coach and continues to hone that perspective. For the most part, he has found it easy; the difficult times come when his team loses to an inferior opponent. In those cases, he looks first to himself to see if he could have done something to prevent the loss, to see if he had let his players down with his performance. "If we lose a game that we shouldn't lose, I feel like I've somehow let people down." He admits that's judging his performance by result, but he acknowledges that the root is in giving his best effort. He believes that now, because of what he learned on that quiet morning in a tiny Catholic school, his motivation is right.

+ + +

As Faith players had suspected could happen, a fast start did deflate their opponent. The Lions scored on three of their first four possessions to take a 20–0 lead by the end of the first quarter. The lead was at 26–0 when a Pantego punt gave Faith the ball at its 29 yard line with 1:14 left until halftime and all three time-outs available.

Although Faith was in control, this situation offered an opportunity to run its two-minute, hurry-up offense. There could be a playoff game down the road, with a closer score, when the offense's ability to drive the length of the field late in a half could mean the difference between the season continuing and ending. Perhaps even winning the state championship.

Anderson worked the offense to near perfection, putting the Lions in the end zone with a 16-yard run with six seconds to spare. Messinger's extra point gave Faith a 33–0 halftime lead.

The drive had Hogan pumped up as he entered the locker room. "The drive at the end of the half—great job. Championship drive," he told his players. "Guys, let me tell you something. There was a minute-fourteen on the clock. Let me tell you something. With our team as we sit today, a minute-fourteen and three time-outs, there's not a field too long in this country. We can be this far from the goal line, a minute-fourteen with three time-outs is an eternity for us. So don't worry about time ever. I hope that drive teaches you a lesson. No field is too long for this team."

Hogan's tone softened, his voice lowered slightly. "Last thing, we're going to be in a position here in the second half to really show our colors. Let me tell you something. They are looking at us right now, and they're remembering 58–0. I just got called on the carpet by one of their fans who knows nothing about football, telling me I should have taken a knee because they can't score on you, and I didn't have any class. Here's the deal. They have a bunch of people over there. And he just kept on saying, 'Class, no class, no class,' as I'm walking off. I don't care what they say about me—if anything, *That guy's a jerk, but boy he's got good kids.* That's fine with me. I want you guys to help them up. Listen, 33–0. They just got hammered last week. They remember 58–0." With the score lopsided, Hogan knew fans' focus in the second half would shift away from plays and strategy. The behavior and actions of both teams would stand out more. Now, he told his players, would be an extra opportunity to demonstrate their Christianity. "Listen, that's a great school. They're great kids, great parents, they're great Christians. Take the opportunity to show your class."

Faith won 47–0. As the teams lined up to shake hands, Hogan told his players, "Pick these guys up. They're down a little bit."

The teams went their separate ways to pray. Hogan briefly addressed his players. "We are going to hang around, intentionally, just a little bit. I want to hang around and kind of intermingle with these guys and love on them a little bit. I don't know why they didn't pray with us. Probably not their decision. But we need to pick these guys up. They're a class program. They do things right. Okay, let's pray. You guys did a great job. Good win. No embarrassment for them, but we got a shutout. Exactly what we wanted to do. Make sure you go over there and love on them before we leave."

Faith's players sought out Pantego players, exchanging handshakes and encouraging words. Nerney asked one about Reicher. "You'll beat them," the Pantego player responded. "Reicher's good, but if you play like you did tonight, you'll beat them."

CHAPTER 14

Lesson in Courage

GAME 8: TEMPLE CHRISTIAN EAGLES

Coaches dislike Homecoming week. There are distractions galore all week, such as working on parade floats, preparing for the Homecoming dance, deciding who to ask to the dance and how to ask. Considering all the potential distractions, Temple Christian made a good Homecoming opponent: the Eagles had lost all seven of their games, with only two decided by fewer than twenty-one points.

To close Tuesday's practice, Hogan made distractions the theme of his exhortation, though not in relation to the upcoming game.

"I want you to consider the law of subtraction," Hogan told his players. "Take a look at your calendar, your day planner, what you do on a daily basis. If there's anything that you can scratch off, you need to scratch it off. Distractions are going to come in, and they're going to affect your schoolwork, your football team. There's only a few things in life that really matter. Just a few that really matter, guys. If I said you could have four things—just four things—you could choose them, you could keep them, what you would put on that list is really all that matters. Four doesn't seem like a very big number, but after securing your eternal destination, everything else is a distant third place after your family. It's way back there, isn't it? Should be, anyway. There's just a few things in life that matter. Just a few. For instance, what other people think about you really doesn't matter that much so long as you're doing what you know to be right. How much money is in your account doesn't matter that much. Just doesn't matter. Life's about relationships."

Hogan instructed his players to determine two or three areas in which to specialize, then give maximum effort in those areas. "All great people exercise the law of subtraction," he concluded. "They commit to a few things, and they're better than everybody else at those."

+ + +

The week's practices were casual. The Lions even worked on a different defense for the Reicher Catholic game three weeks away. There was no need for anything out of the ordinary against Temple Christian. A big talent gap existed between the teams, and Faith should be able to easily win the Homecoming game with its basic offense and defense.

The more serious lessons during the week dealt with life. Wednesday's practice ended with another non-football exhortation. Players were on the game field, on one knee at the goal line. Hogan stood in front of them, facing the practice field.

"I want to talk to you about how you think, in terms of a word," Hogan began. "The word is *courage*. It takes some courage to play football the right way. Because if you do it right, there will be some minor inconveniences of pain. If you're good, it takes courage. It takes courage to be good at most sports, but football's really Spartan-like. You know; you play it every day. And even if you are a super, Division I genetic freak, if you don't have courage, you can't play in college, even at a small level. It's really tough to play this game without courage. I want to talk to you, though, about a different kind of courage that you may not consider."

Hogan asked the players to contemplate the courage it takes to be a Christian. It takes more courage, he told them, to be a Christian than an agnostic, or an atheist, or someone who possesses a live-and-let-live philosophy, who avoids making difficult decisions. There are Christians around the world who are beaten because they refuse to renounce Christ, Hogan said. Christians make a difference; people who are neutral do not. "You have to be different. No great person has ever been with the crowd. Ever. There's not one in history who's ever been with the crowd. They always walk against the flow. Always."

That type of person constantly encounters friction, Hogan continued. He always defends his stance. He gets stabbed in the back. "To me, that's the person with courage. A crowd is where a coward goes to hide, because he can't stand up. You say, what does that have to do with Christianity? Think about some of the things you may consider hard. You might consider it hard to share your faith. Especially with your cool buddies around. You might think that's hard. See, that's not nearly as easy as grabbing a beer and fitting in and drinking. Not *nearly* as easy. Okay?

"What about this one? What about praying for someone that you know hates your guts? When's the last time you did that? That's what Christians are called to do. What about standing up in a crowd of people that you really, really want to fit in with and stopping some action that you don't agree with? Pretty difficult, isn't it?

"So who does have the hard road? Where does it take more courage? I can argue against anyone: it takes a lot more courage to be a Christian teenager than it does to be anything else on this planet. Because you guys are moral wimps most of the time—and I'm talking about your age, not you. But teenagers are moral sissies. They just cannot—because of their need for approval, they just cannot look another person in the eye and say, 'Hey, man, I'm not going to drink. You know I don't drink. Why do you do that?'" Hogan banged his right hand against a player's shoulder pad for effect. "'Quit being stupid.' And then if everybody's against them, they say, 'Oh, okay.'

"You can't do that at this age. You don't do it very well. I know a lot of adults who can't do that. So tell me who you think it takes more courage to be. I'm telling you right now, it's a man of God who can override any crowd. 'I value what God thinks about something more than your opinion of it. Listen, if you have a hard time with that, go be somebody else's friend, sucker.' People can't do that. That's the great thing about where we are and what we do."

Hogan pointed at Nerney to illustrate what it would be like if he could make that type of stand with the knowledge that his teammates would support him, that none would turn their back on him or his actions. "Listen," Hogan continued, "I don't have as many personal friends that are as tight as are sitting in this group. I just have a few because people can't tolerate me. Okay. I don't mind that, because the people that can tolerate me, we are like this"—he held up his thumb and forefinger close together—"and they would take a bullet for me any day. Quantity versus quality. I'd rather have quality any day of the week. If you ever have a support group in your life that looks like this, this big"—he motioned his hand over the team—"you'll be way ahead of the crowd. Way ahead of the crowd. That's why in [First] Corinthians it says don't neglect coming together as a body. You're going to need each other, because most of the time you're by yourself. Go ask your dad who he works with and how they act. Just ask him. I'll bet you he doesn't have a support group like you have."

He went on, "Nerney shouldn't need anybody else, with this group right here around him. That's what makes it so powerful, which is why when a few Christians come together, there's something about it. That's why twelve men turned the entire known world on its head. We don't have to have a big percentage. We just have to have the people who are on board going forward in the same direction. That make sense? Check your coward meter. Where do you rank? What are you willing to do? Are you willing to be different? Because if you won't be different, you'll make no difference. Trust me. You'll make no difference if you're not different. It takes a lot of courage to be the man of God that you dream about being, that you read about."

Hogan asked Clegg to close the practice in prayer. As it happened, Clegg proved an interesting choice that day.

+ + +

Weston Clegg has aspects of a California surfer in him. Ask a question that excites him—his eyes grow big and he begins his answer with, "Dude." The more animated he becomes, the bigger his eyes grow. He highlights his naturally brownish-blond hair and styles it in one of those ways that makes it look as though it is not styled. It takes time to make his hair appear as if he had rolled out of bed and stepped directly onto campus. He is popular because he is loyal. "For everyone in red," is one of Clegg's favorite expressions, and his teammates know he means it, in uniform or not.

Soccer, not football, is Clegg's best sport. As goalkeeper on one of the area's elite soccer teams, Clegg had received scholarship offers from four colleges. The problem for Clegg was that his soccer and football seasons overlapped. He would dash from football practice to soccer practice. Sometimes, he would play football on Friday night, then drive three or four hours with his dad to a soccer tournament. There really was not a reason for Clegg to play football other than that he wanted to. Now something he had feared would happen appeared as though it could: he might be forced to quit one of the sports.

Up until that point in the season, he had managed to juggle football and soccer. When the almost three-hour football practice ended on Monday, he would pull his soccer practice uniform out of his footlocker, change uniforms, and hurry to his car for a ten-minute drive to select-league soccer practice that would last up to two hours. Football practice ended at 6:00 p.m.—the same time soccer practice began. He was always late.

Monday was heavy conditioning day for both of his teams. He would go from the 360s of football to the complex runs of soccer, where the team would circle the large soccer complex in a required time or face extra running. It amounted to double conditioning for Clegg, and he did not want to do it.

The runs at soccer practice were a struggle. His mind would tell him he did not need to run, that football conditioning had him in good shape. Plus, he was a goalie, and keepers do not need to be as much in shape as the other players. He ran less than anyone else on the soccer field during games. But, by the time soccer practice had ended, he had run more that day than anyone else on either team.

Clegg had to run, however, so he found a way to convince his mind that there was a good reason to give his all during soccer conditioning. Clegg would look down to his blue and white soccer clothes and see red. Faith red. "I'll run extra hard just because I know that my teammates are hanging out in the locker room, cleaning up, and I'm over there running sprints with the soccer team," he explained. "You've got to get that in your head—that I'll run the extra mile for Grant, or run the extra mile for Landon, for Nerney, and Reeder. Just have those names in your head and just run hard for them even though you're wearing your blue and white."

Tuesdays were the same—football practice then soccer practice—minus the extra soccer conditioning. Wednesday practices were optional for soccer, and with Faith's practices let out early because of church, that was Clegg's light day. On occasional Thursdays he would have goal-keeper training, but because football on Thursday was dedicated to Open Floor, he at least had time to hang out in the Faith locker room before soccer.

And then there was homework. He still was, after all, a *student* athlete. He arrived home after 8:00 p.m., often exhausted. Especially on Mondays. He would melt into a living room chair for a few minutes, eat dinner, and then, by 9:00 p.m., hit the books. The homework load had been extremely heavy his junior year, and he struggled to keep pace. This year had been better, helped by having an off-period, during which he began his homework. But he could not get it all done. Wednesdays, when he did not have soccer practice, and Thursdays, with occasional goalkeeper training, were his homework catch-up nights. That meant missing church on Wednesdays and sub-varsity games on Thursdays. But that's when he had "a window of study time."

As demanding as his sports schedule was, Clegg did not want it to change. But, the week of Homecoming, he feared it might. One Homecoming week distraction and one decision brought him *this* close to having to choose between football and soccer.

He had been sick Tuesday and stopped by soccer practice to tell his coach he would not practice. On his way home, he decided to check out the senior class float for the Homecoming parade. As a student coun-cil member, he was supposed to help monitor the building of floats. During his short time there, his soccer coach called his home. His par-ents told the coach that their son had been sick during the day, but that he was not yet home. The coach called Clegg on his cell phone and let him have it for missing practice. Clegg knew he had no defense. His coach told him to report to the practice facility Wednesday for goal-keeper training, and to be on time. If he did not, the coach would find a new keeper.

Clegg considered the $3,500 in annual fees and expenses his parents paid for him to play with this club. He did not know what he would tell them. Then he remembered that Wednesday's football practices end at five o'clock. He could be at soccer practice on time.

After closing Wednesday's football practice in prayer, he reported for goalkeeper training. But there would be no training. The coach, instead, told Clegg to practice with one of the club's younger teams. Clegg was annoyed. The coach was obviously making him be there just to be there.

This coach had chewed him out at previous practices, criticizing him for playing football, criticizing him for playing at a small private school, criticizing him for anything else he could think of, Clegg believed, just so the other players on the soccer team could see him getting onto Clegg. Now the coach started in on him again. *"I don't care that you go to a little private school. They're not good at anything anyway. The only reason you're going to college is because of me."*

Clegg is an internalizer. He had watched the coach light into other players, as some coaches are wont to do. Those players seemed to take it as nothing more than a coach letting off steam. But Clegg could not let the words go. He would compare that soccer practice to the football practice he had just left. He would think about how his football coaches tell him that they love him, and how they show him they love him. And now here he was getting yelled at again before practice.

Clegg shook his head. He wanted to hold back, to take it all like he always had. But he remembered Hogan's words on courage from not even a half hour earlier. For the first time, he stood up for why he played football, for his "little private school." Clegg told his coach he knew he had no future in football. He knew he did not have the size or speed to play in college. But, he told his coach, he loved football "ten times more than your team right now. You made me hate it." The coach only looked at Clegg as he continued. "I play football for the ten other people on that field and for that coaching staff there. You made me hate it here. Soccer is my love and passion, and you made me hate it."

If that was the way he felt, the coach said, perhaps he did not need to practice. Perhaps he did not need to stay with his soccer team.

As much as Clegg had not wanted this moment of decision to occur, he had prepared for it. He would keep playing football if forced to choose. The college soccer offers would still be there, he believed. This was his last year to play football, to wear that Lion head on his helmet, to share a locker room with his closest friends. He considered turning and walking away. But as he looked into his coach's eyes, he saw irritation, nothing more. Clegg stayed. He had found a way to stand up for his beliefs and decisions without, in his view, crossing the line of showing disrespect for his coach. It had taken courage to do what he had just done. He was not going to quit now.

Hogan's phone beeped Wednesday night at home. He opened the text message.

Hey coach hogan it's weston. I was just letting you know that i extremely appreciate you and everything you stand for. There is such a dramatic difference between you and my soccer coach. I constantly am worn out physically and mentally by my soccer coach and i know for a fact that he doesn't give a rip about me. You are such an encouraging role model in my life. I can't imagine myself playing for another school. I love you coach! See ya tomorrow!

+ + +

There were forty-seven players in a locker room not built for near that many. For Homecoming, junior varsity players dressed out, and there was a good chance most would get to play in front of the alumni.

The JV players sat on the floor in the minutes before game time, while varsity players sat on their footlockers along the walls. "Guys on JV," Nerney called out. "This is going to be your first time walking out of the tunnel. Don't forget your first time. It won't be your last."

Clegg began making his way around the room, hugging teammates as he did before every game. He hugged the JV players, too. Anderson also was going through his pre-game routine of walking by each player, calling him by name and saying, "I'm playing for you." He called each JV player's name, too. The message the seniors were sending before the game was clear: On this night, there was no varsity and junior varsity. They all were on the varsity. They all were Lions. They were one team.

+ + +

As the players waited along the goal line for the pre-game coin toss, Rost turned and walked to the middle of the end zone. Rost had been sick to his stomach. He took a knee and leaned on the helmet he was holding with his right hand. He could not hold in what was upsetting him any longer.

Kevin Dodd, the father of JV player Corey Dodd, left his place behind the tunnel where players' fathers each week formed a spirit line for the players. Mr. Dodd asked Rost how he was doing. Rost nodded. Mr. Dodd placed a hand on Rost's shoulder and prayed. "What's your name, son?" he asked. "Tommy Rost, sir," came the answer. "I'll be praying for you all night," the father said. "Go out there and tear somebody's head off."

Rost smiled and walked back toward his teammates, holding a cold water bottle to his forehead.

+ + +

The JV players did get to play, and for longer than they expected. The Lions scored three times in the first quarter to take a 20–0 lead. JV players began entering the game early in the second quarter after an Anderson touchdown pass to Nathan Jordan made the score 27–0.

Cale Morris, a sophomore, replaced Hockenbrough at running back after the senior had advanced the ball twenty yards to the Temple 27. Morris ran three yards on his first carry. His JV teammates cheered. On the next play, he broke free for a 20-yard run to the Temple 4. Varsity and JV players cheered. "Give it to Cale!" they encouraged coaches. The coaches did, and Morris moved the ball to the 3. On the next play, he scored his first varsity touchdown. A roar erupted from the Faith players. Morris returned to the sideline to a bevy of congratulatory helmet slaps.

When the Lions took possession again with more than nine minutes remaining in the first half—ahead 33–0 and yet to allow Temple's offense a first down—ten of the players on offense were wearing logoless JV helmets. The only logo on the field belonged to junior backup center Jacob Pruett.

Dexter Cheneweth entered the game in the fourth quarter. He dashed onto the field as a late substitution, barely making it to his right-tackle spot. Roddy, back in at right guard, made sure Dexter knew his assignment. Dexter fired off the line and blocked the defender across from him. Cox carried the ball over the left side of the line for a 3-yard touchdown run. Dexter's block was not a factor in the play, but he made his block, and the Lions scored on his first play.

Faith won 53–12. The JV players had received an extended chance to play against another school's varsity and had fared well. Morris wound up as the team's second-leading rusher, with seventy-two yards on nine carries and that one touchdown. Freshman quarterback Luke Steinmann completed all seven of his passes for seventy-nine yards.

JV players later described their experience as "cool," from the big things—entering the field through the tunnel—to the small ones—having filled cups of Gatorade ready for them in the locker room at halftime. Then there was the Friday night crowd that was much larger than the seventy-five to one hundred fans for their Thursday night JV games.

"There were just so many people," Morris said. "There was more of a rush. I don't want to say there was more pressure, but it was more exciting."

"I know it's just a lot more energized," Steinmann said. "The crowd and all, there was like a hundred thousand more people."

The JV players had gained a sense of what it was like to play on Friday night and experienced the pre-game focus that takes place in the locker room. More than that, though, they had experienced the varsity players' acceptance. That is part of leaving a legacy that Hogan preaches to his players, especially seniors.

"The seniors, this is their last year," Steinmann said, "and they were excited to let us play in their Homecoming game. I thought it was pretty sweet. And Landon was like, 'I really want to get you into this game.'" After this game, accepting the younger players is something Steinmann said he would do when he is a senior. "I'll make sure they feel loved, because I know how it feels."

Morris added that already was taking place on the junior varsity, where the sophomores had taken on leadership roles by accepting the freshmen. "We don't want it to be just on the football field. We want to be friends with them, and develop relationships and friendships. It's about more than just football."

CHAPTER 15

"How Will They Remember You?"

GAME 9: LUBBOCK CHRISTIAN EAGLES

With the way the district's other games had played out Friday night, the Lions had clinched a playoff spot, but not one of the players mentioned that as they took the practice field Monday. Coaches were not even aware a postseason berth was assured. Merely making the playoffs had never been a stated goal.

Lubbock Christian was next on the schedule, and Sells was coaching his receivers on how to get free at the line of scrimmage against Reicher Catholic's physical, man-to-man coverage. Hogan did not like what he was seeing from his players. "Are you guys going to do this on game day? Reicher's going to go to seven in the box because they're going to get tired of having the ball run down their throats. We're going to run it down their throats, and you guys are going to have to get open."

Only three weeks earlier, the Lubbock Christian game looked as though it would be important in the Lions' pursuit of the district championship. The Eagles had finished non-district with a 4–1 record. The Lubbock school was the outsider in the district, almost 350 miles away in the Texas High Plains region. The small public schools on Lubbock Christian's non-district schedule, schools such as Smyer and Anton and O'Donnell, were unfamiliar to Faith's players and coaches. All they could do was look at the results, see that Lubbock was winning those games while scoring twenty-eight points per game, and assume the Eagles would provide a challenge.

But much had changed once district play had started and Lubbock Christian began playing teams Faith knew.

The Eagles had opened district play with a 41–20 win over Temple Christian. Then came a 52–12 loss to Reicher and a 28–14 loss to Pantego. The Eagles were two games behind Faith in the standings, and scores against the teams' common opponents did not compare favorably for Lubbock Christian.

What had once loomed as a big game now became one in which all the Lions needed to do was take care of business. That meant the coaches could devote part of practice time to Reicher's offense. The week before, the coaches had begun installing a new defensive look to counter Reicher's high-powered offense. While Faith was defeating Temple Christian, Reicher was beating Trinity Christian—playing without star running back Dominique Rambo—38–17, to leave only Reicher and Faith unbeaten in district. The Reicher game the final week of the regular season appeared it would be for the district title.

During practice, Clegg walked over to Ford. In the aftermath of the exchange with his soccer coach the previous week, Clegg had made a point to tell every assistant coach how much he appreciated him. Ford was the last he was able to thank.

"Whenever that sucker starts ripping you, think about how much that guy there," Ford said as he pointed to Hogan, "loves you."

+ + +

At the conclusion of practice, Hogan told his players to lie on their backs and place their hands over their eyes to block the sun.

"I want you to imagine sixty years from now," Hogan told them. "Let's just say that you're right at ninety, and it is at your funeral." No matter that his math didn't add up. "It's before they go over to your funeral and your family, your wife, your kids are around the table, and they're eating. And they're about to drive to the funeral and all of your old friends, maybe even some people in this story, and your kids' friends have provided a meal. And your wife is there and your kids are there.

And your grandkids are there. And they're from ages three to fourteen. What would your wife and your friends that are in this circle who are there to give your family support, what would they think about you? When they look back on your life, what would you want them to say about you? Not a ton of stuff. You probably wouldn't want them to say, 'He was never here, but he sure was rich.' Probably not what you would want to be thought of. Because listen, when you're dead, you're dead. The legacy you leave on earth is what you will have done over the past fifty or sixty years.

"So what is it that you would want your wife to think of you? In a day and age when you can go to the computer and instantly go look at pornography, what would you want your wife to think about you when you're in the ground? What would you want your son to think about you? *He sent me to select-league, but he never saw me play.* Or, *Man, he made a point to play catch with me day after day after day.* What would you want your daughter to say? What did she see? How did she see you treat her mom? What would you want your grandkids to say? What would you want your friends to say about your high school days? About your college days? No doubt some of you people will be on the same college campus. It is so early in your senior year right now, for the seniors, you can totally transform what people thought about you by the way you loved the unlovables in your class. By the way you respected adults who may not even deserve your respect, but you gave it to them anyway because that's what you'd want someone to do to your mom or dad. You can totally transform the way someone thinks about your life just in the few months you have left here.

"For you guys who are juniors and sophomores, you have such a long road ahead of you it seems like in high school. In some ways, not very many, because you only have a few football games left. But in terms of days that you show up on this campus, you have a lot of days left. What do you want your friends to think about you when you're in college?

"Guys, you'll come back for a class reunion in ten years. You're going to come over here for a class reunion, and you're going to meet in the gym. You're going to meet in the gym, or you're going to meet on the new campus. Maybe even in the stadium that you'll never get to play in. But ten years from now, you seniors are going to come back, and we'll probably meet somewhere in that new fine arts facility, and you guys are going to sit there and look and see what Clayton Messinger has done over ten years. What Daniel Ackerman has done with his life over ten years. You're going to see what Jeff Kallal has done in ten years. Alex Nerney. Grant Hockenbrough. Every senior in this group. Let me ask you a question: Will you come back proud? Will you come back as a man of God? Or will you come back with petty addictions? Will you come back a spiritual giant because you've spent hours in the Word of God with godly men at early-morning Bible studies, filling your brain with the Word of God? Or will you come back neutral? *I'm in a nine-to-five, I go to church on Sunday, don't teach, just go to church and listen on Sunday. I just go about my business trying to make a lot of money Monday through Saturday.* Will that be you? What ripple effect will you have for the Kingdom? What do you want them to say at your twenty-year reunion? Or your thirty-year reunion? What do you want the preacher to say about your life when they put you in the ground? Because whatever it is, you'd better get started right now, because a week from now is too late.

"Every day you have is a gift. What you do—now listen closely—what you do in a given day, you exchange those activities for a day of your life. If you sit at your house on a summer day and stay inside all day long for ten hours and eat junk food and play video games, that's okay if that's what you want. There's no great sin in that. But you'd better recognize one day of the life that God gave you was traded for ten hours of video games. And if you're okay with that, I'm okay with that. It's your life. Nobody's going to tell you what to do with that. I'm just saying the three or four or five things that you do every day, you just traded a day that God gave you.

"This weekend somebody read me a story about a guy who volunteered in a hospital. He volunteered to rock preemie babies. So he'd go up there, and these babies weighed ounces. Eight-, nine-, ten-ounce babies, little bitty, you could fit in the palm of your hand. You could see their little chests going up and down, barely breathing. And he knew most of them were going to die. But he also knew their drug-addict parents weren't going to be there. So for ten years he rocked babies that you could fit in the palm of your hands, sometimes holding four and five of them at a time, let them listen to soft music and rock them. He's not giving sermons, but there's a verse that says if you've done it unto the least of these, you've done it unto Me. I would say he was doing a great exchange for the time God gave him on earth.

"What do you do every day? What sarcasm do you use with your buddies that maybe you shouldn't use? Not joking around; everybody loves a good joke—most people. There's nothing wrong with joking. But I mean real sarcasm. Something that would hurt somebody's feelings. What 'unlovable' do you pass in the hallway that nobody's going to talk to all day, and all it would take is for a Lions football player to say, 'How's it going?' When they put you in the ground, you don't want people saying, 'You know what, he thought a little bit more about what people thought of him than doing the right thing. He was a little too cool.' People are being buried all the time. All the time. And the preacher has to lie at the funeral about how nice they were. Don't waste one single day that God gave you. Trade it for something meaningful.

"You need to go home this evening, and if you have brothers and sisters at home with you, you need to treat them with love and respect that maybe you don't feel like showing. It doesn't matter if you feel like it. We're not called to feel good about everybody. We're called to love them. I tell you what, you just ask these boys in this circle right here who have had older brothers and sisters what it feels like when they don't show up anymore. I think about Brock and Laramie [Jameson], so close to each other in age, then one day she's just gone to college. There were times when he probably could have gone out to the car and carried her bag for her. Times when he felt sorry for her when she hurt her shoulder as the best catcher on a great softball team. You've got people at home. You'd better take care of them and love on them while you're there, right now. Nobody in this circle can pay back their mom and dad. You might as well forget that. But you can make them proud. And you can make your mom and your dad, when they lay their head on their pillow at night, you can make their heart totally at ease and think how blessed they are to have a son who looks them in the eye and says, 'Yes, sir' and 'No, sir,' 'Yes, ma'am' and 'No, ma'am.' Takes out the trash before being asked. Guys, you can make your mom and dad's life if you'll be the young man that they've dreamed about you being.

"Life is too short to not have reflective moments like this. It's too short. You've got to think about where you're going. Try driving somewhere without a road map. You can't do it. Habit number two from the Covey principles: begin with the end in mind. What would you want people to say about you when you're gone?"

After Messinger prayed, the players broke their huddle and headed off the field. Cheneweth walked up to Hogan. "Thanks for saying that, Coach. I was crying the whole time." Hogan smiled. "You're going to be a great dad," he told Dexter. "I'm sure you're already a great son."

✦ ✦ ✦

By Tuesday's practice, Lubbock Christian's offensive and defensive schemes already had been broken down. Plus, Faith held a significant talent advantage. Friday looked to be a frustrating night for the Eagles, and Coach Sells was getting an early taste of that as he played quarterback for the scout-team offense against Faith's defense. The defense was stuffing every play, and Sells sounded rather defensive coming out of the huddle and approaching the line of scrimmage.

"You know what the Bible says," Hogan called out to his assistant. "'The guilty flee when no one pursues.' I've got a Scripture for every occasion."

Hogan then turned to Clegg and Steven Little. "He looks like a calf you're trying to catch to brand and he knows he's about to get burned."

✦ ✦ ✦

Hogan opened Open Floor Thursday by saying it would be an extremely short session. There had been a lot of talk during the week with Hogan's end-of-practice admonitions, and he does not like to "overtalk things." Life is about doing, he said. The players had done a good job during the week in preparing for this week's opponent—and next week's, too. But there was one more thing he wanted to talk about.

"This is more about your spiritual life and your future," he told them. "So let me tell you something, and you can do with it whatever you want to. If you are going to be what God intended you to be, if you're going to have any impact at all spiritually speaking, you must meet with God as a lifestyle. You must take the time to put that on your calendar and schedule everything else around it. If you don't, you will not have spiritual impact on this planet. You're just not going to do it. It's like taking a car and not putting gas in it. It doesn't matter how many horses the engine has, it ain't going to go without fuel.

"Meeting with God is to your spiritual life what food is to your mortal body. It will shut down and cease to function. It's not that you'll lose your sonship or relationship, but you will lose your fellowship with God, and you will be spiritual midgets. You will not impact your kids. You may think you will, but you won't. They will only hear you talking, then they'll go out and say, 'Okay.' And they will learn from the school of hard knocks, and the reason why is because the words you spoke did not have the anointing of God, so they're going to fall on deaf ears. An uneducated person, such as Peter the fisherman, can get up and speak with the guidance of the Holy Spirit and three thousand can run to join the church. But an educated man like Nicodemus, without the anointing, can speak and everyone will say, 'That's nice' and go on about their business.

"Your resources and mine are not enough to function in the Spirit and make an impact. Oh, they might be enough to do some certain job, if that's what you want your life to be. But you will have no impact spiritually if you don't make it a priority to meet with God over and over and over and over and over as a lifestyle. Will you always feel like it? No. Will you always be on cloud nine spiritually? No. But listen: uncommitted adults and little kids do what they *feel* like doing, and they're driven by their current circumstances. But a man of God does the right thing all the time, whether he feels like it or not."

+ + +

Chance Cochran was in the locker room before Friday's game. His Grapevine Mustangs had played a Thursday night game on regional television. A group of players and coaches, wearing their Faith sweatshirts and jackets, had sat on the Grapevine side of the stadium and cheered Cochran in his last home game. The next day, Hogan was telling his coaches about a text message he had received from Cochran: "My last home game was in the wrong uniform."

Cochran sat between Clegg and Hockenbrough, his two best friends on the team. In the coaches' office, Sells shook his head. "That kills me now even more that Chance isn't here. Maybe it's the look on his face." Then the coaches entered the locker room to instruct the players to take the field. "See it, boys, see it," Postema said. "Let's go." Hogan walked in behind him. "Okay, let's go."

As the players began to exit, Anderson walked over to Cochran. "I love you, number 7," Anderson said. "I'm playing for you." On the way out, Cochran reached up with his left hand and slapped the "Tradition Never Graduates" sign.

✦ ✦ ✦

The game proved to be an even bigger mismatch than anticipated. Faith led 21–0 less than seven minutes into the game and 44–0 at halftime. Unlike the previous week's Homecoming game, there were no junior varsity players on the sideline to put into the game. Coaches were sending in backups where they could, but the Lions kept scoring. Fifty points. Fifty-seven. Then sixty-four points early in the fourth quarter.

Lubbock Christian hit on its biggest play at that point, a 58-yard pass play to Faith's 14. But that drive stalled near the Lions' end zone. Hogan wanted to move the ball out into a little more comfortable area, then hold the ball and chew up the final seven minutes on the clock and get the game over with. Fearing a bad snap in Faith's shotgun formation with backups in, Hogan sent Hockenbrough back in at running back as a safety net. The snap to Ashton was perfect, as was the handoff to Hockenbrough. Hockenbrough took the ball up the middle, broke a tackle at the line of scrimmage, bounced to his left, and broke another tackle as he cut toward the Faith sideline. By the time Hockenbrough had reached the Faith 40, there was only one defender left that could prevent a touchdown.

"Block in the back! Block in the back!" Ford yelled from the sideline. He hoped the words would be heard by Reeder, the receiver who had been teased, sometimes unmercifully, for drawing penalties with illegal blocks downfield. Now Ford wanted such a penalty, to bring the play back. Reeder did not hear him and delivered a textbook block near the Lubbock Christian 35. As Hockenbrough dashed what remained of the ninety-four yards to the end zone, he quickly considered slowing up and allowing one of the defenders some ten yards back to catch him, or perhaps stepping out-of-bounds. But in the short time it took Hockenbrough to cover the distance, he thought that would embarrass the other team. He crossed the goal line and thought, *Man, I wish I hadn't scored.* His teammates and coaches shared that thought as the scoreboard reflected the new score of 70–0. Messinger's extra-point kick made it 71–0, and there was no hint of a celebration on the Faith sideline. In fact, the mood darkened with that score, because 71–0 looked horrible.

After the game, Hogan said softly to a fan that he had never felt so bad after a game, win or loss. There had been games when he felt bad for a player who had made a play that lost a game, but he could not recall ever feeling as empathetic for a group of players' feelings as he had for Lubbock Christian's players. He had been on the losing end of blowouts, and he understood the feeling.

Back in 2004, unbeaten Lubbock Christian had a team with state championship hopes, and coach Hutch Haley's Eagles routed Faith 54–33 in the final game before the playoffs. Most of Faith's points came late in the game after the outcome had long been decided. Haley apologized to Hogan for the final score. Hogan said he understood and wished Haley's team well in the postseason. The Eagles went on to win the state title.

On this night, the roles had reversed—and then some.

More than half an hour after the game, Hogan and Sells stood outside the field house near the Lubbock Christian bus. Most of the Eagles players had boarded, with brown-bag meals provided by the Faith Booster Club, for their six-hour ride. Sells leaned with a shoulder against the wall. Hogan stood with arms crossed. Both looked like they had just lost the game. They said little as they waited until Haley stepped off the bus. "You wanted to see me, Kris?" the coach asked. Hogan apologized for the score. His counterpart told him not to worry about it, and that he was more concerned about his players' tackling than anything Faith had done. "I know who you are," Haley told Hogan, "and I know how you are."

The coaches shook hands, and Haley stepped back onto the bus for the long trip home.

+ + +

The mood was brighter Saturday morning as players and coaches attacked the stacks of pancakes in the school cafeteria. They passed around the local sports sections, reading through the box score from Pantego Christian's 8–2 upset of Trinity Christian. The players were happy for Pantego's players. When all had had their fill of pancakes and it was time to stretch and lift weights, Ford stood from his seat. "Let's go," he said. "It's Reicher week."

CHAPTER 16

Perfect Ending

GAME 10: REICHER CATHOLIC COUGARS

Reicher Catholic spoiled Hogan's weekend. But after an extended session of game planning, he had determined late Sunday night: "We're going to kick their tail."

Reicher's offense resembled Faith's. Both teams employed the Spread offense. Both liked to run from that formation behind strong, physical linemen. Both featured a quarterback equally adept at running and passing. And both possessed sure-handed receivers capable of producing big plays in an instant. The Cougars were 8–1 overall and had won all four district games by at least three touchdowns, averaging 39.6 points per game. For one weekend, Hogan had a taste of what opposing defensive coaches faced in trying to draw up a way to slow Faith's offense.

On a typical Saturday, Sells would meet a coach from the next week's opponent early in the morning to trade game films. Faith coaches would get a start on breaking down their opponents' films before the players arrived at 9:00 a.m. to eat the pancakes their fathers made, then when Ford took the players for stretching and weight lifting, the other coaches would resume film work that hopefully would be finished by midafternoon. The rest of the work, mainly diagramming formations and defensive strategies, could be handled at home. The time at the field house on Saturdays was all about efficiency: Hogan did not want any member of his coaching staff to work on Sundays.

There is not much family time for coaches during football season. Sunday, Hogan expects, is a day his assistant coaches could spend with their families. They might pop in a game film at home, but at least they are at home and on their own time. Hogan works Sunday afternoons at home, putting on paper what would be in the scouting report players would receive Monday.

Reicher's offense, though, made this an atypical week. Hogan went home Saturday evening with DVDs of Reicher games. He watched through the night. Sunday morning, he went to church and returned home. On Sunday afternoons, his son, Deuce, would want to watch NFL games, especially the Dallas Cowboys. Deuce would watch while his dad sat and schemed on paper for the next game. Kris would glance at the game and pay enough attention to be able to answer his son's questions or acknowledge his comments. He admits he may not pay as much attention to the Cowboys game as his son thinks he does, but as far as Deuce is concerned, he is spending Sunday afternoon watching football with his dad. That, Kris said, "is not the worst thing in the world."

This Sunday, however, Hogan retreated to his bedroom and projected Reicher's offense onto a wall. A friend, knowing the district championship was at stake, picked up the two older Hogan kids to play with her kids. Kris's wife, Amy, also cleared out of the house with their two-year-old, Zeke. She had been married to a coach for eleven years and understood that times like this are a part of football season. Although her husband's job demanded that he not be around much on Saturday, even that he miss some of Deuce's soccer games and Jerilyn's softball games, things definitely were better now.

When Hogan took his first head coach's job at Sacred Heart, Amy would drive then-one-year-old Jerilyn an hour to the Metroplex on Saturday mornings and stay with family for the weekend so Amy could sell Mary Kay products there for extra income. For Friday night away games, instead of spending the night at home, Amy and Jerilyn would leave for the Metroplex after the game. Hogan would spend Saturday, from 7:00 a.m. to midnight, watching game film, formulating a game plan, and then double- and triple-checking that plan. He would join his family Sunday morning for church. Hogan did not have to work Sundays then, but the cost was not spending Saturdays with his family. That Saturdays-apart routine continued when Deuce was born and throughout the four years Hogan coached at Sacred Heart. During the week, because he lived two blocks from the school, Hogan would go home for lunch to see his family. Amy and the kids would often head over to the school and sit alongside the field and watch practice, just so they could all be at the same place. The Hogans made efforts to "steal moments" together when they could.

So Amy knew that not having the kids around not only would give Hogan a quiet house to work in, but it also would keep his mind from wandering out into the family room, where he wanted to be and felt he should be. Yet he also felt obligated to give his players their best opportunity to win. For the Reicher game, that meant completely changing the defense, and he knew that Reicher's coaching staff would find and exploit any weakness in his scheme.

At 6:00 p.m., Amy and the kids returned home. "How's it going?" Amy asked. "I've got them 70 percent stopped," her husband said. "I need about another forty-five minutes." So Amy took the kids out again. Hogan sat at the family table and watched through the front window as little Zeke, the last one out, happily made his way up the sidewalk to the car. Hogan felt tears forming in his eyes. Now he would need fifty-five minutes, because for ten minutes he sat there and cried. Hogan rarely uses the word *hate*, but that was a moment he said he hated. "That killed me," he said. "It was just terrible."

+ + +

Hogan informed the players during Monday's scouting report of the defensive changes. He then clued his players in on something he had picked up while watching hours of Reicher game film. Reicher's offensive tackles tipped off whether the play would be a run or a pass. Hogan had watched the Cougars run 168 plays, and on all 168 he had accurately predicted run or pass by watching the two tackles.

"Reicher is the best team you've played," Hogan said. "They're tenacious, and they never quit. You can't make them quit." Unless, Hogan added, Reicher's players' ribs were broken. "Are you promoting breaking ribs?" Roddy asked. "I would not promote rib breaking," Hogan answered, "unless you're talking barbecue sauce."

Before the players left for the practice field, Ford gave a final scouting report. He had missed the Temple Christian game to watch Reicher play Trinity Christian. "Reicher loves football," Ford said. "They eat it up." The Cougars, he concluded, were "high speed and hard hitting."

Inside the Lions' locker room, three printed Internet pages had been taped on the whiteboard. The third sheet had Reicher's Homecoming schedule; Reicher traditionally schedules its Homecoming for its final home game. Lions players loved the thought of winning the district championship on Reicher's field in front of its Homecoming crowd. Highlighted on the Reicher schedule was "10:30: Post-Game Celebration."

+ + +

The mood had been light during the week's early practices, and coaches made sure it stayed that way Wednesday. While players stretched, with temperatures in the mid-sixties during the first full week in November, Ford walked around squirting cold water on them. "I'm in a great mood today!" he declared. Hogan would add, "It's a *fabulous* day!" Their moods remained that way throughout practice. In fact, the practice felt like most of the others throughout the season. There was little mention of Reicher specifically. Players maintained a business-as-usual approach, which for them meant mixing good execution with jokes and laughs.

At the conclusion of practice, with players on a knee around him, Hogan talked about a common attribute he has observed in championship teams: poise. Watch New England Patriots quarterback Tom Brady, he told them. He always keeps his emotions under control. Watch NFL cornerbacks, he said. They get beat by a player like Patriots receiver Randy Moss, and they bounce back to play well. Reicher had led Trinity Christian 15–0 at halftime when they played two weeks earlier, Hogan told them, but Trinity Christian tied the score 15–15. Reicher players remained poised and came back to win 38–17.

"How well do you come back?" Hogan asked. Other than the Trinity Christian game, the Lions had not had to answer that question. "What if they get back-to-back-to-back good plays? What if they get the ball on their 10 and drive all the way to our 10? Can you come back and make a goal-line stand? It's huge for a football team. You've got to be able to get back to the moment. It's a sign of maturity. If you're in a college classroom or an upper-level CEO seminar, they can tell a good joke or do something funny, something can happen, everybody can bust out laughing, and then they can all come back to the topic at hand. But if you go to a seventh-grade classroom and something happens and some kid falls down or something, they'll laugh the entire class. You can't get them to come back. It's like, your lesson plan's done. It's because they're immature little kids. They don't understand you can have a great time, but then you can come back to the task at hand.

"Same thing with mature football teams. Something good, something bad, whatever, we're going to come back, and we're going to kill you because we have poise and focus. That make sense to you? That's what champions do."

+ + +

"We're finally at Reicher week, Open Floor Thursday," Hogan said from his chair in his customary Thursday spot at the opening to the locker room. "Nine and oh—right where we wanted to be a long time ago." Skit night at Mt. Lebanon seemed so long ago, he said, yet in some ways it seemed as though the season had sped past. But now it was Week 10. The last game of the regular season. District championship on the line at Reicher's Homecoming.

Hogan wanted to share a quote for this week; he couldn't recall where he had read it. "'Men are judged on planet Earth not by what they start. Men are judged by what they finish,'" Hogan recited. "Now just think about that for a second." The players reflected on the quote. Then Hogan shared another. He told how Thomas Edison had failed many times before inventing the lightbulb. As one author had concluded, Hogan said, "'Most failures have no clue how close they were to success, they just quit.' They had no clue how close they were," he added for emphasis. "That kind of goes with [the first] quote, because you only know people who finish stuff." Those who come close to finishing, he said, are remembered in a negative way. He offered the Buffalo Bills and their four consecutive Super Bowl losses as an example. "So I want you to think about that as you go through this football season. I don't think this football season will wrap up the way you want it to in your mind if we don't finish like we're supposed to. So that's how I want to start us off today. Okay, who's next?"

Dunnington was next. He told how at church the previous night, they had watched video clips of John Weber, the chaplain of the Dallas Cowboys, who had passed away the previous week. One thing Weber said, Dunnington told his teammates, was that a goal in life is not so much to be spectacular, but to be faithful, because spectacular things come from being faithful. "So, I just think that if we go out and are faithful to our responsibilities, faithful to working our ground, faithful to everything we have established as precedents this past season," Dunnington said, "then we'll have spectacular things happen tomorrow and throughout the rest of the playoffs."

"That's pretty good, pretty good," Hogan said as he nodded. "He was a great man."

O'Neal talked about the need for every player to be willing to fight for the district championship. Dunnington talked about how goals produce motivation, and motivation produces passion. Nerney talked about how no more than five games remained, telling juniors that even though they still had another year, "life's faster than you think." Clegg recalled how past Reicher teams had talked trash during games and that the players needed "to protect our brothers against a pack like this." Nerney spoke again to suggest his teammates begin thinking now how they would deal with any adversity that might arise during the game, to have those planned responses Hogan teaches.

The conversation worked its way around the room, through players and coaches. Postema said the word *courage* had been jumping out at him, and he referenced C. S. Lewis in describing courage as a defining mark of a Christian and a testing point of all other virtues. "We're big about virtues, and those are good things to have," Postema said. "But what it takes to manifest those things is courage. I've been a little bit surprised by our group this year, especially that Cedar Hill game. We just rose up."

Postema said he and his wife, Cory, Faith's volleyball and girls' track coach, had talked about that type of courage they had seen displayed in Faith's athletes in their little more than a year at the school. "What I see from you guys more than anything else is the virtue of courage,"

Postema continued. "Our virtues manifest in that one virtue of courage. That's what I would love to see [tomorrow], and that's what has just enraptured me and captured me—to be a part of this group, and this team, and this school. It's been pretty neat to see that."

Hogan closed the session by pointing to the signs that read, "PASSION . . . Without It, Nothing Else Matters!" and "Tradition Never Graduates." The coach related the origin of those signs. The seniors from the 2004 team started playing with passion at the end of their final season, and they begged Hogan to put up those signs. They saw how well the junior high teams—and some of the players listening to Hogan's story had been on those teams—were playing. Those seniors, Hogan said, believed that those junior high teams were going to be better at football than they had been. "And they had no pride issue in admitting it." They felt that they had begun to turn around Faith's program, and they wanted to leave something behind for all future teams. Because they realized that they had not played with passion until late that season, they chose the "PASSION" sign. And because they wanted to be remembered for recording the school's first playoff victory, they chose the "Tradition Never Graduates" sign.

"Bottom line is," Hogan said, "this is what I think an appropriate sign would be for you guys. I think if we put up a sign that said, 'Focus and Finish,' it would define you. Let me tell you why. If you win the state championship, if *we* win the state championship, you will have been the first Faith football team [to do so]. Because there will be others, but this will be the first one that finishes it. You will be the beginner of the finishing groups. I would love to have a sign up that says, 'Focus and Finish,' somewhere in here, that never comes down, and at the bottom of it, we can put '2007 Lions.' For everybody who ever plays to come through and see that, and I can then look at that and say, 'Let me tell you what *focus* means. And this group put it up here because, listen guys, they went 14–0. Not 13–1, because that would suggest at some point they lost focus. They went fourteen and zero. They knew something about focus.' And then I could explain to them the highs and the lows. Wouldn't that be a sweet legacy for you to leave? *Finish* would be, obviously, a self-explanation. And that's where I think we are. So before we get to that, let's make that our battle cry for the next five weeks. As long as we focus, I promise you we'll finish. But if we don't focus, we may not finish. So let's dedicate the last five weeks to 'Focus and Finish.' Can we do that?"

"Yes, sir," the players responded.

+ + +

The sub-varsity teams concluded their seasons Thursday night by sweeping Reicher in the seventh-grade (28–0), eighth-grade (34–12), and junior varsity (47–12) games. Combined, the three teams had a 27–2 record and had outscored opponents 989–267, or by an average score of 34–9. From top to bottom, the program was churning out victories.

Between the eighth-grade and JV games, Anderson had gone out onto the field with old teammate Cochran and was throwing passes to Cochran as Sells covered him. Hogan watched from an unoccupied section of the stands and laughed at Sells's defense. Then Anderson and Cochran huddled, broke the huddle, and ran Option Right. The last time they had been on the field together in a game was against Regents in the state semifinals. The last play they had run was Option Left. Hogan's face dropped at the sight of Anderson pitching to Cochran and Cochran sprinting easily through the open field. "I didn't need to see that," Hogan said.

+ + +

A district championship *and* a Homecoming game. The atmosphere around J. J. Kearns Field in Waco was so exciting that Hogan slapped even the team manager, Chris Wicker, on the backside during pre-game. "Are you ready?" Hogan asked him. Wicker nodded. "This is gonna be fun," Hogan said.

Faith's fun started on the opening kickoff. The Cougars' Ben Crenwelge fielded Messinger's kick at his own 10 and returned past the 20, where he was hit hard by Anderson and Wright. The ball popped free, and Nerney dived ahead of a Reicher player to recover the ball. Nerney stood with football raised in his right hand. The Faith sideline and stands erupted. Players hopped and slapped hands and bumped chests as the offense replaced the kickoff team on the field. One play into the game, the Lions had the ball at the Reicher 22.

The Lions came out throwing, but Anderson's pass for Reeder in the corner of the end zone was well defended and incomplete. On the second play, Anderson rolled right toward the Faith sideline, where Reicher defenders chased him down and sacked him for a 7-yard loss on a loud hit. "That was a good hit," Wright said from the sideline. "That was a good hit." A third-down pass also failed, leaving Faith with fourth and seventeen from the Reicher 29. To not score after receiving a turnover on the opening kickoff would have shipped the momentum across the field to Reicher. The distance was too much for a field goal attempt, so the Lions went for the first down. Sells sent in a running play. With the Cougars defense expecting a pass, Anderson scampered for the needed seventeen yards plus two more. First and goal just inside the 10. Three runs moved the ball to the 1. On fourth down, Roddy motioned from his right-guard spot for Hockenbrough to follow him into the end zone. Hockenbrough did just that. Messinger's extra point gave Faith a 7–0 lead with 9:20 remaining in the opening quarter.

On their first possession, aided by two Faith penalties, the Cougars moved the ball to just shy of midfield, where running back Ross Rasner converted a fourth and one with a 10-yard run. Both head coaches were showing go-for-it aggressiveness early. Reicher soon faced another fourth-down play, this time needing eleven yards from the Faith 43. Anderson picked off quarterback Kenneth Cluley's pass to set up Faith's offense at its 38. Six plays later, the Lions' big-play ability showed when Anderson hit Nerney over the middle for a 50-yard scoring strike and a 14–0 lead late in the first quarter.

The defenses dominated the next three possessions with all ending in punts. After the final of those punts, Faith took possession at its 47. Anderson threw incomplete on first down. On a second-down handoff, Dunnington broke through the middle of the line, darted outside to the right, squirted through three Reicher tacklers, and sprinted to the end zone. With 8:11 left until halftime, Faith led 21–0.

Although Reicher's crowd seemed stunned, Cougars players were not. Behind the running of Cluley, they marched to Faith's 26 before turning the ball over on downs. The Reicher defense then forced Faith to punt without gaining a first down. With 1:06 left until halftime, the Cougars had the ball at their 29. Intent on cutting their deficit before intermission, they advanced the ball to their 43. From there, the Lions' defense delivered three hard-hitting messages. Three times Cluley threw incomplete passes downfield, and three times a Faith defender laid a big hit on the intended receiver—the first two by Jameson, the third by Anderson. "We're bringing the lumber," Ford said on the sideline. "My goodness."

With time enough for one play and on fourth and ten at Reicher's 43, Cluley called one more pass play in the huddle. But junior defensive end Justin Huffman sacked the quarterback before he could release the ball. The defense's final series of the half had the Faith players fired up as they ran toward their locker room. "That's the way to finish the half!" Ford yelled as he jogged off the field. "Bring the lumber!"

"Hey, listen," Hogan told his players as he concluded his brief half-time talk. "I don't have a whole lot to tell you at halftime other than this: let's put the pedal all the way down, just like we're doing. Listen, I'm proud of you guys. You deserve a few yells at halftime because you shut out a great team for one half. But remember, it's focus and . . ." Hogan stopped.

"Finish," the players said for him.

"Focus and finish," Hogan repeated.

The players stood to return to the field. "Focus and finish!" they encouraged each other.

The Lions had the ball to start the second half and gained one first down before punting. Reicher opened its possession with two huge plays—a 41-yard run by Cluley on an option keeper and a 30-yard pass from Cluley to Crenwelge—that moved the ball to Faith's 5. Three plays later, Cluley scored on a 1-yard run. O'Neal blocked the extra-point attempt, but Reicher had managed to put points on the board and close the gap to 21–6 with 8:18 left in the third.

Faith could not answer with a score, but it did the next best thing: chew up clock while moving the ball into Reicher's end. The Lions ran off ten plays before stalling at the Cougars' 20. They regained possession, though, when Anderson intercepted his second pass of the night, at Faith's 34.

What followed was a district championship–clinching drive. Anderson started off with two short completions to Clegg and Reeder, respectively, that moved the first-down sticks. Dunnington followed with a 20-yard run up the middle to the Reicher 34 and a run for no gain. Anderson and Nerney then connected for an 11-yard completion, and a 5-yard face mask penalty moved the ball to the 18. The Lions narrowly avoided a turnover on the next play. Anderson made a bad pitch to Dunnington, and Dunnington picked up the ball, circled to reverse his field, and was hauled down back at the Cougars' 33. The 15-yard loss set up a second and twenty-five. Anderson cut that distance in half with a 12-yard run before the horn sounded to end the third quarter.

"Let's go! Hustle up!" Kallal shouted as the Lions moved to the far end of the field for the final quarter, championship within their grasp. "Let's go! Let's go! Let's finish!"

During the time-out between quarters, Sells relayed through Hogan a pass play intended for Nerney.

"Hey, make the play," Ford said to Nerney.

"Hey, make the dang play," Hogan added.

Nerney did make the play. Anderson sidestepped a blitzing linebacker and lofted a soft pass to the end zone. Nerney leaped to grab the ball, both hands over the defender's outstretched arms. Hands raised all along the Faith sideline when Nerney came down with both feet in bounds and stepped backward out of the back of the end zone. With 11:53 to play, Faith led 28–6.

Reicher made one serious scoring threat, reaching the Faith 8 with under five minutes remaining, but the Lions' defense held. The celebration did not begin, however, until Reicher's final play when Anderson intercepted his third pass of the night. Anderson and the offense had to take a knee one time from the Victory formation to run off the final twenty-four seconds.

Players and coaches rushed onto the field and embraced each other. They had finished the regular season 10–0, and the district championship was theirs.

+ + +

At midfield, after the teams had congratulated each other on a hard-fought game, Faith campus pastor Jon Brooks stepped into the team huddle. Most of the three hundred or so Lions fans who made the trip had remained and gathered around the players.

"Coach," Brooks said, "I want to say congratulations. Two thousand

and seven, perfect season, district champs, right here." Brooks handed Hogan a trophy with a large, gold football atop the base. Players and fans whooped and hollered as Hogan held the trophy aloft. When the noise had subsided to where Brooks could be heard, he added, "A lot more to come."

Hogan admired the trophy. "Isn't that pretty? I've got to tell you guys, listen—I had no idea we were going to hold them to six points. You did a great job. Great execution. You deserve it. You are the district champs. Listen to me: how many weeks do we have left?"

"Four!" the players answered. Their regular season was over, but their season was not.

"Four more," Hogan said. "I told you guys at camp, doesn't matter if it's spiritual-wise, grades, what you're going to do for a living, marriage—nothing comes at an easy price. There's a real Satan that stands in the way. And there are real opponents always vying for what you have. They're good, aren't they?" Hogan asked as he motioned toward Reicher's huddle. "They're the best team that we've played. And do you think you'll see them again?"

"Yes, sir," the players responded.

After Hogan finished and Dunnington prayed, the players gathered in a circle, index fingers raised. They remained number one. "Hey," Anderson said. "Let Reicher know who we are! Let Reicher know who we are!"

"We are Faith!" O'Neal shouted.

"Sold Out," the players and fans declared with one voice.

CHAPTER 17

The Postseason: Grade Expectations

BI-DISTRICT PLAYOFF: CORAM DEO LIONS

The players were stunned. They had arrived for Wednesday's practice to learn practice was canceled.

It was the first round of the playoffs—the first of four steps on the path to the state championship—and on the last day of the week with a full practice, they were being told that instead of putting on their helmets and pads, they needed to grab their notebooks and pens.

Coaches had learned that about ten players were either failing or close to failing a class. Those in danger of failing were sent to meet with their teachers. The rest were told to help their teammates and to push them to raise their grades.

The coaches meant business. After all, way back on the first day of practice, when Hogan had introduced the "Sold Out" theme, school had been one of the four areas in which he had told his players they must give sold-out effort—behind God and family and before a state championship.

"Sometimes," Hogan explained in his office, "people get their priorities out of whack, and you have to help them with that." He had never before canceled a practice because of grades—but he had never had this many players this close to ineligibility. Canceling Wednesday's practice, he calculated, would be a preemptive strike before the end of the grading period the following week. Any players failing a class then would technically be ineligible for the championship game. But Hogan would hold them out of the semifinal game, too. He would not go into a state championship game with first-time starters. The season goal was not to play for the state championship, but to win the state championship. So he was sending the message that selling out for the championship included selling out in the classroom. "Canceling a practice leading up to a playoff football game generally gets everyone's attention," he said with a smile.

Hogan's decision did get everyone's attention—everyone at the school, elementary on up.

"The whole school knew about it, so it was a big deal," Kallal said. "It's pretty embarrassing when three kids come up to you, 'Are your grades up? Are your grades up?'" Rost told of students he did not know who stopped him in hallways and asked if the team would practice Thursday. Teachers were asking the same question. Hogan delivered the answer that afternoon: no. There was no walk-through on Thursday. Not even everyone's favorite time, Open Floor Thursday. Once again, the coaches told the players to forget about football and go study.

It irritated players such as Wright and Messinger, who had kept their grades up, when they heard of eligibility concerns arising as the playoffs kicked off.

"I was kind of mad at everybody else that they didn't hold up their end of the deal," Wright admitted. Messinger, who was projected to be the senior class's salutatorian, expressed frustration as well. During Commitment Night, he had offered to help anyone needing assistance with any classes. Teammates had taken Messinger up on his offer a couple of times, but now there were ten players flirting with ineligibility at the worst time possible. "It's really not that hard to pass. As long as you go to your classes, listen, and turn in your homework, it's real easy to pass," Messinger said. "It's frustrating that they were sacrificing grades for football. That was not thinking of their teammates first, because if they were thinking of their team, they'd be passing their classes."

But the situation provided another opportunity to witness the togetherness of this team. Despite the frustration, no split developed between those in danger of failing and those not. A small group of players without grade problems met and decided to help fix the problem instead of continuing to complain about those who created the problem. As they had done throughout the season on the field, the players worked together off the field. Taking care of your brother included academics, too.

"It should be 'Sold Out' all the time, field and classroom," Rost said. "The classroom comes first. You have to be 'Sold Out' academically before you can be 'Sold Out' athletically."

+ + +

Not practicing Wednesday and Thursday kept another important question unanswered: could Anderson throw a pass?

Near the end of Tuesday's practice, Anderson lowered his right shoulder to make a tackle on Gesek as Gesek carried the ball into the secondary during first-team defense. The practice had grown intense, and from his safety spot at the back of the defense Anderson had tired of watching the scout-team offense break through tackles at the line of scrimmage. So he lowered his right shoulder to deliver a message to his fellow defensive starters. Anderson's shoulder pads met Gesek's knee. Anderson immediately felt a hot sensation in his throwing shoulder. Then pain. *Oh, no,* he thought.

+ + +

The red cups in the chain-link fence in front of the field house spelled out "PLAYOFFS 07." Red paw prints had been painted on the sidewalk leading around the field house to the main walkway in front of the concession stand, where a large red Lion head had been painted onto the concrete. "We are Faith" was spelled out underneath the Lion head, with "Sold Out" to the right.

It was playoff time, and for the first time the Lions were playing a postseason game in The Jungle. The highest-seeded teams in the playoffs are rewarded with a first-round home game. In previous seasons, Hogan had chosen to rent a larger stadium in the area to give his players a special playoff-game feel. This year was different. Holding a game at home would bring in revenue that could be used on chartered buses for possible trips to the Houston area in the third round and for the state championship game in Central Texas.

The players, especially the seniors, relished one more chance to play at home. In an area brimming with shiny, new, multimillion-dollar stadiums for the large public schools, The Jungle—from its size to its name—brought a small-community feel to games. It was home to the players, and had been since they first put on a Lions uniform in seventh grade. Some had played their first football game here in youth leagues.

As the coaches walked out of their office to head to the locker room, they passed the long whiteboard on which the sixteen-team playoff bracket had been written. "Okay, let's go," Hogan said upon entering.

The place was crowded. The nineteen junior varsity players who had not already joined the basketball and soccer teams had joined the team for the playoffs. With no extra room and the visiting team using their locker room, the JV players had to dress standing in the middle of the floor. Inconvenient, but worth it to be on the sidelines during the postseason.

For this game, though, if things went as planned, there could be an added bonus: a chance to play in a postseason game.

Coram Deo Academy did not figure to present much of a challenge. Coram Deo, located in Flower Mound across Grapevine Lake, is a young school with a strong academic reputation. Also nicknamed the Lions, they had been playing football for four seasons and were working their way into being competitive. They had barely made it into the TAPPS playoffs for the first time as the fourth seed in their district. "We're just happy to be here" is a too-often-used cliché in sports, but in Coram Deo's case, that seemed appropriate.

At the conclusion of pre-game warm-ups, the varsity and junior varsity split into separate groups. Hogan told the varsity players along the goal line that this game and the next would reveal whether they were ready to be state champions. They would not have any problem getting ready to play an undefeated Bay Area Christian team in the third round if that matchup materialized, Hogan told them, but these first two weeks of the playoffs, when the Lions would be heavily favored, would reveal their maturity level.

Over in the corner of the end zone, JV coach Matt Russell had circled his players around him. "This is something that's going to stick with you through your entire high school career and beyond," Russell told them. "I remember some great moments that I had. Even above the ones I had in college. But the big message tonight is this might be the last chance you get to see the field. Some of you might get some opportunities, but let's be real—this game right here could be your last snaps in a live game." Russell issued a final warning. "Hey, at all moments, you guys need to be ready to go in. When Coach calls for you and you're not paying attention, that's really going to hurt you. Don't do that, because you might not get a second call."

+ + +

With one group preparing to play its final home game ever and another hoping to actually see postseason playing time, the Lions headed toward the door. "Seniors, this is the last time you walk out of this locker room," Anderson said. "Come out hard. Come out hard." Nerney, as before every game, took a slight detour to pound his fist on the metal sign that read, "PASSION." He pointed to the sign. "This one's my favorite."

"Last game on this field!" one father shouted as the players gathered behind the inflatable tunnel. Jameson walked over to his own father and gave him a hug. Moments like that are why Hogan asks players' fathers to be the last people the players see before taking the field. After the players had walked through the smoke and jogged to their sideline, Nerney sought his pre-game father-son moment: he walked up to Hogan and embraced him.

+ + +

Anderson could not toss more than perhaps a 5-yard pass because of his shoulder injury, and even that short throw was painful. But he still was on the field as the starting quarterback. Hogan wanted everything to feel normal for his team when the game started, and having Anderson barking the snap cadence from the shotgun behind that big offensive line was normal. So no passing plays would be called, and Anderson would not be asked to run the ball. Anderson's assignment for the night was to hand the ball off every play on the first series, lead the team to a touchdown, then turn the offense over to the freshman Ashton.

Faith's defense forced Coram Deo to punt on its first possession. Faith set up shop at its 36 yard line. Nine plays later—all running plays, none with Anderson keeping the ball—Hockenbrough was in the end zone and the offense was Ashton's.

Ashton took over from there. He threw a 5-yard scoring strike to Shivers on the Lions' next possession. He threw a 4-yard touchdown pass to Nerney on the third. Then he returned a punt fifty-four yards for a touchdown, and Faith was in control 27–0 with 1:01 still to play in the first quarter.

The JV players did get to see the field. Ten different Lions carried the ball in the game. Five caught passes before the passing game was abandoned because of the big lead. In the end, Faith had notched a 54–0 victory.

Hogan had few words for his players at midfield after the game. They would learn something about themselves this night, he had told them before the game, and now they did not need their coach to tell them what had been learned. They proved themselves ready to make a run for the state title.

"We are not coming in in the morning. Not coming in to watch film in the morning," Hogan announced. "So, we're going to break it out right here, and then I'll see you guys Monday with a scouting report ready to go. No coming in tomorrow."

The players balked.

"What, you guys want to come in?" he asked. Yes, they replied.

"Okay," Hogan conceded, "you guys come in in the morning."

The players cheered. Hogan shrugged as he looked to Sells.

"I tried to give them a day off," he said.

"They want to win," Sells answered.

"No," Hogan said, "they want pancakes."

+ + +

After the players broke their huddle, the realization began setting in for the seniors that they would never play on this field again.

Nerney walked to an open spot on the field and sat alone. When teammates gathered on the painted Lion head for pictures, he joined them. The players laughed and hugged and posed with teammates and parents. After a few minutes, Nerney left the pack. He shared a brief word with his girlfriend, then walked over to the goalpost behind the east end zone. He dropped to his knees.

His first thought was, *Good-bye*. He began running through his memories of playing football here. The Friday nights. The "brothers" he had practiced and played alongside. The Jungle, where they had showed what they were made of. He could not believe that now it was over. He leaned forward, head dropping onto his forearms. Then he thanked God for using football to shape him, to turn him into the man he had become, even if it had not always been under the best of circumstances. Without football, Nerney believes, he would have been lost. As tears flowed, he clenched the grass with both hands, as if he did not want to let go. A sudden peace came over him, and he released the grass from his grip. Because of what he had experienced on this field and in this sport, he could let go. Faith football had prepared him to move on.

"Thank you, God," Nerney said as he stood and walked to the spot in the end zone where he had scored his first touchdown as a sophomore. He could still feel the hit of the defender as he caught the pass. And he'll never forget how he hung on to that ball with all his strength, how he could hear the fans cheering, and how his teammates had rushed to celebrate with him.

"Our Father, who art in heaven," he began. "Hallowed be Thy name. Thy Kingdom come. Thy will be done, on earth as it is in heaven. Give us this day our daily bread. Forgive us our trespasses as we forgive those who trespass against us. And lead us not into temptation, but deliver us from evil. For Thine is the Kingdom and the power and the glory forever. Amen."

Then he walked off the field for the last time.

CHAPTER 18

Passing Marks

STATE QUARTERFINALS: PANTEGO CHRISTIAN PANTHERS
Landon Anderson slowly made his throwing motion. The ball floated five yards. Anderson winced.

The second-round playoff game, a rematch against district opponent Pantego Christian, sat four days away, and Anderson's warm-up throws before Monday's practice left little hope that he would be able to throw a pass Friday. During passing offense, freshman Peter Ashton took all the snaps. He looked sharp before throwing back-to-back interceptions.

"It's ball responsibility," Hogan told Ashton. "You're entrusted with it. It's your job to protect the ball."

A few minutes later, Hogan walked up to Anderson. "Okay, here's the question: What do you think, percentage-wise, is the chance of you playing [next week] against League City and saying, 'Aw, I can throw fine.' What do you think the percentages are?"

"Percentages?" Anderson asked.

"Mm-huh," Hogan answered. "You think it's a 50 percent chance you'll be able to throw and you'll just say, 'Hey, I can go'? If it's a 30 percent chance? What do you think?"

"If it hurts," Anderson said, "I'm going to shoot up with something.

I'm going to throw through that pain until my shoulder falls off. I've worked way too hard to let that stuff go to waste."

Hogan nodded and walked away. An Ashton pass sailed wide of its target. "Stop thinking," Anderson called out to his replacement. "Just throw. You have a great arm."

+ + +

This was a big week for Peter Ashton. Not only would he likely play a significant role in the outcome of the Lions' second-round game, but he also needed to have a quality study week. Ashton had been one of the players in danger of failing a class, and his situation might have been the most perilous. He needed to make a 100 on his World History test the following week to pass. At home this week, Ashton would spend two to three hours per night studying for the test. At school, he would spend his lunch periods with Sells, studying for both upcoming tests: in World History and in football.

Schoolwork had always required extra time for Ashton. Over the years he had been diagnosed with Auditory Processing Disorders, memory retention deficiencies, dyslexia, ADD, and ADHD. What most students could memorize by going over four or five times, Ashton would need to go over up to fifty times to memorize.

Even football plays presented difficulties: Faith's system of reading numbers flashed in from the sideline, and then matching that number to the plays on a wristband presented opportunities for short circuits and mistranslations for Ashton.

During preseason practices, Ashton would write "80" on his right hand and "90" on his left so he could match the called pass protection with the play call. Teammates had helped him throughout the season when he had played quarterback late during blowouts. On an "80" play call, wide receiver Nerney would sometimes indicate that the play was called for his, or right, side of the field. Linemen and running backs would also help make sure Ashton knew the correct play.

But Ashton had greater weaknesses that were converted to strengths on the field. Off the field, he had always possessed an ability to sense a weakness in other kids—and he would make those kids targets of bullying. He also tended to act out impulsively, doing something as random as throwing a sandwich and Skittles across a classroom just to see how others would react. On the field, his instinct for detecting weakness was given appropriate outlet. Ashton was no tiptoeing quarterback. He relished contact, and if an opponent seemed to shy away from being hit, Ashton would deliver a memorable blow. Along with his natural athletic ability, he had a football instinct that cannot be taught. That was especially evident as he produced big play after big play in JV games, often by impulsively jittering away from would-be tacklers. And he had displayed those same abilities in the opportunities he had received during varsity appearances.

Fans talked excitedly about their future quarterback. But away from the crowds, during practices and meetings, coaches wondered whether Ashton could be that quarterback. Hogan holds his quarterbacks to higher standards than other players. With the position comes leadership and responsibility. While Ashton had an ability to create trouble for opponents, he also had a knack for creating trouble for himself in school. From his younger days, Ashton had struggled with his self-worth. He learned early that by acting up, he could elicit a negative reaction that he enjoyed.

Ashton was a third grader when his family moved to Texas and enrolled their children at Faith. By seventh grade, a particularly difficult year, his behavior had earned him a thick file in the principal's office. His father, Bill, traveled extensively with his job at that time. He laughed as he recalled almost a weekly routine of talking to principal Jeff Potts after getting off a plane on Monday about something that happened involving his son that day, then again on Wednesday, and possibly on Friday.

One by one, Ashton's closest friends—his partners in mischievousness—left Faith. "Peter could have found trouble himself," his mother, Anne, reflected, "but when there was somebody else who could lead him down there to find trouble, it was double trouble."

His parents look back on seventh grade as a pivotal time. From that difficult year came an awareness of Ashton's problems, medication to help with the impulsiveness, an educational partnership with school administrators and teachers for the Ashton family, and principal Potts's determination to bring out the good he could see in the kid with the low self-worth and the thick file. Potts helped start the process of putting together the right group of people around Ashton to help with his learning disabilities. The hope was that by stopping the downward spiral of either Ashton's academic or behavioral issue, the other issue would improve.

Sports, which begin in the seventh grade at Faith, became a great motivator for Ashton. "If he didn't have sports, I would hate to think of where he would be," his mother said, "because he'd feel horrible about himself because there would be no place for him to shine." Ashton had learned, in his father's words, that "as easily as you can do an activity, it can as easily be taken from you." His eighth-grade year, he hoped to play baseball on the junior varsity. But Ford, the baseball coach, did not extend an offer. The Ashtons disagreed with the decision, believing Ford had made his decision based on what they considered "old information," or how their son had acted during seventh grade. They met with Ford and Hogan, but still their son was not allowed to play. That, Bill Ashton said, showed his son that choices bear consequences.

The lessons would continue into this football season.

On the first morning at Mt. Lebanon, Hogan had learned that Ashton had told another freshman to put a big hit on his backup JV quarterback during a kickoff drill. Immediately after lunch, Hogan went upstairs in the dorm and told Ashton to put on his shoes. He took Ashton to the practice field and gave him the option of quitting football—offering him a cell phone to call his father—or completing a long series of front rolls. He chose the front rolls. Ashton's lunch did not remain in his stomach for long. About forty yards from the end of the 300-yard field, Ashton looked ready to quit. "What's your dad's cell phone number?" Hogan asked. Ashton shook his head, muttered something Hogan could not understand, and finished the front rolls.

On the way back to the dorm in the golf cart, Hogan told Ashton he was being tough on him because he loved him. "Has anyone been hard on you before?" Hogan asked. "No, sir," Ashton replied. "I'll do whatever it takes to get you to the next level," Hogan told him. "If you develop character, I will be your number one supporter, behind your parents."

There would be other small on-field "detentions" for Ashton during the season. But in the process, he began to understand the leadership role that comes with being a quarterback for Hogan. "If I do something [bad], other people will do it," Ashton said he had learned, "and he doesn't want that."

Those gradual lessons were taking place behind the scenes. What the fans saw on Thursday and Friday nights was their future quarterback. They would tell Anne Ashton how great her son was playing. She did not know how to respond, because few knew everything about the family's journey to this point. "I know the appropriate response is 'Thank you,' but I wanted to say so much more about the whole—" She did not complete her sentence. "This is a miracle. You just can't go into all that."

"If we told everybody what we've been through," her son interrupted, "we'd have to spend all day doing it."

The mother laughed, and then recalled the game when she was sitting next to Dunnington's mother, Lydia. Anne Ashton turned to her and said that her son struggles in all areas of life except on the playing field. He might have two weeks, or sometimes two months, of reprieve. But there always is something that comes up involving his learning and his impulsiveness. "And when I see him on the field," she explained, "that's how I see how God has wired him, and the beauty of it all. It makes sense then."

+ + +

Tuesday was an early-release day from school for the Thanksgiving holiday. It also was an early-release day from practice. Practice went so well that Hogan ended the session forty-five minutes early.

A day after practicing in a record-high temperature of 84 degrees, Wednesday morning's practice began with the temperature at 60 degrees and a strong north wind producing a windchill in the 40s. Forty-five minutes into practice, with jackets on and hands in pockets, the coaches had seen enough. Their team was ready for Pantego, which had won its four games since playing Faith, including upsetting Trinity Christian in Week 9.

There would be no practice Thursday, the coaches announced. The game plan was the same as the first meeting with Pantego, and the players were executing almost flawlessly. But the news drew mixed reactions. In Texas high school football, there exists a certain status from practicing on Thanksgiving Day, because only teams advancing through the play-offs have that opportunity. Hockenbrough, for one, thought it would be cool to say he had practiced on the holiday. Plus, some players were concerned that skipping practice the day before a playoff game could result in a loss of focus.

The coaches believed skipping a practice before playing an opponent they had crushed 47–0 five weeks earlier would put the onus on the players to ensure there would be no loss of focus.

+ + +

"Sweet," Dunnington said as he walked into the locker room of the Birdville ISD Fine Arts/Athletics Complex. Red nameplates bearing players' names had been placed on the lockers. "It's awesome."

Sells made a quick trip to the coaches' booth, where he would spend the game. He took an elevator to the sixth floor to get there—a far cry from The Jungle, where he would climb a ladder inside the press box through an opening in the ceiling to reach his chair atop the roof.

This stadium had become a standard-setter in this part of the Dallas/Fort Worth Metroplex. Opened in 1999, the stadium cost $11.9 million to build and included a $300,000 scoreboard with full-color electronic replay capabilities. Nearby high schools had since built more-costly stadiums in what seemed to be a contest, with the philosophy "Any stadium you can build, we can build better." But this 12,000-seat stadium less than ten miles from The Jungle still carried a big-time feel for Faith's players and coaches as they checked out the short blades of the artificial-grass playing surface. It was a fast track, they kept saying, and that should increase their speed advantage.

Hogan was uncharacteristically nervous, even more so than before the teams' regular-season meeting. Although Faith had easily won that game, Hogan again cited his respect for Pantego coach Steve Hohulin and an offensive scheme that matched up well with Faith's defense. Hogan also knew that Panthers players would view this game as an opportunity to pull off an upset like they had against Trinity Christian–Cedar Hill during the regular season.

So Hogan called Hockenbrough over. "You might want to walk around and make sure everybody's focused," Hogan told him. "I guarantee you they're looking at this game as Cedar Hill Part 2. It might even be worth a trip into the locker room, too."

Hockenbrough made his way around the field, dropping a brief comment about focus to his teammates. He then headed to the locker room to address the rest of the players. "I'm telling you, Pantego's going to be ready for us," he said. "They came back and beat Cedar Hill. They look ready to go after us. Make sure everybody stays focused and thinks only about football. All right? I want to make sure this isn't my last game."

+ + +

Only five plays into passing drills, with Ashton and third-stringer Shivers making all the throws, Hogan called for an early end to the drills. He did not want a Pantego coach to see that Anderson was not throwing. Anderson had thrown 15-yard passes shortly after the team had arrived, but stopped and shook his head to Sells. He would not be able to throw today. "They need to figure it out as late as possible," Hogan said.

But Pantego had figured it out. On the first play, Pantego's defenders ignored Faith's two inside receivers, putting seven players directly on the line of scrimmage in an all-out commitment to stopping the run. Still, Faith took the opening possession and marched sixty-one yards for a touchdown, running on all nine plays, for a 6–0 lead.

The Panthers' first three offensive plays netted eight yards, and Pantego punted. Faith, with Anderson remaining at quarterback, ran on seven consecutive plays to reach the Panthers' 8. There, on fourth and eight, with Pantego wise to Anderson's inability to throw, Ashton entered the game to throw a pass that fell incomplete in the end zone. That would be the only possession of the first half on which the Lions did not score until throwing an interception with seventeen seconds remaining in the second quarter. Faith led 24–3 at halftime.

During intermission, Hogan took Ashton to a whiteboard and drew a couple of adjustments to plays for the second half. Hogan then gathered the players and sent them back out for the second half with these words: "Let's drive a nail in them. Let's finish this game."

Faith did, scoring four second-half touchdowns and winning 52–3. Ashton finished the day completing eleven of eighteen passes for 150 yards with two touchdowns and two interceptions. Again the defense suffocated Pantego, holding the Panthers to forty-four yards rushing and 140 yards total. In two games against the Panthers, Faith had outscored them 99–3 and outgained them 747 yards to 260.

"You guys did a great job," Hogan told his players after the game. "Especially defensively. Good job by the O-line."

With the Lions having completed their part to set up a third-round meeting between undefeated teams, Hogan could turn full attention to playing Bay Area Christian, if Bay Area could win its game the next night. "I watched some films on Bay Area. They're never out of position, guys. Ever. We've got some advantages on them, and we'll show you about that stuff next week, show you some film. One thing is, teams we've played have been gambling all year. Even Reicher played seven in a box. But Bay Area is never out of position."

Nerney led the team in prayer, asking that what the players hoped would be a two-week ending to the season would honor and glorify God, and then Hogan dismissed the players.

"Make sure you go hug your mom and somebody else's," he told them. "Unless you're sweaty."

CHAPTER 19

The Dream Comes True

STATE SEMIFINALS: BAY AREA CHRISTIAN BRONCOS

There was that August moment, during the first practice, when Ford had pointed to a spot on the practice field where he witnessed players letting up on the final steps of a 360. He told the players that spot represented the state semifinals. "We finished here last year," Ford had said. Just short, in other words.

The Lions had been in the semifinals twice before. Both times, the season had ended here. That was on players' and coaches' minds as preparations began for the much-anticipated matchup of the 12–0 Faith Christian Lions and the 12–0 Bay Area Christian Broncos from League City, between Houston and Texas's Gulf Coast.

Bay Area had marched through its twelve opponents much as the Lions had theirs. Not since the first game of the season, a 33–14 victory, had an opponent stayed within twenty-eight points of the Broncos. Three times they had scored at least sixty-eight points. Their average margin of victory was 50–7.

The day after defeating Pantego Christian the second time, Hogan and Sells had made a four-hour trip to College Station with Mark Jameson, the booster club president and father of Brock, to scout Bay Area. Clegg and his father, Ron, made a two-hour detour to join them when Weston's soccer tournament in San Antonio had been rained out.

On a cold, windy night with rain pelting a muddy field, they watched Bay Area's powerful run game easily dispatch Hyde Park Baptist, 46–0.

So back at school on Monday, players were immensely interested in Clegg's and the coaches' observations. Hogan provided his when the team gathered in the classroom that afternoon. Bay Area, he told them, was disciplined, big, and strong. "They throw the ball only out of dire necessity," he said. "They just want to run it, and I think that plays into our hands a little bit."

Hogan warned them about one player in particular. "Number 33," he called him. That was running back Alex Hooper. The roster listed Hooper at six-foot-four and 235 pounds; Hogan said he easily could weigh 240 or 245. "He's like a train. He runs north and south." Hooper does not rely on speed to get outside, or shifty moves to slip into the open field. He runs straight ahead, often accumulating defenders on his way. "You have him in the open field and you're by yourself, you'd better hang on and pray for those white jerseys to get there, because he's going to drag you." The key, Hogan said, would be to force Hooper to run sideways. "We've got to make this kid run east and west. He runs at a lot less than 240 pounds when he's going sideways."

Hogan wanted to beat Bay Area at its own game. He had read in South Texas newspapers on the Internet that Bay Area's coach had talked about the teams in Faith's side of the playoff bracket that ran the Spread offense, and how the Broncos' district featured teams that play smash-mouth football. "Let me tell you what he's telling his kids right now: 'They're a bunch of fast kids,'" Hogan said. "They're going to say, 'Okay, guys, we're going to smash them in the mouth. They're a Spread team. We're going to wear them down and do what we do.'"

At least, that's what Hogan hoped the Bay Area coach was saying.

"I will say this," Ford said as Hogan began to dismiss the players to suit up for practice. "Last year this week, we had a big letdown. All of you, coaches included. We took somebody lightly that we didn't need to."

There was that Regents loss again. It just would not go away.

+ + +

Anderson made a prediction as he walked across campus to the field house: "I'll be 21-of-30 for 265 yards." The first pass he would throw against Bay Area would be his first in the playoffs. Yet Anderson was optimistic about his shoulder injury. There were other injury concerns, however. Dunnington, who had hurt his back against Pantego, was late getting onto the field because he was being wrapped by trainer Auggie Gomez. Although Dunnington was late to the field, at least he was there. Roddy was not.

Five weeks earlier, before the Temple Christian game, Roddy had started feeling weak, as though all his energy had been drained. He left school early a few times to grab a nap. Then two weeks ago, he had begun feeling worse, and his throat felt like it was trying to close. Roddy felt even worse during the previous Friday's game. After the game, his temperature spiked to 103 degrees, and his parents took him to a clinic. Mononucleosis, the physician told him. No football for six months although, the doctor added, he did tend to be ultraconservative with his timetables.

Six months? All Roddy cared about at that point were the two weeks remaining in the football season. He visited a sports doctor on Monday, who sent him to an internist for blood work. The results would be back Wednesday, but mono appeared to be a certain diagnosis.

+ + +

The playoff bracket on the coaches' office whiteboard had been updated. What had started as a sixteen-team bracket had been erased to four teams: Reicher and Regents on the left side, with a line drawn for the winner to advance to face the Faith–Bay Area winner from the right side.

+ + +

When the Lions hit the field in full pads for Tuesday's practice, Wright was filling in at right guard for Roddy. Anderson was on the field, but at C receiver instead of quarterback. Reeder was at home, throwing up and suffering migraines. Coaches had planned on getting Anderson some work at Reeder's position anyway, but there were head shakes about another player being unable to practice the week of the semifinals.

Early in practice, all offensive plays featured Anderson at receiver. Nerney, from his receiver spot at the far right of the offense, called out to Clegg across the formation in a mock coach's voice: "Weston, you're very good at blocking. Get in there and block." Players laughed.

When practice switched to first-team defense, a new player suited up. Coach Postema grabbed a JV player's shoulder pads and red practice jersey, slipped them on, and then pulled a helmet over his head and buckled the chin strap.

Meet number 33.

At six feet and 205 pounds, Postema offered the closest look at what the Lions could expect when Hooper lined up in the Bay Area backfield—except for Postema's salt-and-pepper goatee. This was the first time Postema, who played two years of minor-league baseball after being drafted by the Detroit Tigers, had padded up for football since 1983 when he was a high school senior in Michigan.

"You guys need to wear his butt out!" Hogan yelled to the defense.

"That's number 33," Ford followed. "Get after his stinking tail."

On the first play, Sells, manning the scout-team quarterback position as usual—without pads and away from contact—handed the ball to Postema. "Number 33" carried the ball off right guard, was hit by a defender, and bounced off the tackle and through the line of scrimmage.

"We can't tackle him!" Hogan cried out. "You're right, Coach Postema! These guys are a bunch of wimps!"

Hogan's face showed his disgust as he turned and walked away. Loud enough for all to hear, he said, "These suckers don't remember that that little Regents team came out and kicked their butt. Okay, it'll happen again [against Bay Area]."

Postema then broke through the defensive line again. Nathan Alcantara came up from his safety position to make the tackle, and right before he did, he noticeably pulled up—this was Coach Postema he was about to tackle. Postema lowered the boom, drilling Alcantara, who hung on to make the tackle but only as Postema continued straight ahead over the top of him.

That would be what the Lions could expect to see from Hooper on Saturday.

After the scout-team offense ran twenty-five of Bay Area's plays, the players took a water break. Beads of sweat were running down Postema's face as he talked with a small group of players about the five or six helmet-to-helmet hits he had endured.

One of the players suggested Postema's IQ dropped each time he had banged helmets with a defender. "It can't drop much more if I'm out here doing this," Postema said.

Tuesday's practice ended with little positive to be taken away. "You think that was a good practice?" Hogan asked. The players did not. There was little of the usual laughter and playfulness as the players left the field. A few stayed behind.

"The off-tackle stuff, I'm just trying to explode," Postema explained to some who remained.

"Yeah, you were doing good," Nerney said. "I'm just frustrated with the team."

"Yeah," Postema replied. "That wasn't real good."

"Coach? Sells? Sells?" Nerney got Sells's attention. "Is Curtis not going to be back?"

"I don't know," Sells shrugged. "He looked pretty good today. He came up here today. He's skinny, though. They'll find out tomorrow. Listen, we're fine with Greg, too."

"I know," Nerney said.

But still, everyone would rather have Roddy healthy and in uniform.

"He sounded better, and he looked better today," Sells said. "But he has Wednesday, Thursday, Friday, four more days to suck it up. Landon's getting better. We'll be in good shape."

"He was able to bring his arm back," Nerney said. "That's killing us, though."

"Listen, no," Sells interrupted. "He'll be fixed. Don't you worry."

"Okay," Nerney nodded.

"Seriously," Sells said, sensing a need to continue the conversation. "There's things we can do."

"Sells," Nerney said, "I've got to tell you, it's pretty rough when like—like we all know, like me, Brock, Grant, and Weston—we all know that Landon's a really good athlete and stuff. But it's really rough when you like just throw him in there and you just throw him the ball the whole time. I didn't get one pass. Brock got one."

"Because I know you can catch," Sells explained. "Would you feel comfortable if we got out there and ran 800 Slide and Landon's never run it?"

"No," Nerney answered.

"You think we're really going to stick Landon in the B [receiver position] for one play, just to run Reverse Right? No."

"No."

"We've just got to practice things. We don't run it without practicing it. That's why we went from Buckeye to Bearcat to Landon at B to Landon at C. I know you can catch 800 Slide every time we throw it. That's not the problem. I don't need to sit there and throw it to Brock on 90 Wheel every time. He can do that stuff. Landon needs to get out here and see if we can run this play, and see if we can run that play. That's why we did that."

"Yeah, that's fine."

"Also, for us to win, we need to get Landon the ball."

Sells then placed a hand on Nerney's shoulder and motioned away from the other players listening in to their conversation. The two walked away, still talking.

Behind them, Wright was lying on the field, thinking about the game ahead, thinking about what could be, and wondering—with all that this team was playing for, and what had happened in this round of the playoffs the past two years—how today's practice could be so lousy.

✦ ✦ ✦

Dana Stone wondered whether she should stop answering the athletic department phone.

In successive calls on Wednesday, Hogan's assistant had learned that Ackerman had been throwing up all night and missed morning classes, that there had been an emergency recall on the school's detergent and the team's water bottles could not be washed, and that Roddy's blood work confirmed the mono diagnosis and Roddy would have a sonogram to see whether his spleen had enlarged.

By the time practice rolled around, Reeder was back from his illness. Ackerman had made it to afternoon classes, but he was not participating in practice. Neither was Dunnington. Roddy was still out, too, so the starting offensive line during practice included backups at center and right guard, the starting quarterback (Anderson) was at running back and the starting running back (Hockenbrough) played a receiver position.

It was no surprise, then, that the offense portion of practice was so-so. When the defense took over, Ford hollered, "You guys are going to have to pick up the pace! We're another day closer to the state semifinals!"

Postema was not number 33 this day. He said he felt fine, as he displayed the welts on his right arm and told of icing the arm the night before. Garrett Cox, at five-foot-eight and 170 pounds, was playing the role of the much bigger Hooper.

The defense responded to Ford's words with a spirited workout.

"Now we're playing defense!" Hogan yelled at one point. Ford was particularly animated, slapping helmets and shoulder pads after each play. At least for the defense, Wednesday was much better than Tuesday.

Reeder filled Anderson's safety spot as Anderson stood behind the defense, with Ackerman and Dunnington. "Don't talk to him; you'll get sick," Hogan told Anderson, pointing at Ackerman. Then he pointed to Dunnington. "And don't talk to him; you'll get hurt."

+ + +

The semifinal losses came up during Open Floor Thursday.

"I've been thinking about it for, I guess, this whole week until today," said O'Neal, leaning forward as he sat on his footlocker. "I want to say in light of how far we've gotten and how far we got the last two years, making it to the semifinals—we can't allow ourselves to say, 'Oh, we've made it this far. We've accomplished this already and it's cool. We made it back. We knew we were as good as we were the last two years.' You can't look back on anything that you've already accomplished, because you know what you truly deserve: the state championship. So you can't look back and say, 'Oh, we've made it this far before, so it's okay if we don't make it further.' We should still have our heads down and be moving toward our goal. You can't say, 'Oh, we made it this far, so we're good.' No, we've made it this far, so now let's go even further because we can. So don't look back and say, 'We're just as good as we were last year, so we're good. Now, if we lose, it's not like we got worse.'

"We have to win, or we didn't get what we deserve, or what we put the time in for, what we worked for. Don't allow yourself to be satisfied with what you've already accomplished, because you haven't accomplished what you deserve yet."

Hogan took over from there, telling of a conversation he had had with a reporter from *The Grapevine Courier*. "He said, 'Do you consider this season a success right now?' And I said, 'In terms of what, wins or losses?' He said, 'Well, let's just say you get to the state game and lose. Will it be a successful season?' And I said, 'In terms of wins and losses or other things?' And he said, 'What other things?' I said, 'There are other things beside wins and losses.' He said, 'Okay, tell me what those things are.' So I told him, 'For instance, this team is a very tight team. We had an unbelievable experience at camp and as we've gone through the season.'"

Hogan told the players that they were on a team with relationships that most would never have again. Only in college football could they have the opportunity to have this many relationships on one team. And even then, that team would have to have the level of vulnerability that existed within this locker room. Hogan continued telling about his conversation with the reporter.

"'So in that aspect,' I said, 'yes, it's been a successful season. In terms of wins or losses, nothing's acceptable except for a state championship.' I wish they would have printed that. But, anyway, that's the way I feel. I think that's what Josh is saying, and that's good, because you need to get what you are capable of getting."

+ + +

The Mel Gibson movie *Braveheart* played on the charter bus television monitors as the Lions made the three-hour bus ride to Round Rock, near Austin in Central Texas. The players notified the coaches at the front of the bus when they should skip past a couple of inappropriate scenes during the movie.

A little more than two hours into the trip, the bus was sailing down Interstate 35 through Temple. On the left side of the road, the TAPPS Division IV state championship game was being played at Wildcat Stadium. That stadium also would be the site of larger-classification title games the following weekend. The players who were awake looked toward the stadium as they drove by. "We'll be there next weekend," came one voice from the back of the bus.

+ + +

The injuries and illnesses that had kept Ackerman, Dunnington, and Reeder out of practices during the week no longer were a concern when the team took the field for warm-ups. Roddy had been cleared to play and, though thirty pounds lighter, he said he felt strong. The adrenaline of meeting another undefeated team in the semifinals more than made up for the lost weight. Anderson warmed up his arm, lobbing passes almost twenty yards. He was throwing, but he looked nothing like a quarterback capable of making good on his prediction of passing for 265 yards.

Bay Area's fans created much of the pre-game atmosphere, blasting air horns and shaking or clapping noisemakers a full hour before kick-off. Faith's players appeared loose and confident as they worked crisply through pre-game drills. There was more pep than usual, with more back slaps and rhythmic head nods from the players.

When the quarterbacks and receivers went near their end zone, Anderson threw a few short routes. Ashton and Postema, however, were throwing the longer passes.

On Ashton's helmet, for the first time, were two Lion-head stickers. He had played all season with a blank white helmet because the JV had been his primary team and, in the interest of morale, Hogan does not like having a sometime-varsity player standing out on the JV team. Nor does Hogan want a player wearing a helmet logo for varsity games and then taking it off for JV games. "You have to work kids where they are," Hogan said. This week also had marked the end of a six-week period for which Hogan had challenged Ashton to not have any behavior problems in school. On Tuesday, Ashton reached that mark. And that World History exam he needed to ace to remain eligible? He answered correctly all the questions plus the bonus questions. So here he was Saturday evening, with those Lion heads on his helmet, preparing for a vital role in the state semifinals.

"That a boy! Great shot!" Hogan exclaimed after one perfectly thrown ball by Ashton. Hogan turned to Sells. "He can throw that pass." Hogan continued to encourage the freshman. "Good ball." "Good shot." "Looking sharp." At one point, Hogan placed a hand on Ashton's right shoulder. "You're doing a great job."

Hogan sensed that Ashton needed the encouragement. Hogan knew he had handed an enormous assignment to a kid who had turned fifteen six days earlier, by asking him to take over—in the playoffs, no less—the quarterback position. Ashton's passes would matter much more against undefeated Bay Area than they did the week before against Pantego, and Hogan wanted to show Ashton he had faith in him. "I knew he needed it," Hogan said, "plus, I wanted him to know I was on his side. My philosophy has always been to tell the player, 'You're my guy no matter what. You make a few mistakes, fine.' Because I think that people play better like that."

Hogan gathered the players before heading back to the locker room to make final preparations for game time. "We ready to fly tonight? Let me tell you something. We did a little research. I have never, ever, ever lost a game to a running back who weighs over 200 pounds. Anybody want to guess why? Speed. Speed. That's your best asset. When that ball's snapped, I want them to see something that there's no way they can adjust to. That make sense? Let's get after their tail."

+ + +

Bay Area received the opening kickoff and gave the Lions a heavy dose of straight-ahead Alex Hooper. The big running back ran for three yards on his first carry, five on his second. On third and two from the Broncos' 34 yard line, Hooper advanced the ball just enough for a first down. Hooper carried again on first down, for three yards. Fullback Will Weeks, a big runner himself at six-one and 215 pounds, carried for a 3-yard gain on the next play. On third and four, though, the Lions' defense rose up to stop John Wade for a 3-yard loss, forcing Bay Area to punt to the Lions' 38.

Anderson started Faith's first possession at quarterback. As was the case in the previous two games, Sells called only running plays with Anderson in. And as was the case in those two previous games, the Lions marched to an early touchdown. They ran the ball eleven consecutive times to cover the sixty-two yards to the end zone, with Hockenbrough running the final five yards and then kicking the extra point for a 7–0 lead.

Bay Area's next possession lasted only three plays—without Hooper touching the ball—before a punt gave Faith the ball a yard inside the Broncos' side of midfield.

The Lions needed less than two minutes to take a 14–0 lead, with the speedy Dunnington breaking through the line of scrimmage and outracing Broncos defenders for a 42-yard touchdown run. In its first two possessions, Faith had already matched the most points Bay Area had yielded in any game for the season.

A long kickoff return allowed the Broncos to start their next possession at Faith's 41. Bay Area pushed the ball to the Faith 8, but the threat ended there on a fourth-down incompletion.

Neither team mounted much of a scoring chance until late in the first half. Faith had designs on scoring when it took possession on its 36 yard line with 1:17 left in the half and Ashton having taken over for Anderson during the previous possession.

Ashton directed an efficient drive, completing four of six passes to lead the Lions to the Bay Area 9. From there, and with only six seconds showing on the first-half clock, Ashton threw a scoring strike to Nerney. Hockenbrough's extra point gave Faith a 21–0 halftime lead.

"Listen to me, guys," Hogan ordered at halftime. "This team is good. The beginning of the third quarter in any big game is very important, because they are looking at 21–0 and they're thinking it's now or never. So let me tell you what's going to happen. Just trust me on this. I've seen it a lot of times. The first eight minutes of the third quarter, you're going to get every bit of adrenaline, every bit of pride, every bit of fear, every bit of anger—everything that they have bottled up from a 12–0 season, you're going to get it in the first eight minutes. And the way to deal with it is to match the surge, and it'll be a discouragement.

Listen, there is no time to relax. You see their crowd is good. They get a little bit of momentum, and they'll be ready to fight. All right? Let's close the lid."

Bay Area did get some momentum on the second play of the second half, when Ashton lost a fumble on Faith's 34. But again, Faith's defense held on a fourth-down play, handing the ball back to the offense at its 27. The offense responded by taking the ball to the Bay Area end zone, with Ashton hitting Reeder for a 32-yard touchdown pass. The momentum had swung back to Faith's side in the form of a 28–0 lead with 6:26 left in the third quarter.

That "every bit of everything" that Hogan predicted the Lions would receive came out when the Broncos took the ball back. Bay Area drove ninety yards, getting on the scoreboard when quarterback Josh Morgenroth connected with fullback Wade for a 9-yard scoring pass. Wade had sprung wide open when Hockenbrough blitzed the quarterback from his linebacker spot.

"That was totally my fault," Hogan told his players during a time-out after the scoring play. "I blitzed Grant because I thought they were going to do a drop back. That was his guy. That was my fault. My fault."

Although Bay Area had scored, the good news for the Lions was that the Broncos had needed twelve time-consuming plays to do so. As the Broncos failed on the two-point conversion attempt, the scoreboard showed only thirty-four seconds remaining in the third quarter, with Faith ahead 28–6. Bay Area's running offense was not built to overcome such deficits in that amount of time.

Indeed, the Broncos advanced into Faith territory only once more, reaching the 31 before that drive ended with an interception by Jameson.

As the final seconds ticked off the clock, players doused Hogan's white dress shirt with a Gatorade bath. Hogan's teams had remained unbeaten against 200-pound running backs. Hooper had finished the game with twenty-eight yards rushing on only nine carries. Faith's early lead had forced the running Broncos into a passing mode, and they had completed only ten of their twenty-two pass attempts.

The semifinals hump had been cleared. As campus pastor Brooks presented the team its semifinals trophy at midfield, he declared, "Hey, you are state finalists for the first time!"

Word made its way to the field that there would be no rematch with Regents. Instead, the state title game would be a rematch with Reicher, which had defeated Regents 15–9. Although the players had hoped for another chance at Regents, there was no disappointment in playing Reicher again. The opponent did not matter. Being in the championship game was most important.

"This is all I've been dreaming about for four years now," a happy Reeder said.

"I can't tell you how intently I'm going to be looking over that scouting report," Clegg said. "That's all I'm going to be thinking about. I'm going to tell all my teachers, 'Listen, there's one thing I'm focusing on this week, and it is *foot . . . ball.*"

The next week for sure, win or lose, would end the season.

"It feels good that we finally made it to state," Ackerman said as he walked off the field. "But it's sad in a way, because it's our final week."

CHAPTER 20

"Remember Why You Play"

STATE CHAMPIONSHIP: REICHER CATHOLIC COUGARS
It was time for coaches and players to finish what they had started seventeen weeks earlier. The words across the bottom of the first page of the Monday scouting report carried Hogan's admonition for the week:

The person who gives their best, you can ask nothing more. What does your best look like? Let's finish with our best.

Unlike the final practice week of the previous season, that week the Lions did give their best. There were no flat practices like the ones leading up to last year's season-ending loss. The players were sharp. They were confident and focused. And they were loose. On Tuesday, as Wright played middle linebacker for Reicher's simulated defense, he sang, "Rum, pum, pum, pum," even though temperatures in the high sixties did not indicate it was time for Christmas carols.

By Thursday, the final practice, temperatures had reached beyond 70 degrees, and a deep blue sky shared space with the bright sun. "Seniors, this is it for you," Hogan said as the team assembled on the practice field. "This is the last time you'll wear a Faith practice jersey. This is the last Faith practice. God blessed us with a beautiful day. It's perfect weather. Tomorrow's Open Floor, and you're playing in the last—likely the last—football game you'll ever play. But the last high school game. So this is it. Seniors, I love you guys. I've had a great time coaching you. Make your last practice a sharp one."

They did, all while maintaining the relaxed atmosphere of the week's practices. The players laughed as they practiced defending Reicher's Swinging Gate, the trick play they like to attempt for two-point conversions. Clegg would look away from time to time toward the game field, where the soccer team was playing Coram Deo. He and four other members of the football team would be joining the soccer team Monday.

The linemen had been off at one end of the field, doing a sit-through instead of a walk-through. They carried their chairs over to the rest of the team, but before taking their seats, they expressed mock sentimentality over the final practice by interrupting the pass offense to give a group hug to Sells. There certainly was no anxiety in this group.

Roddy plopped down in his chair. Coach Rivera walked over to Roddy, who was celebrating his birthday on the practice field like he had so wanted to do the previous season. "Last one, big boy," Rivera said. "I know," Roddy answered. "It's depressing."

When the Swinging Gate appeared to be sufficiently defensed, Hogan called the team together. He would dismiss everyone except the players involved in pass defense because he wanted them to see a few more of Reicher's plays. The rest, however, would be free to go after Hogan prayed.

"See ya," Hogan said, after concluding his prayer, and saluted his players.

The members of the pass defense, with a handful of players running routes against them, stayed for five more minutes before they, too, left the practice field for good. Nerney walked slowly off the field as he chatted with Hogan. Roddy, who had stayed to watch the pass defense because he had not wanted to leave, was the only player on the field as Sells filled a milk crate with offensive players' wristbands.

"I want to run one Post pattern," the lineman told Sells.

"Okay," Sells said, as he picked up a football.

"How do I run a Post pattern?" Roddy asked.

Sells demonstrated the route with his right hand, and Roddy took off lumbering down the field. When Roddy angled toward the middle of the field, Sells launched a perfect, 25-yard spiral. The ball hit Roddy's hands. Then it hit the ground. In his last action on the Faith practice field, Roddy finally played a skill position, and he dropped the ball.

Hogan and Nerney, who had stopped to watch, laughed and turned to resume their conversation.

+ + +

Hogan held up a piece of paper to start a championship-week Friday edition of Open Floor "Thursday." He read the headline from the *Waco Tribune-Herald*: "Reicher gets shot at trophy it wants most." When the Cougars had won their second-round playoff game two weeks earlier, the article said, coach Mark Waggoner had held the trophy up for his players to take. They let him keep it. "We told Coach Waggoner this isn't the trophy we want," senior running back Nick Fung said in the article. The only trophy the players wanted was the one up for grabs the next day against Faith.

"So they will definitely be ready," Hogan told his players. As he had done many times throughout the season in assessing an opponent, Hogan warned his players that they would get Reicher's best game. "They'll be ready," he concluded, then opened the floor for players.

Kallal spoke first, telling of text messages from a former Faith player who wanted him to tell the players that he was proud of their accomplishments and that he loved each of them. "I just want to say," Kallal said, adding his own thoughts, "it's been an honor to play with you guys this season, and I will give my heart for you guys tomorrow."

Wright shared two quotes regarding determination: "The surest way not to fail is to determine to succeed" and "Determination gives you the resolve to keep on going in spite of the roadblocks that lay before you." "Since Reicher's such a good team," Wright said, "there are going to be roadblocks. They're going to get a big play here and there." But, Wright added, if the players could maintain the determination described in those quotes, the defense could answer Reicher with a big play of its own and prevent Reicher's offense from putting a good drive together.

"I just wanted to start off by saying," Nerney began, "that it's the same thing as that first Commitment Night. It's that I love you guys more than anything. For the entire summer and the past 360 days, there's nothing else I've thought about that was bigger than football. I care so much about each and every one of y'all." He spoke of all the 400s they had run, especially the ones they had not wanted to run. Those were, he said, for this moment. "I just want each and every one of y'all to be thinking about that tonight. Thinking about what it's going to be like to walk out there at Wildcat Stadium with your brothers, people who have gotten down there in the grit and grime with you every day. When you didn't want to. I know for a fact that you're going to get my best effort that I've ever given and that I think I ever will give to a football team, tomorrow. And I love you guys."

Those types of thoughts continued, as players seemed eager to speak in the last Open Floor. Of course, it would not have been an official Open Floor without inspiring words from O'Neal. "Muhammad Ali said this," O'Neal began. "He said, 'The fight is won or lost away from witnesses, behind the lines, in the gym, out there on the road, long before I dance under those lights.'" O'Neal took the players back to Mt. Lebanon, when no one else was there to give the players credit for their work. All that work, all that sweat, all that pain, he said, was done solely for each other. "We have four quarters left of football. Probably forever, for most of you seniors. Just four quarters. How are you going to play those four quarters? When everything you've done for the last four years comes down to the last four quarters, what are you going to do with them? What better way is there to leave than with a state-championship ring? So you can say, 'I've done all this work, and I have accomplished my goal. I worked when no one was looking. I threw up when no one was looking. I ran that extra 400 when no one was looking.' What better way to end it all than with a state-championship ring?"

Clegg fidgeted as he began telling his teammates about playing soccer while also playing football. Especially the soccer conditioning right after football practices. "It was bad, guys. It was just so hard. I would be the first one to jump in and do the conditioning, and I'd be the last one to finish it." He told of how he would be running around the soccer complex, but as he would look down to the soccer team name on his practice jersey—and at this point he began to cry and would cry even harder as his story progressed—"I was running for you guys. Every time. Every time. Every bit of conditioning, I had this team in my head. My coach would just wear me out for being late or just not being good enough and other stuff, and just wear me out. I had everyone here in my mind because I knew I was working for every single one of you guys. And I knew, I knew that you guys were going to state."

He told of the time when the coach suggested Clegg should quit the team and he had almost walked away, but how he instead had told his coach how much his football coaches and teammates meant to him. "I love you guys so much. Looking at this team, I'll never be a part of another team with the dedication level and the commitment and the love like you have here. I told him, 'You don't know what it's about.' It's about having brothers, it's about having people working as hard as you, loving the others, giving 100 percent for them. To know, I won't have another football game ever. Ever. Like Josh said, four quarters. I'll have a lot more soccer games, and I'll have a lot more coaches. But it will never be like this. Ever. Ever. Every word that my coach was screaming, just tearing me apart, guys, it was all for you. And now we have four quarters left. So knowing all that stuff, know—know for a fact!—I'm not taking any plays off. I'm not taking anything off. I'll finish what, this season, I started. And I want to go to the next practice I have and say, 'Yeah, we won state. And I know you don't give a rip about it, but I do. Because you don't know what it's about.' Let me be able to say that. Let me be able to think that. I want it so bad. I love you guys. I'm not holding anything back."

As player after player spoke up—O'Neal again, on living out their commitments instead of merely speaking them; Hockenbrough on being thankful he could spend this part of his life with the guys in this locker room; Messinger on the thrill of walking, hand in hand with teammates, through the tunnel each week—emotion flowed in similar fashion to Commitment Night.

John Ashton, a junior and Peter's older brother, had played in only two games because of injuries and grades. He spoke little, if at all, during team gatherings. But today there was something he had to say. "It's just been amazing watching you guys play," he said. "And I'm so proud of everyone." His voice became unsteady. "And I'm proud—" He couldn't finish the sentence, taking two deep breaths then looking down. He took another deep breath. "It's been kind of cool to see you"—he looked across the room to his brother, Peter, tears beginning—"step in for Landon and you get the spotlight as a freshman and all that. It's kind of brought me down a little bit, but you're my brother, and I'm so proud of you. I just wanted to let you know that."

"Embrace!" Nerney said to break the silence. The players picked up an "Embrace!" chant until the brothers met in the middle of the locker room and hugged tightly.

O'Neal had said he had a quote to finish the session. That had been at least six or seven minutes earlier. But the time had come for a closing thought.

"'Let others lead small lives, but not you,'" O'Neal read from a sheet of paper. "'Let others argue over small things, but not you. Let others leave their future in the hands of somebody else, but not you.' Let's go win state tomorrow."

"Let's do it," one player stated with determination as the players stood to gather in a circle and dismiss in prayer.

+ + +

The coaches looked across the artificial surface of Wildcat Stadium as Anderson began throwing passes to Cochran and as other players began going through their pre-game routines, looking for clues as to how well Anderson would be able to throw. Coach Matt Dowling walked over to Anderson and asked how his shoulder felt. "Sweet," Anderson replied. Still, Anderson was throwing soft passes as the offense ran through its key plays.

Shortly, the players returned to the locker room for the final time before the game's start. Cochran, who wouldn't miss this game for anything, painted two strips of eye black below Wright's eyes. But for this game, Wright wanted more. Cochran smeared the eye black down Wright's cheeks, in *Braveheart* warrior fashion.

"I love you," Clegg said to Nerney as they embraced. "Let's get us one."

"I love you," Messinger told O'Neal. "Let's finish it."

Anderson, sitting next to Cochran, wrote a red "7" on his right

forearm. Wright, Clegg, and Hockenbrough all had written Coch
old jersey number on their taped wrists.

"Remember who you're playing for tonight," said Roddy, pac-
ing around the locker room. "You're playing for the guy next to you.
Remember waking up early every day in the summer so you could play
for a state championship at the end."

Hogan emerged from the coaches' meeting room to address the
players. "All right, listen. I'm reminded of what the apostle Paul said to
a group he wrote a letter to. He said, 'Hey, we didn't come to you with
a bunch of fancy words.' You remember what he said he came with? In
demonstration. That's what he said. He said, 'We did it.' We didn't just
say it. We didn't tell you what to do. We showed you what to do. We
showed you. That's what people—I don't care if it's an apostle, a pastor,
a business owner, a football team, it doesn't matter. People who win in
life demonstrate things. They don't just talk about it. They demonstrate
it. How bad do you really want to win the football game? That's the
question. I think I know how bad you do. That's why this is not a rah-
rah speech. This is just a reminder. I know how bad you want to win.
And I wouldn't like to be wearing light blue tonight. I really wouldn't."

Then, almost position by position, Hogan detailed how players
could demonstrate they wanted to win. "You demonstrate it with perfect focus for four quarters," he concluded, "and you'll finish what you
started in Mt. Lebanon. You with me? Let's get after their tail."

+ + +

"Everyone in red!"

"Nobody touches your brother!"

For the fourteenth game, players declared who they were playing for
as they rocked side to side inside the inflatable tunnel. As always, when
the front flap opened, the senior offensive linemen walked out first,
hand in hand, through the smoke. The seven rows of players walked
between the cheerleaders for the first ten yards, then in unison chanted,
"We are Faith!" and ran to their sideline.

Reicher's players huddled on the opposite side as Faith's kickoff-
return team prepared to take the field. Hogan hoped for another quick
"get off" like his team had managed when the teams had played four

good kickoff return by the Lions would be a great
ut a strong wind at the back of Reicher's kicker
over Anderson's head at the 7 yard line. Anderson
ect the kick and gathered the ball near the goal
enough to disrupt the timing on the blocking, and
by four white-shirted Cougars at the 17.

The first play Sells relayed down from the press box called for
Anderson to carry the ball. Right away, Sells saw something different about Reicher's defense. Faith's no-huddle offense, with each play
relayed from the sideline through coded numbers, provided Sells time
to survey the opposing defense before sending in his play call. It had
worked that way in the first Reicher game, as it had in every other game.
But that was not the case on the first play. After Sells called in the play
and the numbers were flashed to the offense, Reicher's defenders looked
to their sideline and picked up signals from their coaches before set-
tling into their alignment. Reicher's coaches called a perfect defense for
Faith's play, and Anderson was stuffed for a 2-yard loss.

Sells next sent in a pass play in case Reicher expected Faith to
stick to running plays only with Anderson at quarterback. Again, the
Cougars' defenders looked to their sideline after Faith's play had been
signaled in. The play was a short pass to Clegg, one Sells was confident
Anderson could complete after watching him make that pass at least
thirty times in practice that week. Clegg had a defender in front of him
and a second defender behind him on the route, and Anderson's pass
was soft and well out of reach of Clegg's diving attempt.

Reicher stopped another Anderson run on third down, and Faith
sent out its punt team. For the first time all season, Faith did not score
a touchdown on its first possession. Only a fine, athletic play by Wright
kept his punt from being blocked, but the low, scrambled kick gave
Reicher its first possession on Faith's 45.

That was field position Hogan knew his team could not afford to
give Reicher. Although far from easy, the Cougars took advantage to score
a touchdown. Four times Reicher faced third down on the drive. Of the
four hundred or so Faith fans, about seventy-five—mostly students—
stood along the rail at the front of the stands, encouraging the defense
each third down to make a big stop and end the drive. But three times,
twice with runs and once with a pass, Reicher quarterback Kenneth

Cluley gave his team the first down. After the fourth third-down failed at the Faith 1, Cluley carried the ball across the goal line on fourth down for a 7–0 lead. Reicher ran fourteen plays and kept the ball for eight minutes and twenty-three seconds in scoring. Almost ten minutes into the game, the Lions had possessed the ball for ninety-three seconds.

Reicher's kicker booted the ensuing kickoff through the Faith end zone for a touchback, giving the Lions the ball at their 20. On the first play, Anderson broke a momentum-shifting run that, even with a 10-yard penalty enforced from near the end of the run because of an illegal block downfield, put the Lions in a good spot near midfield. Jameson pumped his fist at the end of the run and turned to the Faith stands, motioning with both arms for the fans to make more noise. But up in the press box, Sells again had observed something that concerned him.

Anderson had started left on the play, toward the Faith sideline. As he neared the sideline, boxed in by three Cougars, he reversed his field. When Anderson began to retreat toward the far sideline, ten of Reicher's eleven defenders were on the near side of the field. Only Anderson's athletic ability had allowed him to escape one tackle in the backfield, and only his speed had allowed him to outrace the defenders across the width of the field.

Somehow, Sells suspected, Reicher's coaches knew what plays he was calling.

Three running plays netted Faith nine yards, setting up fourth and one at the Reicher 46. The first quarter ended there, with Faith trailing by seven points and having run but seven plays on offense.

Hogan elected to go for the first down rather than punt, and when Hockenbrough was stopped for no gain, Reicher took over at that spot. On the second play, Reicher's strong-running quarterback broke two tackles in the backfield and three more downfield en route to a 24-yard run. "Dadgummit! Dadgummit!" Roddy yelled from the sideline.

Hogan called time-out. As his players took a knee around him and gulped water, he told them, "Here's the bottom line. Listen to me. I'm going to shoot straight with you like I always have, ever since you've known me. Here's the bottom line. They're mad, and they're playing at the top of their game, and for some reason, some of the people in this group think they're scared of your red jersey. Cluley wanted to make a first down a *lot* more than you wanted to tackle him. That's the bottom line. He whipped your butt. That's the bottom line." And, in a rarity, Hogan pointed to individual players and said "you and you and you" to indicate a half-dozen defenders who were not working to fight off blockers. "They want to win more than you. Go."

The defense returned to the field, only to have running back Ross Rasner carry the ball another twenty-four yards to the Faith 4 on the next play. Cluley scored from there, and Reicher led 14–0 with 10:35 to play in the second quarter.

As Faith defenders jogged to the sideline following the extra-point kick, Kallal met them halfway, encouraging them with, "Let's go! Let's go!" then slapping Nerney and Messinger on their backsides.

The Lions trailed by two touchdowns, and the defense had yet to stop Reicher's offense. So Sells decided to go to plays from the new Bearcat formation. Anderson, his first pass had demonstrated, was not throwing as well as he had earlier during the week. So Ashton was sent in at quarterback and Anderson moved to running back. The coaches wanted to get the ball to Anderson in the open field, because they did not think anyone on Reicher's defense had the speed to keep up with their biggest playmaker.

The first play called for Ashton to throw a short pass to Anderson behind the line of scrimmage. As Anderson reached up for the pass, Rasner planted his helmet square into Anderson's chest. The collision knocked the ball free from Anderson's hands for an incomplete pass and drew "oohs" from both sides of the stadium. Anderson bent over, the front of his helmet on the turf for a moment before slowly rising. He took three steps, leaned over at the waist and unsnapped his helmet before staggering to the sideline.

Faith fans watched both the game and Anderson lying on the sideline. After an incomplete pass, Ashton connected with Nerney for completions of twenty-two and twelve yards that moved Faith within striking distance at the Cougars' 27. On the next play, however, the threat ended with an intercepted pass. Any hope that Anderson had suffered nothing more than having the air knocked out of him disappeared when EMTs began wheeling a stretcher around the track toward the Faith bench.

By the time Anderson was loaded onto the stretcher, Faith had finally stopped Reicher's offense, but also had given the ball right back with an interception on Faith's side of the field. A quick touchdown put Reicher up 21–0.

Even Hockenbrough, the player O'Neal had cited in that Open Floor Thursday as the one who would best carry the legacy of Faith football, felt the game slipping away. It was not the score as much as how Faith had played to that point and how Reicher seemed to know every play that was coming. After only a dozen or so offensive plays, Sells was convinced Reicher coaches had broken Faith's numbering code for relaying plays. When the coaches changed the set of numbers players were to read, Ashton read a wrong play and threw an interception. With so many players playing both offense and defense, there would not be sufficient time to communicate a new method of calling plays until halftime.

Hockenbrough did not see a way the Lions could overcome that deficit, especially with his best friend in an ambulance headed for the emergency room. When Anderson left, so had half of Faith's offensive game plan, including all those new plays from new formations the Lions had been working on for more than a month.

The deficit grew to 28–0 when Reicher recovered an onside kick and scored five plays later. The snowball was rolling and growing. Another interception, which gave the Cougars the ball at Faith's 37, led to another touchdown. With 2:44 left in the first half, the Lions trailed 35–0.

With thirty-four seconds on the clock, Ashton gave the Lions their first positive play since Anderson's long run when the freshman broke free down the right sideline for a 65-yard touchdown run. "Go Peter! Go Peter! Go Peter!" teammates yelled as they chased Ashton down the sideline toward the end zone.

But that play further confirmed coaches' belief that Reicher was calling defenses based on Faith's offensive signals. Ashton had run the wrong play. The coaches on the sideline with the numbered cards had sent in a pass play to the left; Ashton misread the numbers as a running play. After he started left with the ball and stopped in the backfield, nine Reicher defenders were on that side of the field. As Anderson had done earlier, Ashton reversed toward the other sideline and, with good blocks from receivers and few defenders on that side of the field, found an open lane to the end zone.

+ + +

Deuce Hogan was waiting for his dad by the locker room door at the start of halftime. With tear-filled eyes, the seven-year-old grabbed his father. "Daddy, what's wrong?" he asked in a squeaky voice. "Deuce," his dad said, "it's okay. Whether we win or lose, I'm still going to come home, and tomorrow you and I are going to play football." Asked Deuce, "Are we going to lose?" "Well," came his dad's answer, "we could. There's a good possibility that we may lose." Again, Hogan told his son that they'd be playing football together at home the next day. "We're going to have a great time," he said. Deuce then told his dad that he loved him and squeezed his thumb. Hogan smiled, bent over, gave his son a kiss, and entered the locker room.

"I know you guys are disappointed, but don't you dare quit," Hogan told his players. "There's a lot of time left." Hogan then headed into the coaches' meeting room with his assistants.

The players showed no signs of quitting. The game was still winnable despite the 35–7 deficit, they told each other. Roddy took his teammates back to the September morning during athletics period when they had gathered around the Lion head at midfield and created all those scenarios and planned how they would respond to each. One of those scenarios, he reminded them, was trailing by thirty points to Reicher at halftime. And then, another player remembered, Anderson would get hurt. "Yeah, and Landon gets hurt," Roddy remembered aloud. "Everything is like that. And you know how we said we were going to respond? We said we're going to play to our full potential and come back and win this freaking ball game!"

The coaches came out of their meeting room, and Hogan stood in front of the players. First, he said, the offense would huddle during the second half because Reicher knew their signals. The running backs would alternate bringing plays to the huddle. Second, he detailed defensive adjustments that he thought would be effective. Third, he told his players they were getting beat on speed and effort. There was plenty of time left to play, however. They had needed only twelve seconds to score their first-half touchdown. He had seen plenty of second-half comebacks like he knew this team was capable of making.

"Don't quit on me, Red, don't quit on me," Messinger said as the players stood to return to the field. "Let's go."

✦ ✦ ✦

The locker room door opened to a thunderous noise. The Faith stands had practically emptied. Most of the four hundred fans had left their seats and crossed over behind the end zone—much to the displeasure of outnumbered security personnel—to form a long tunnel leading from the field house to the field.

The amazed players jogged through the tunnel as fans chanted, "We are Faith! We are Faith! We are Faith!" Later, Hockenbrough would recall thinking fans had formed "a small line, and like ten minutes later, I was still running through it. . . . It was a cool feeling of no matter what happens at the end of the game, everybody still loves us."

The coaches were the last to leave the locker room, and they were more stunned than the players. Sells started through the fans and made it three or four steps before cutting out of the tunnel. He had become so emotional that he did not think he could make it through all the fans without breaking down and crying. Ford and Hogan, who trailed Sells, veered left and walked around the fans. Tears welled up in their eyes.

The fans had successfully charged up their players for the second half. After reaching the sideline, Roddy shoved Nerney. "They didn't go to Lebanon! I did!" he screamed into Nerney's face mask. "I ran all day!"

But comeback hopes were short lived. Cluley, who media would vote the game's Most Valuable Player, took the third play of the half fifty-nine yards for a touchdown run and a 41–7 lead. Hogan had been right about the offense being able to drive the ball when it huddled. The Lions followed with a long drive that ended with Ashton's fourth interception of the game, this one in the Reicher end zone.

On that drive, Ashton had been hit hard on the helmet near the Reicher sideline. He remained on the turf as Gomez rushed across the field. After a couple of minutes, Ashton rose and began walking toward the Faith sideline. Nerney, the senior, stepped into his path to embrace him and tell him that he would be all right and to express encouragement for Ashton's three remaining years wearing that Lion decal. Ashton missed one play as Gomez continued to check him on the sideline, then jogged back to the Faith huddle.

On Faith's next possession, however, Ashton went down again. This time, he had been hit straight on by a defender after pitching the ball on a reverse. Ashton started toward the sideline, then dropped to his knees before rolling over on his back.

The referee walked over to Hogan as Gomez again checked Ashton on the field. "He won't tell you this," the referee said, "but he's really in pain here." Hogan nodded. When Ashton told Gomez that he felt pain running up and down his back rather than from side to side, Gomez called for another stretcher as a precaution. With Ashton's father there on the field with him, he was loaded onto the stretcher and taken to another ambulance. Both the first- and second-string quarterbacks would finish the game in the emergency room. (Anderson would be diagnosed with a bruised sternum and a bruised pancreas, Ashton with a sprained back.)

Faith would finish the game with juniors Wright and Shivers rotating at quarterback. Wright had run one play at quarterback late in the playoff blowout of Pantego. It had been two years since he had had serious reps at quarterback in practice. Shivers, who had warmed up his arm in pre-game on "a gut feeling," had not thrown a pass since the third game of the regular season.

Hogan watched as the offense continued to move the ball, although not enough to sustain any scoring drives, with untested third- and fourth-stringers at quarterback. At one point on the sideline, he thought about the character Wright and Shivers were showing. "It was real affirming for me," Hogan said. "Affirming that what we do on a daily basis, it's going to translate when life crunches."

Out on the field, in the game's final two minutes, Dunnington preached one of Hogan's messages. "We don't have the right to give up and not play our hardest to the last second," he told teammates. "We're playing for all those fans. We're playing for Faith."

With 1:15 remaining, Reicher called time-out. Hogan motioned his players around him. From the Reicher sideline, a horn blared in celebration of the pending state championship. Faith fans countered by repeating, "We are Faith!" throughout the break. "Hey, don't quit,"

Hogan told the players. "Keep playing till the end. I know it's not what you wanted. But don't quit. You're Faith. Represent. You've got great fans. Go play hard."

As the huddle broke and the defense returned to the field, Hogan saw tears through Clegg's face mask. Hogan walked out to Clegg. "You're a winner in everything you do," Hogan said. Clegg looked his coach in the eyes. "Weston," the coach said, "I hope my son grows up to be just like you." The two embraced on the field as Clegg began to cry even harder.

It was Clegg who had stood at the front of that chapel on Commitment Night and said he would do "whatever it takes" to make sure that this season would not end with an opposing quarter-back taking a knee as the clock reached all zeros. But that was what happened again.

Unlike the previous season's loss to Regents, the outcome of this game had been known for a good hour now. But the finality hit with the final kneel-down. Emotions released.

Roddy bent over, sobbing. Coach Rivera put his arms around him.

Jordan Adams, a freshman on the junior varsity team, grabbed Nerney by the arm, and the two stepped down the sideline. Nerney had become Adams's off-field mentor during the season, and now the freshman sought to console the senior.

Sells, down from the press box, embraced Clegg, who squeezed his big brother–type coach so hard he almost choked him. Sells looked into Hockenbrough's eyes and saw a look of pain he says he will never forget. Sells told the seniors that he would not trade them for anyone on the other sideline.

Then Wright came up to Sells, crying. Sweat had erased almost all the eye black Cochran had smeared on his cheeks. Tears were finishing off what remained. "I'm sorry, Coach Sells," the junior said. "You shouldn't be," Sells told him. "You're a winner."

Hockenbrough was sobbing as Dunnington embraced him—the player he had looked up to since his freshman season. "I'm sorry I couldn't get it for you," Dunnington told him. Then Dunnington realized something. He actually was sharing in a season-ending loss like he had only watched the previous year. "As much as it hurt," Dunnington later recalled, "I was glad to be there with them this time."

+ + +

Hogan accepted the runner-up trophy and handed it to Deuce. As Reicher received its championship trophy across the field, reporters huddled around Hogan to collect his thoughts on the game. With players still crying and embracing behind him, Hogan summarized for the media: "For the district championship at their place, we got some big plays early, and we were healthy. This week, they had some momentum and big plays early, and they were healthy, and that's the difference in the game."

After the interview, Hogan gathered his players. Because fans would not be allowed on the field after the game, Hogan had planned on taking his players to a spot outside the fence around the field for what he had hoped would be a state championship celebration. He pointed to that area. "We said we were going to get with the parents after the game, and that's what we're going to do. We're going to walk out this end so they can crowd around you just like they need to. So you can see the people, about four hundred of them, that are lined up right over here for you. We're going to go out there, and you guys circle around and take a knee where your parents can be here with you. Let's go. Hold your head up. Let's go."

When the fans saw the players gathering outside the fence, they began to move toward them. Hogan considered what to tell his players. The coach who prepares for everything, who teaches his players to do the same, was not prepared for what to say to his players after a 41–7 loss. At no point during the season had he envisioned this scenario.

Most players, on one knee in front of their coach, had ducked their heads and were openly crying as fans formed a circle around them. Parents that could reach players placed hands on their shoulder pads. After the end of the line arrived, Hogan spoke.

"You'll find out in life you don't always have to be viewed as the best to be the best to somebody. It wouldn't have mattered if you would have lost in the first game of the playoffs. It wouldn't have mattered. In fact, I'd say you probably have more people because of the outcome of the game than if we had won. Life's about relationships. You guys don't play football just to win on the scoreboard. What's the number one thing that's on your scouting report every week? What's number one?" The players answered in low voices.

Hogan continued. "The first, greatest commandment: 'Love your teammates.' That's why you play football. If I would have said we would have went 0–10 and we didn't have a very good football program at Faith, you would have all played anyway, wouldn't you? You don't play for the scoreboard. I know you want to win. I know you're hurt right now. I understand what your goals are. Let me tell you why I like football. Because if the score were reversed now, you would have to still, from the beginning of the season, demonstrate all of the biblical qualities that make a great husband, and make a great Christian, make a great dad. It's perseverance. It's commitment to other individuals. Commitment to a team. You're going to have to do that one of these days when you don't like what's going on in your church, aren't you? You don't just bail when things get tough. You go to your pastor and you tell him you love him and you fix it from the inside. Are you with me?

"You live life for a purpose greater than yourself. That's what sports are about. When two teams get together that are about equal talent and you have some momentum early in the game, this could happen. It happened in Week 10. We got momentum, they fumbled the kickoff, and we were healthy, and we won. [Tonight] they got momentum, they got good field position, we lost our first quarterback *and* our second quarterback, and you guys who came in played great, with no fear. You're [not always going to get] what you even deserve in life. On a work scale, you probably deserved to be the state champions. You don't always get what you deserve. I don't deserve my wife. I outkicked my coverage when I married her." Players and fans briefly laughed. "So maybe she didn't deserve what she got with me. You won't always get what you deserve. That's not what life is about. Life is about how you deal with what you get. You understand what I'm saying? I know you're hurt, but you've got to listen. You've got to listen."

A horn blared from Reicher's celebration across the field.

"The sun's going to come up tomorrow. And your best friend is still going to come to school Monday. Just take a look around you at these guys. If you had it to do over, knowing the outcome, I bet every one of you would sign up to go to Lebanon, wouldn't you? Remember why you play. And you play for an even bigger group than is wearing a jersey. You play for all these cheerleaders, all these drum lines, all these moms, dads, aunts, uncles, all these alumni I see back here. You play for all of them. And they love you just as much as if that score would have been reversed. I promise you. That's why they're standing right here."

Hogan stopped and dropped his head. The only sound was that of players crying and sobbing. Those circled around Hogan wondered what their coach would say next. They wondered what was going through his mind as his silence grew longer. Hogan wanted to end his speech in a way that would let his players know how he felt about them, win or lose. Then he looked up and addressed his players for the final time as a team.

"I love you guys."

CHAPTER 21

Faith in Action

Six and four. The disappointment of 2006 had served as motivation for the '07 team. But coming off the program's first state-championship-game appearance, the heavy loss of players to graduation, and a significant step up in competition diminished expectations for the next season. So as the 2008 season opener approached, and with preseason workouts having gone better than expected, Hogan and Sells said a 6–4 record looked achievable. But the team would have to keep progressing, and the season would have to go really well for the program's postseason streak to stretch to five years. All eleven of the 2007 season starters on offense, and seven on defense, had graduated.

The most athletic senior class in Faith history certainly left a legacy. After the football team reached the state-title game, the seniors helped produce state championships in soccer, baseball, and track and field. Hogan would have liked to squeeze one more football season out of the most talented team he had coached, because the 2008 season would have offered a challenge even for that team.

TAPPS realigns its divisions every two years based on school enrollments. Faith had grown just enough since the previous realignment to be moved up one classification, from Division III to Division II.

Hogan shook his head when he saw the new alignment. Faith had been moved into a district with a school from Midland in West Texas, and also Lubbock Christian for all sports other than football.

With gasoline prices nearing four dollars per gallon, and factoring in hotel costs for games in Midland and Lubbock, Hogan estimated an extra $100,000 in annual travel expenses for the athletic department because of the new district. Then there was the amount of school time athletes would miss because of travel. Hogan considered asking TAPPS to move Faith up into Division I, for the state's largest schools, where there were more teams geographically closer to Grapevine. He analyzed the competitive levels of the two largest divisions, found the difference to be surprisingly small, and recommended to school officials that Faith make that request.

"We had to balance the concern we had for both stewardship of resources—talent, time, and treasure—as well as the competitive arena that we'd put our kids in," Hogan explained. "In other words, setting them up for failure or success." Once it was determined that the school could be competitive in the largest classification, Hogan said, "then it seemed like an automatic no-brainer to let stewardship make the call." TAPPS granted the request, and Faith stepped up as the smallest school among the state's largest.

That decision set the stage for a season that would put the Lions in the national spotlight—not for how they did, but for what they did.

+ + +

Despite having jumped up two divisions, despite having lost eighteen starters, the Lions made it to the second round of the playoffs and finished with a surprising 9–3 record.

Along the way, they opened the season by winning all their non-district games and took a 4–0 mark into their district opener at unbeaten and state number one–ranked Nolan Catholic, the Division I state runner-up the previous season. In its preview of the game, the *Fort Worth Star-Telegram* noted that Nolan Catholic had more students in its senior class than Faith had in its entire high school. The Lions pulled off a shocker, winning 21–13 in what Hogan called the biggest victory in school history.

Two weeks later, Faith took on the new state top-ranked team, Trinity Christian Academy of Addison. Faith lost that game by six points. The Lions lost once more in the regular season, again by six points—in four overtimes—against Bishop Lynch. Those three opponents all reached the final four of the playoffs, with Nolan Catholic defeating Bishop Lynch in the state-championship game.

But when Hogan would summarize the season at the team's post-season banquet, those football highlights made up only five minutes of his twenty-minute review, and the final five minutes at that. What made the season successful is what Hogan talked about in those first fifteen minutes—in fact, what had people all around the nation talking about Faith. The 2008 season was one in which the Lions truly had put their faith into action.

+ + +

In the final week of August, Faith had been preparing to host Grace Prep in the season opener, and also a team from suburban New Orleans, John Curtis Christian School. Grace Prep would be visiting The Jungle on Friday to kick off the season, and the John Curtis Patriots would arrive the next day. The Patriots, owners of twenty-two Louisiana state championships, would be playing the following Monday at Texas Stadium against the Texas public-school powerhouse and national top-ranked Euless Trinity Trojans. Hogan and Sells had visited the John Curtis campus during the off-season to learn the Patriots' old-school Split Back Veer offense, which Faith coaches decided would better suit their personnel for the 2008 season than its Spread offense.

Hogan and Sells quickly struck up a friendship with the John Curtis coaching staff and offered to let the team use Faith buses and facilities for practices while in Texas. And as they prepared their team for its season opener, Faith coaches also discussed with their players ways to reach out to the Louisiana team during its visit. John Curtis had had to work through the aftereffects of Hurricane Katrina three seasons earlier, and now Hurricane Gustav was pointing toward the Gulf of Mexico. A mind-set of becoming involved in others' lives began developing among Faith players. Within a week, that mind-set transformed into action.

The Lions defeated Grace Prep 20–8 on the first Friday night of the season. On Saturday morning, as the team watched film of the game, Hogan kept pointing out how his offensive linemen had failed to contain Grace Prep's number 74. The opposing player's number stuck in the Lions' minds.

Later that day, the John Curtis team flew into North Texas amid forecasts that Gustav would make landfall along the Gulf Coast early the next week. Patriots coaches and players, monitoring the weather back home and staying in touch with family members, were receiving reports that the New Orleans airport might soon shut down. The coaches, with lessons learned from Katrina still fresh, had developed two game plans—one for Monday morning's game, and one for the scenario in which they would not be able to return home as planned. On the Texas Stadium field the morning of the game, less than two hours after Gustav's eye reached Louisiana's coast and with a mostly cloudy sky visible through the stadium's hole in the roof, John Curtis coaches told Hogan they had to find a way to get the hurricane out of their players' minds.

Meanwhile, news was spreading quickly among Faith players that Grace Prep's number 74, Shane Allen, had died in a car accident Sunday. "He was especially in our minds from that game," Wright said. "He had had a big impact on that game, so we remembered him." Said Shivers: "It really hits home when someone your age dies—when it's someone you played against, the same age." Alcantara said that as a teenager, he felt invincible until learning of Allen's death. "It makes you stop and think, Wow, that could have been me," Alcantara said. Faith players appeared distracted during their Monday afternoon practice. Afterward, they met and decided they wanted to attend the funeral to express their support to Allen's family and to his classmates and teammates.

While the players were reflecting on Allen's death, parents were working quickly to help the members of John Curtis's traveling party— coaches, players, and family members—who were unable to return home. They raised money to help cover the costs of the extended stay. A cookout was thrown together for that night, with Faith players serving the guests and then sitting at tables and talking with grateful John Curtis players.

"I think the John Curtis situation was the catalyst for them starting to be aware of just how much they could influence just by stepping into people's lives," Hogan said.

The potential for influence became even more evident to the players in the wake of Allen's death. Hogan called the Grace Prep coach to ask if it would be okay for his team to attend the funeral. The coach checked with the family and gave their approval to Hogan. The day of the funeral, Faith players slipped their red jerseys over their white dress shirts and ties and rode on a school bus to the service. After the funeral, as the players were about to board the bus across the street from the church, the casket was carried out of the church. The players lined up near the bus and stood in silence. Soon, Grace Prep players came across the street to thank the Faith players. Players that had opposed each other on a field less than a week earlier began embracing one another.

Parents of Grace Prep students began sending e-mails of appreciation to Faith. "They showed that football is more than a game, that there are important things other than the outcome or the score," Grace Prep coach Dale Meinecke said. "It's about people, it's about relationships."[1]

The following Friday night, in a home game against the North Side Steers, a public-school team from the Fort Worth Independent School District, opposing player Martin Rodriguez suffered a scary injury to his neck and back near the Faith sideline. Faith trainer Gomez and the North Side trainers immobilized Rodriguez, and an ambulance was summoned. With the ambulance near midfield, Faith players looked across the field and saw the concern of Rodriguez's teammates. Of their own volition, Faith players walked as a group to the other sideline, knelt with North Side players, and prayed for the injured player. Faith cheerleaders then did the same, crossing the field to pray with the visiting cheerleaders.

A few Faith parents accompanied Rodriguez's family to the hospital. Throughout the night, at least one person from Faith remained with the family. When Rodriguez was transferred to a Dallas hospital the next morning, Faith parents made sure the family was not alone there, either. Rodriguez was diagnosed with a pinched spine and recovered to play for North Side a few weeks later and earn an opportunity to play at Ouachita Baptist University.

"Our coaches teach us to focus more on other people, not just within our little world of Faith," Alcantara said.

It is that attitude taught by Faith coaches that the nation learned about when Gainesville State School came to Faith.

+ + +

When Faith had moved up into Division I and Hogan looked at the new schools his team would be playing, one opponent stood out: Gainesville State School, a prison school.

Hogan could vividly see the looks of despair on inmates' faces in adult prisons he had visited, and it was easy for him to envision those same looks inside Gainesville State. But these faces would be much younger, and these inmates had to wonder whether their futures could offer anything positive.

"I imagined sitting there at their age, missing my mom. I imagined missing my dad, and my brother," Hogan recalled. "I tried to imagine how it feels to believe that life is slipping away. I imagined cars passing by, with people driving home from work, and seeing them through that security fence. And I imagined the time lost with the people I love. I felt hopelessness because I could see those kids sitting there, alone in a small cell, feeling as though they could do nothing about their situations. They could not rewind the clock and correct the mistakes and decisions that had landed them there."

The words of Jesus came to Hogan's mind: "I was hungry and you gave me something to eat, I was thirsty and you gave me something to drink, I was a stranger and you invited me in, I needed clothes and you clothed me, I was sick and you looked after me, I was in prison and you came to visit me." Next, Hogan recalled Jesus' oft-quoted statement a few verses later: "Whatever you did for one of the least of these brothers of mine, you did for me."[2]

Hogan knew immediately that playing Gainesville State would present a ministry opportunity. "I said, 'Now that's going to be special.' Because I knew we were going to do something. I just didn't know what."

+ + +

Gainesville State School, about sixty miles north of Grapevine, is a maximum-security correctional facility for males ages twelve to nineteen. The razor-wired fence surrounding the campus runs along one side of the hardpan football practice field and behind the lone, rusted goalpost. The other goalpost had been removed to make room for a solitary-confinement building.

The football team has no realistic hope of being competitive among TAPPS' largest schools. With the students' daily school and on-campus work schedules, practice time is limited. Equipment is bare minimum. The Tornadoes had lost their first eight games of the season, scoring only two touchdowns total.

Football at the facility is a teaching tool and a motivator to make good choices. Only students who have served at least half of their sentence, have maintained good grades, and have not committed any behavior offenses are eligible to play. "We're not here to build football dynasties or win championships," said coach Mark Williams, who was hired at Gainesville State in 2003 after more than twenty years in public schools. "We're here to get these kids back home with their families."

Each Friday afternoon, the few who have earned the opportunity to play football and the off-campus privileges accompanying that, board the bus, pass through the double security gate, and depart for a few hours' sampling of the free world. Every game is a road game. Rarely will they have any fans other than a couple dozen school personnel and volunteers. Then after the game, the players will step back onto the bus—usually with a post-game meal courtesy of the school that had just defeated them—and, while the teenagers they just squared off against head off with friends to eat at a local restaurant or hop in a car and cruise around their hometown, the Gainesville State players return directly to their campus, back through that double gate, and back into their cells.

School officials pause when asked to describe a typical student. The facility's population hovers a little below three hundred, and the coaches and teachers and administrators who see the inmates every day, who have read their personnel files, who have seen so many come through here and too many return, know that each is an individual teenager with individual problems that require individual solutions.

"There's three hundred sad stories out here," welding teacher Chris Styles said.

There are general trends, though, for those sentenced here. Most students come from dysfunctional families, raised by a single parent or grandparents. They come from low socioeconomic backgrounds and live in high-density neighborhoods in large cities. They perform poorly in school. That is, if they're still attending school. Not only are they behind in academic performance, they're also behind in emotional maturity. Much of their development has come on the streets, with drugs and alcohol and gangs. Many have children of their own, and some of those have never seen their children, caught in crime before their girlfriends gave birth.

The students represent a wide range of offenses: theft, burglary, drugs, aggravated robbery, sex crimes. Many times, they have been through detention centers, halfway houses, and community outreach programs but continued to build up a rap sheet until one day a judge declared, "No more." Sometimes, it was just one poor decision, one offense, such as driving drunk and committing involuntary manslaughter, or choosing to run with a friend who draws a gun while robbing a store.

Whatever the circumstances, whatever the background, they typically spend between nine months and three years at Gainesville State. Freedom forfeited. Behind a fence, no longer in control of their schedule. The students are told when to go to bed and when to wake up, when and what to eat, when to go to the restroom, marched to class in rows of two, and keeping time the whole way. They walk through the school building's hallways with hands behind backs, one hand holding the other wrist. Every move is monitored.

"It may not seem like a big thing, but going to the restroom is a big thing, just whenever you want to without having somebody tell you to do something," A. Castillo said.[3] (For confidentiality purposes, the school does not release students' full names.)

Outside the fence, they know, other students their age are enjoying their freedom, and probably taking their freedom for granted. "We're missing a lot by being in here, because the world is still going on," M. White said. "A lot of people are missing their high school prom and stuff like that, stuff that really means something. So I wouldn't encourage nobody to come here and miss out on that, because you don't get too many proms. After your high school years is over with, that's it. You can't go back to it."

But they will be going back into society. Back to what is often referred to as "the free world," or "outside the fence."

"We look at the end in individuals," superintendent Gwan Hawthorne said. "Our main purpose is, How can we get them back to where they were? We're only their keepers for a little while. Our main focus is to get them better."

That is a daunting challenge. The key for school personnel is to keep looking for, as Williams said, a glimmer of hope in each individual, even if it comes from one conversation or one short answer that indicates that there is a reason to hope. "Because once we find that little cornerstone," Williams said, "we'll build a whole foundation on it."[4]

The teens need adults to play guiding roles in their lives. Lucinda Scott, who teaches modular technology education that allows students to discover their interests for future occupations, has been at Gainesville State for ten years after teaching twenty-seven years in public schools. "I had the most wonderful assignment when I left public school," she remembered. "I had all honor students, and everything was perfect. It was what I worked for twenty-seven years to get, and when I got there, it was like, 'These kids don't need me. They go home and they have the most wonderful parents and the most wonderful families and just everything they could ever want or need.'" At Gainesville State, she knows the kids need her. "I'm helping them. I'm one of the little things, but these kids need role models. They need people that care. And they need to see there's good people."[5]

"Some of them haven't seen what true love is," said Hawthorne. "They sometimes associate it with beatings, whippings, cursings, or things that's not really typical of what love is. But that's what they associate it with. I think the biggest need for them is to know and see how the other world and how other people feel about them, and how they should feel about themselves. Because low self-esteem plays a big role in them."[6]

Once teachers are able to gain students' trust, to let the students see that they are there to help them—and that is teachers' biggest challenge, Scott says—the students invite them to be a part of their lives. The students begin asking for advice on day-to-day life issues and, for those with children, on how to be good fathers when they get out. The potential for teachers to impact students goes far beyond the classroom topics.

Still, Scott says teachers must keep emotional distance from the students. "They've done some bad things. And I mean bad. What I try to do is, I want to assume that what they're here for is very serious. But I try not to go into their file and see exactly what it is, because I don't want to prejudge or anything like that. [I] don't think for one minute that they're here for anything other than a crime. But they're still people. You know, it's just—. They're just people."[7]

+ + +

Joe Perry, a minister and former coach, has a heart for boys who are without positive role models. That is why in 2000 he started a mentoring program for such boys, and that also is why he had made two or three trips to Gainesville State School as a minister with Prestonwood Baptist Church in Plano, Texas.

On the first Saturday of November 2008, he went to the facility as part of his church's annual outreach into various prisons for juveniles and adults. For the outreach on the Gainesville State campus, small groups are allowed to visit each dorm and speak to inmates. Perry asked to speak in his group's designated dorm. He knows most teenage boys like football stories, and, as a former coach, Perry loves to talk football. Especially if he can work his son, who played college football and coaches at one of Arkansas's most successful high school programs, into the conversation.

After Perry spoke to the thirty or so in the dorm, he and his group hung around to just chat with the kids. "They love talking because it's someone new to talk to, and they don't get that a lot," Perry explained. A football player Perry remembers only by the name of Alex approached and asked if Perry had any advice he could pass along to his teammates. The Tornadoes had suffered another blowout loss the night before— this one 52–0—and Alex was looking for anything that could help his team. Perry shared a little bit about football techniques, although he admits today's game is more complex than back when he coached. A second player joined the conversation.

"It is really tough for us," Perry recounted Alex saying. "We never win. We never have anybody to cheer for us. We never have any people in the stands. We show up in a bus, guards with us. We never get to run through a banner. We never get to do any of that. We go to the sideline and we play. If we get a positive affirmation, it's from another player or coach. Nobody ever hollers for us in the stands."

Perry didn't know what to say at first. Then he felt led to say to these two, "Because you know for sure you have Christ in your life, I want you to understand that you're only playing, really, for an audience of One—and God is cheering for you."

"Ohhh, that's good," Alex replied with brightened eyes. "I like that. I'm going to tell the whole team that."

Inwardly, though, Perry wished he could provide more than words. He thought perhaps he could have his son visit sometime and work with the team's coaches and players. Even more, he wanted to put together a group of people to attend a Tornadoes game and cheer for them. But he knew that Gainesville State's season was ending the very next week, so that idea would have to wait for another year.

"You never know what might happen," Perry told the two players. "Maybe someday there will be people pulling for you."

+ + +

Two days later, never having met Joe Perry and unaware of his conversation with the two players, Kris Hogan sent this e-mail to all Faith parents:[8]

> This Friday night the Lions end their regular season schedule by hosting Gainesville State School. Gainesville State school is a fenced, maximum-security facility within the states juvenile corrections agency. Youth in the agencys care and custody receive individualized education, treatment, life skills and employment training from positive role models. The young men earn the privilege to participate in outside activities such as sports, by demonstrating an impeccable record in behavior and effort in their studies. The stories of some of these kids would break your heart. They have very few people on their side. I view this as an incredible ministry opportunity for Faith, and would like your support and help in touching the hearts of these young men and those who are called to work with them.

These young men will not have any fans outside of the faculty from their school. Their parents will not be there.

Here's the message I want to send: We love you. Jesus Christ loves you, intentionally created you, and has a plan for your life. You are just as valuable as any other person on planet earth. We are supporting and affirming the effort you have made by earning the privilege to play.

Here is our plan: I want as many people as we can get to come down to the west end of the football field at 7:15 pm and make a spirit line for the Gainesville players to run through as they take the field. I want some LION fans to sit on the visitor's side and cheer for the Gainesville team throughout the game. We will get a roster with their names and numbers, so the folks cheering for them can call them by name. We will have the JH cheerleaders go to their side lines and cheer for them. We will send them home with some sort of post game goody bag.

We look forward to your participation Friday night.

ONE HEART,
Kris Hogan

CHAPTER 22

A Game of Hope

Seventy-five minutes before game time, the Gainesville State bus and an accompanying white van entered through the gate to The Jungle parking lot and pulled alongside the field house. The bus door opened, but the coaches and players remained inside while security personnel made their way to the visitors' locker room.

One rumor down: the guards were not armed. They were not even dressed in the uniforms some onlookers expected, garbed instead in light blue polo-style shirts, dark pants, and nonmatching black jackets. The guards entered the locker room directly behind the home bleachers, and the slams of footlockers banging shut resounded through the open door as the guards inspected the room, then the shower and restroom. Locker room secured, they lined the path from the bus to the locker room, and the all-clear signal was given for coaches, players, and student managers to unload.

Players exited the bus five at a time, picking up their football equipment from beside the bus and walking in a loose single-file line directly to the locker room. When the fifth player in a group left the bus, the nearest guard would look toward the locker room entrance and raise five fingers above his head. When the last player reached the door, the guard there would raise five fingers back toward the bus to signal all were accounted for and the next group could unload.

The players were silent, and most walked with their chins lowered, making little eye contact with the handful of Faith fans near the path. Other fans looked on curiously from a distance.

Forty-five minutes before game time, the guards blocked off a path from the locker room, around the bleachers, and onto the field. All fourteen players, suited up in solid black helmets and pants and plain white jerseys that read "TORNADOES" above the numbers on their chests, made their way to the field, this time in a tight single file, and began stretching exercises.

Guards at the four corners around the team watched players and fans and the surroundings, but the security presence—while unmistakable—was less rigid than expected.

There was little spirit as players worked through their offensive plays under the watchful eyes of coaches and security guards. As before every other game, Faith players looked across the field to measure up their opponents. "They looked like they didn't even want to be there," O'Neal recalled.[1] As Tornadoes assistant coach Walt Scott would later say with a chuckle, the team entered its final game of the season fully expecting to be "thrown to the Lions." The Tornadoes were not only winless in their eight games, but they also had been outscored 325–12. This was the first game in November, and they had not scored since September.

On the other end of the field, Lions players were more business-like than usual in warm-ups. The Lions had a 7–2 record and already knew they would be entering the playoffs the next week as the third-seeded team from their district. There was nothing to play for in this game. The attitude was one of keeping everyone healthy for the playoffs and winning this game quickly for an early arrival with friends at the post-game hangouts. If not for this being Senior Night, with the team's eleven seniors being honored before the game, there would have been little to look forward to this night.

As game time approached, activity began to build on the field's west end, near where the Tornadoes were finishing warm-ups. Fans in red-and-gray sweatshirts and light jackets began gathering near the corner of the field and then, a few minutes before kickoff, forming a spirit tunnel for players to run through. Faith's Dana Stone made sure their fans knew, as Gainesville State security personnel had requested, to form the tunnel wide so that they could not come into physical contact with the players.

As the tunnel took shape, more fans in Faith colors made their way across the field to join in. The line quickly grew from the goal line to stretch out beyond the 30 yard line. As more fans joined, they took up spots at the front of the line in the end zone, making the beginning of the tunnel run through part of the end zone before curving onto the playing field. About fifty Cub Club members from Faith's elementary school grouped together near the front and playfully chased each other around their spots.

Hawthorne, Gainesville State's superintendent, had walked to the front of the visitors' bleachers and noticed Faith fans and cheerleaders setting their belongings there. "When we first arrived at the game and we began seeing all the people walk past us and go sit down in the stands, I just kind of thought, *Oh, this is going to be a really big game. They're using our side as the overflow.*" She soon saw a sign that something different was taking place: "Then we saw a little girl who showed up with a sign with a tornado drawn on it, and she was passing out fliers to other people on the side. And then another cheerleader started passing out the [game] program that actually had our kids' names listed on it, and that kind of shocked me."[2]

Tornadoes players also were in for a shock. They could not help but notice the number of fans gathering near their end zone, and they assumed their opponents would be entering the field from that point. Odd—but what other explanation could there be?

When the players completed their warm-ups, they gathered in the back of the end zone near the scoreboard for their customary jog across the field to their sideline. Except this week, they figured, they would have to run *around* the opposing teams' fans. But then a Faith dad at the opening to the tunnel began motioning for the Tornadoes to run in the fans' direction. The players were confused.

Hogan, who had left the field house earlier than usual, found a spot next to the far side of the home stands where he could watch the Gainesville State players without being noticed. He hoped to see some of the players' faces as they came through the tunnel.

"When I saw the Faith dad motioning their players to run through, that got me," Hogan said. "I will never forget that moment, because it seemed like it was happening in slow motion. As I earlier had watched Gainesville State players walk with their heads down, and how they avoided making eye contact, it was easy to recognize that they battle inferiority complexes. Seeing that dad compel those players toward him made me think of how God had compelled me toward Him. God does not qualify you and then call you. He calls you and then qualifies you. It is as though He says, 'Trust me, you're worth it. Let's go, buddy.'"

+ + +

A few of the players realized that the spirit line was for them. Williams remembered seeing four players with eyes bulging: "My quarterback goes, 'Coach, aren't they on the wrong end?' I said, 'Uh-uh. They're on the right end. They're here for you.'" Williams instructed his players to run through the tunnel, telling them to "go have fun." The first group of players jogged toward the fans. The next group, still unsure what to do, paused and then followed.

When the players reached the turn in the tunnel toward the field, a huge tear-through banner reading, "GSS Go Tornadoes," awaited them. For most, this was their first time to run not only through a spirit line but also through a banner. The first player ripped through the paper, opening the way for teammates to follow. The first wave of players bursting through cued the Faith junior high cheerleaders to start their run ahead of the players, leading the way to their bench, pom-poms raised and waving. Faith fans roared as the Tornadoes ran past. But the players did not merely run through the tunnel—they sprinted through it. And they didn't just sprint through the tunnel—they sprinted all the way to the far end zone. One turned a cartwheel after crossing midfield.

"It was like we didn't wanna stop," Castillo recalled with a big smile. "Even some of the staff, they were like, 'Y'all quit, y'all quit running,' because I guess they thought we were gonna run over the fence or something. But it was, like, we didn't know where else to run. It was just a rush. Like you couldn't stop."[3]

When the players had run as far as they could, the fans began to leave the field. Coach Williams, who had jogged down the middle of the field, outside of the tunnel and well behind his players, struggled to process what he had just witnessed. Hogan had asked Williams if Faith fans could form the spirit line, but Williams never imagined that the tunnel would be so long and so loud. So emotional for his players—and for himself.

Williams clapped with his hands high, in front of his cap, as he passed the fans. "Thank you, thank you," he said to anyone who could hear him.

It was a first, too, for Hawthorne, who was no stranger to the energy of a football game. Her son, David, is a linebacker for the Seattle Seahawks. "I had been to many, many high school games before," she said, "but even the games I've traveled with our team, I never, never had seen something of that high magnitude. And to see the expressions on their faces, the fact that they were running and, you know, they were smiling."[4]

O'Neal said Tornadoes players' demeanors changed after the spirit tunnel. "It seemed [like to them] it was a state championship game," he said, "and they were coming out to play."[5]

+ + +

As the teams sent their special teams units onto the field for the opening kickoff, Faith fans occupied both sides of the stadium seating—about two hundred on each side, with more still walking around the field's perimeter toward the Gainesville State seats. Fans on both sides stood and cheered as Lions' kicker Wright took five steps to the ball and booted the ball high and into the Tornadoes' side of the field. X. Taylor slid to his right to field the kick, briefly bobbled the ball inside his team's 10 yard line, and set out on his return to the Gainesville State 27.

"Go Tornadoes, go! Go Tornadoes, go!" Faith's junior high cheerleaders began chanting from the Gainesville State sideline as the Tornadoes' offense huddled. The first play was a handoff to L. Fautner, who managed to gain two yards before being brought down. On the next play, the ball dropped to the grass after an awkward handoff. Faith's Justin Huffman corralled the loose ball. Faith fans on the Gainesville State side moaned.

"Defense!" the cheerleaders quickly encouraged the Gainesville

State players. "Let's go, defense!" a man's voice rang out from the visitors' bleachers. Despite the support, Gainesville State's defense could not stop the Lions. Four plays resulted in an easy, 1-yard touchdown run for Dunnington and a 7–0 Faith lead.

Gainesville State defenders disgustedly unsnapped their chin straps as they returned to their sideline. But the fans from behind their bench shouted encouragement as the kickoff return team once again took the field.

"Let's get it going!"

"Run it back!"

"Hey, come on, guys! Come on, guys! Let's go!"

Wright sent a line-drive kick into the Gainesville State end. "Mitchell," the stadium announcer said as number 58 fielded the ball and returned it ten yards to the Tornadoes' 32.

On the first play, I. Else, the quarterback, fumbled, and once more the Lions claimed possession of the ball. The Lions' ensuing play was an incomplete pass, and Lions fans on the Gainesville State side cheered the result. Among those fans were Bill and Anne Ashton, the parents of Peter, the quarterback who had just overthrown an open receiver.

On the next play, Corey Dodd burst through the middle for a 9-yard run. A penalty flag followed Dodd to the ground. Face mask penalty against the Tornadoes, the referee signaled. Boos rose from the visitors' stands in disapproval of the call.

Coach Williams, who had been deep into game mode and unaware of the wall of red behind him, heard the protests. "I turned around to figure out what was going on," he recalled, "and here they are booing— and they're booing [a penalty for] their team, their own team. Well, it wasn't their team. That night, *our* team was their team."[6]

Three plays later, Faith running back Gesek stepped into the end zone from the 1 yard line. Touchdown, Lions. Gainesville State's fans-for-a-night went silent.

"Block that kick!" one parent then shouted to encourage the Tornadoes players lining up for Faith's point-after-touchdown attempt. "Block that kick!" other parents joined in. The Tornadoes did just that—blocking the kick to keep the score 13–0. Fans roared as the players ran off the field clapping their hands and patting each other on the helmet.

White, a Gainesville student manager who had played quarterback the previous year, celebrated his team's play with the coaches and reserves on the sideline. "For the crowd to chant and then for us to get on and set the goal and then accomplish something that you really don't see happen too much," he said. "I felt like it just motivated them to keep on going the rest of the game."

"They were more juiced up than they had ever been," Williams said. "Normally, when we start the game, they're real juiced up. That's what they see on TV. That's their fantasy: this is what we see, this is what we want to be. By the middle of the first quarter, they're already tired because you've got fourteen kids playing both ways and in no time at all, they're gassed. This night, they were still bouncing."[7]

The Gainesville State players, unaccustomed to such support, were hearing more than just cheering for their team. They were also hearing cheers with their own names attached. Faith fans would watch a play, glance to their rosters that had been distributed before the game, then yell out the last name of the Gainesville State player making the play. "They just called me by name," a stunned player told a coach as he came off the field to the sideline.

On one play, a Gainesville State defender delivered a big hit on a Faith ball carrier, and Faith fans shouted the defender's name in approval. "We thought [Faith] had another player with the same name," White said. But then a coach showed him a copy of the roster the fans were holding. "When we found out," he said, "it was just another good feeling for us."

"Everyone was so loud, just cheering," Alcantara said. "I know that for those kids it was a first-time experience, and it must have felt wonderful—just as it did for me the first time I ever experienced something like that. As the game went on, you could tell that their intensity was up just by what we had done for them, and the night wasn't even over."

Along with the players, a handful of other Gainesville State students who had earned off-campus privileges allowing them to attend the game began to experience the welcoming atmosphere. Like the players before the game, the students had kept to themselves, remaining quiet and acting shy. Amy Bronson, a fifth-grade teacher at Faith, had a stack of blankets sitting at her feet that her kids were not using. As the sun and temperature lowered, she offered a blanket to a Gainesville

State student. He declined, Bronson noticed, while also looking over to school personnel nearby. A few minutes later, she offered again. Again, the student declined. Bronson looked at the student and then over to the school staff. She smiled at the staff members as if to ask if it was okay for her to offer the blanket.

"Look," Bronson finally told the student, "why would you deny a mother the privilege of putting a blanket on a child? I know you think you're a big ol' teenager. I've got all these blankets, and I don't need them to sit at my feet. Would you take a blanket from me? You're making me uncomfortable." The student relented and reached out for the blanket. Soon, all of Bronson's blankets were warming Gainesville State students. And, slowly, the students in the stands were warming to the fans from Faith.

On the field, the excitement may have been too much for the players to handle from a football standpoint. The Tornadoes lost four fumbles in the first half. Each led to a Faith touchdown. The fourth gave Faith a 26–0 lead early in the second quarter. "They were just amazed by how much attention they were getting," Williams noted, "and how positive it was."[8]

Three women who had arrived late in the first quarter quickly recognized the Tornadoes' enthusiasm. The women attend Gainesville State games to support the school and players, and they had never witnessed this much enthusiasm from their team. As they watched the events of the first half unfold—on and off the field—they talked excitedly among themselves. They exchanged looks of disbelief. Finally, they turned to the Faith fans seated behind them. Tears were in their eyes. "Y'all don't know what you're doing, do you?" one asked the fans. The three then told the fans that they could have no idea of just how much good they were doing for the Gainesville State kids.

With the fans on their sideline still cheering loudly and still calling them by name, Tornadoes players answered with their most inspired offensive possession of the half. On first down, quarterback Else kept the ball for a nice gain that was wiped out by a holding penalty. Again, the Faith fans on the Gainesville State side greeted the referee's call with loud boos. Tornadoes assistant coach Lee Miller turned and looked to the crowd. "I love them," he said to his fellow coaches. "This is awesome. Best crowd I've ever been in front of."

On the next play, Else kept the ball again for a 28-yard run along the Gainesville State sideline. He might have gained more if he had not stumbled when his feet appeared to be motoring faster than the rest of his body. The fans erupted. Miller turned back to the crowd and clapped. The drive soon stalled, however, and Faith took the ball back and—aided by a Tornadoes pass interference penalty, again jeered from behind their bench—scored on the last play of the first half for a 33–0 halftime lead.

The Gainesville State players, both tired and energized, formed a single-file line on their sideline and walked across the field and around the home stands toward their locker room. Fans from both sides of the stadium stood and applauded the visitors. As they left the field, the Tornadoes players walked with chins up, looking directly into the faces cheering them, smiles shining.

+ + +

In their locker room, Tornadoes coaches determined one thing needed to happen during the second half to make the night complete: Gainesville State needed to score a touchdown. Over in the Faith side of the field house, Lions coaches had exactly the same thought. But how to make that happen? After all, the Tornadoes had scored only two touchdowns all season.

Williams challenged his players to set the goal of scoring one touchdown in their final half together. Faith coaches had a more delicate line to walk. They wanted Gainesville State to score, but they did not want their players to let them score. They wanted the Tornadoes to *earn* a score.

Faith backups and junior varsity players had begun replacing starters late in the first quarter. The rest of the game would belong to them. For most, this was their first experience of varsity football. But this was also their chance to show coaches what they would be capable of doing next season in place of the graduating seniors.

"It was understood that those JV kids were going to fight," Sells said. "They weren't going to go down." Faith coaches never mentioned their desire for Gainesville State to score before sending their players back to the field, but they began planning to play even their backup defensive players out of their normal positions.

In order to give the Tornadoes one more possession in the second half, Hogan decided to have his team kick off instead of receive to start the second half. Fautner darted thirty-one yards up the middle of the field with the return, quickly hopping to his feet after being tackled at the Gainesville State 46. His run drew loud applause.

On the next play, however, Fautner fumbled while working hard to gain extra yards in a crowd of Lions tacklers. Faith's Eean Cochran picked up the ball and returned it to Gainesville State's 15. But Faith returned the fumble on its first play, with Tornadoes defensive end C. Brown claiming the loose ball at his team's 12.

Gainesville State fumbled again on its next play—its sixth fumble of the night. But for the first time, the Tornadoes recovered their own fumble. Then, just like that, the Gainesville State offense began to click. From near his team's goal line, Fautner broke through the line and into the Faith secondary for a 28-yard run. The three reserves on the visitors' sideline applauded along with the fans. Else took the next play a determined sixteen yards around left end for another first down near midfield, breaking three tackles along the way.

"I was dead tired," Else said. But J. White, a receiver, went over to Else and encouraged him to stay in and keep giving his all. "I was like, 'I can't go,'" Else said. White reminded Else of how Williams had taught the players to be "whistle players," to play hard from the first whistle to the last on every play. In response, Else said he would play one more quarter, but he was not convinced he could. "Then I started playing with my heart, playing the way I know I was taught to play by Coach Williams."

Else and his teammates kept pushing the ball through the Faith defense and into Lions territory. On third and twelve from the Faith 31, Else flipped a pass to J. White at the line of scrimmage, who broke back toward the middle of the field, fought through two attempted tackles, and dragged three tacklers the final four yards to the Faith 20.

Fourth down, one yard to go.

The Tornadoes' first scoring opportunity of the game hinged on one play.

Hogan hurriedly grabbed Huffman, said something into the ear hole of his helmet, and pushed him onto the field. Huffman dashed to line up at nose guard, directly across from the Tornadoes' center. As he looked at the group of mostly freshmen and sophomores around him on the defense, he noticed almost a look of relief, as though they believed the senior had been sent in to help them prevent Gainesville State from scoring.

The rest of Faith's benched starters, long ago relegated to the sideline, wondered aloud why Huffman was allowed to return to the game while they were not. Even Sells looked at Hogan with a questioning expression. Hogan looked back to Sells and winked.

Huffman jumped through the gap between the center and right guard, making slight contact with both before the snap.

Whistles blew, penalty flags flew. Offside against Faith. Five-yard penalty. First down, Gainesville State.

Hogan didn't want to give the Tornadoes a touchdown, but he didn't mind discreetly giving them this first down so they could have the chance to earn a touchdown.

"You just know it all, don't you?" Sells said to Hogan, then turned away from the field and laughed. Wright was standing next to Sells. "That's pretty cool," the senior said.

Freshman linebacker Logan Cornelius, making his varsity debut, would not find out until after the game that Huffman had been under coach's orders to jump offside: "I was like, 'What is your problem? What are you doing?'"

With the first down gained, Else kept for ten yards on a quarterback keeper, again slipping through would-be tacklers to set up first and goal at the Faith 5.

Then it happened.

Else took the snap, faked a handoff left to the fullback, and handed off right to Fautner, the tailback. Fautner skirted around one defender and eased into the corner of the end zone.

"Touchdown, number 28, Fautner!" the public-address announcer declared.

Faith's Gainesville fans roared. The handful of Gainesville State students in the stands jumped and yelled. Coaches and players on the sideline raised arms to signal touchdown, then high-fived one another. On the field, one player jumped on Fautner's back. Another ran over to embrace him. Else, the quarterback, stepped in front of Fautner to deliver a congratulatory slap to the side of his helmet.

"They all had huge smiles," Cornelius said. "You could tell that they were happy."

The offense remained on the field for the two-point conversion. Although the try for two failed, the players ran off the field toward the sideline—Faith's fight song playing over the loudspeakers in celebration—with index fingers raised.

Tornadoes players may not have been number one, but on this night they felt as though they were.

The celebrations continued as the coaches assembled the kickoff team. One player frantically searched the sideline for the kicking tee. He found it still inside the team's equipment bag. They had, after all, yet to need the tee that night.

After the kickoff, the Lions took possession to start the fourth quarter. They ran six plays before punting to the Gainesville State 9.

The Tornadoes again overcame a nearly lost fumble on their first play of the drive. Else had a great series of plays. He scrambled twelve yards for a first down on third and eight. Twice, he hooked up with receiver J. White for big pass plays—one for thirty-seven yards down the right side, the other for twenty-one yards to the left. After the second moved the ball to the Lions' 6, White jumped up, faced the crowd, stood with arms spread out wide, then chest-bumped offensive lineman T. Mitchell. The players' shyness had evaporated: now they were playing up to the crowd.

On the next play, Fautner raced around left end untouched for his second touchdown of the game. After a successful two-point conversion this time, the offensive players again sprinted off the field. Again, they had their index fingers raised. Except for Fautner. He held two fingers up as he dashed past his teammates and coaches on the sideline and directly to Junior Corrections Officer Patrick Jenkins. The two laughed and embraced.

Fautner and Jenkins had made a deal before the game. If Fautner scored two touchdowns—and Jenkins said there was no way he thought that would happen—Jenkins would let the hair grow out on his shaved head. Jenkins shook his head from side to side at the thought. "When I let my hair grow out," he explained, "it looks like George Jefferson's hair."

That possession turned out to be the last time the Tornadoes would touch the ball, as Faith received the ensuing kickoff and ran out what remained of the game clock.

As players from both teams removed their helmets after the final play—and for Gainesville State players, it would be their last play of the season and, for most, their last play in a football game ever—the 33–14 score shining in the background on the scoreboard said the Tornadoes had lost.

The joy on their faces said otherwise.

+ + +

"I don't know about the Tornadoes, but I had fun tonight!" Williams shouted as the teams gathered at midfield, with fans all around.

"Did the Tornadoes have fun tonight?" Williams asked.

"Yeah!" his players shouted.

Hogan thanked the Gainesville State players for coming to Grapevine and said a gift had been prepared for each one of them. When they boarded the bus, the players would receive a goodie bag that included dinner and a devotional Hogan instructed the players to read first thing the next morning. Then he placed a first grader from the Cub Club in the middle of the circle to pray. "I know when I'm beat," Hogan said after the kid's prayer. "I can't beat that one." Those in the circle laughed. Hogan intended to close with his own prayer, but he was interrupted by Williams.

"We got one," Williams said.

"Who you got?" Hogan asked.

Williams called out his quarterback's name, Else. "He's been our preacher all year, Coach Hogan," Williams said.

What Else lacked in eloquence, he more than doubled in sincerity. He thanked God for the sun coming up that day. For the air to breathe. For the opportunity to play football. And for simply having another day. "Lord," he concluded, "I don't know how this happened, so I don't know how to say thank You, but I never would've known there were so many people in the world that cared about us."[9]

With hands all around the circle wiping tears, fans and players spontaneously broke out in applause. The players began shaking hands and exchanging greetings one more time, then one of the guards called out, "Okay, let's line up." Gainesville State players started back toward their sideline as Faith fans cleared a path. There were pats on backs and high fives as the smiling players made their way through the fans.

Off to the side, Williams talked with a reporter. His players interrupted the interview, sneaking up from behind and dousing him with water from their Gatorade squirt bottles. The photograph of Williams ducking and players smiling as they celebrated their 33–14 "loss" would appear all over the Internet as the lasting image from the game.

Williams turned to finish the interview. His players, he said, were "one step from heaven. A lot of these kids don't have hope because they've taken a wrong path, somebody's told them that they're going to be negative. They're not negative. They were very positive tonight. They were just like the other kids."[10]

Outside the locker room, Else said again that he never knew that so many people—people he had never seen—cared for him so much. Fautner said the Faith fans made him and his teammates feel like family. A Tornadoes coach stopped Hogan. "This is the greatest experience," the coach said, "they've ever had."

The players' demeanor as they left the locker room for their bus, again in groups of five, stood in stark contrast to when they had arrived. They walked with chins up. They looked around, making eye contact with the fans that remained.

About a dozen Faith fans stood alongside the field house and waved. Tornadoes players crossed the aisle on the bus, their faces filling nearly every available spot in the windows facing the fans, to smile and wave back.

As the bus headed toward the stadium gate, a player at the back of the bus motioned to the Faith fans with his right hand, as if to say, "Come with us." The bus exited the gate and turned left, leaving the fans behind. But in the players' hearts and minds, the fans did go with them. Their cheers were heard for much more than one night.

CHAPTER 23

More Than Football

Chris Styles walked into the Gainesville State guardhouse at 7:30 a.m. Monday, and the teachers and administrators waiting for their shifts to begin all were smiling and talking excitedly. "What's the deal?" Styles asked. "You missed it," he was told.

Styles quickly received an overview of Friday's game. When the twelve students in Styles's first-period agricultural-science welding class arrived, all they wanted to talk about was the game. Same with the students in second period, and third period, and all through the day until Monday's final class. "Everybody had a different take on it," Styles remembered. "Everybody thought it was so cool. Everybody wanted to play football all of a sudden."

In his five years at Gainesville State, Styles had never heard a football game or the football team discussed this much. He had never seen the campus like this.

"The culture," he said, "just switched."[1]

Tornadoes players had chowed down on the burgers and homemade cookies they received after the game. They were used to that; many opponents provide a meal for the players. But Faith's goodie bags included Bibles and devotionals. Each also contained a handwritten note of encouragement from a Faith football player. The players read their letters on the bus ride back to the facility. They talked almost non-stop about the spirit line and the fan support, about memorable plays, about hearing their names called by the public-address announcer and by the fans behind their bench. When they arrived back inside the fence, they returned to their dorms to the same old question: "How bad did y'all lose?"

This Friday night, though, the players could not wait to answer. "We told them straight up, 'Naw, we didn't win, but we learned a lot tonight,'" Else said. They had learned, he told his dorm mates, "There's a lot of people out there who care about us and want us to do right in our life and want us to achieve something." All weekend, players told stories from the game. And all weekend, the ones who had remained on campus listened.

The change began immediately.

"Usually, people, when they wake up, they're all down. Like they ain't got nothing to live for," Else said. "But when we came back from that game, after we told everybody, you could see a light in their faces. It was, like, in the atmosphere. You could feel it. It was, like, they weren't down. They were feeling up. Like, 'I can achieve something.'"[2]

+ + +

Two and a half months after the game, Hawthorne, the school's super-intendent, described the difference: "It's like people's hearts really have changed."[3]

Students changed.

Hawthorne had delighted in watching the players sitting proudly, heads up, smiling, at their own postseason banquet. With all the excitement of the season-ending game, school officials and volunteers decided to hold the banquet off campus for the first time as a special reward. The players' manners represented what Hawthorne was seeing campus-wide. In social settings such as this, the chatter had become less dominated by street language and more grown-up. Across the board, students were looking for ways to do something for others. There were more expressions of thanks, words of gratitude and appreciation. At a recent spaghetti dinner hosted by the local Lions Club, a group of students had asked if they could clean up so their hosts would not have to. One dorm earned a pizza party by completing thirty consecutive days without one of its students being sent to security for a behavioral offense.

Administrators and staff members changed.

Hawthorne said the game's timing could not have been better. The school had recently implemented a treatment program emphasizing earned privileges and rewards that come without monetary value. Seeing the way the players, and indirectly their peers, responded to the encouragement from the Faith fans invigorated administrators and staff. They started coming to meetings filled with ideas. More started attending the school's basketball games.

Those outside the fence changed too.

Opposing schools in basketball followed Faith's lead and stepped up their support for the Tornadoes, with some providing cheerleaders sporting Gainesville State's colors. One couple introduced themselves to Hawthorne at a basketball game. Their preacher had talked about the game in his sermon the previous Sunday, and the couple decided to drive almost an hour and a half to a basketball game so they could give the Tornadoes two more fans. They were not the only ones. For one game, Williams estimated that fifty to sixty fans—including a group on Harley Davidson motorcycles—showed up to cheer the Tornadoes.

There were several hundred e-mails, too, all offering encouragement, some offering help. An appellate judge volunteered to visit Gainesville State and talk with students. A man from a sporting goods manufacturer wanted to design and donate new uniforms. Another man said he could afford only one helmet and one set of shoulder pads, but he wanted to purchase what he could to help. An assistant pastor and members of his church wanted to sign up as mentors. Eventually, more than twenty people from his church began visiting two hours every other week with inmates, including a few who had not had a visitor since being incarcerated.

Witnessing what the football players had received from their visit to Grapevine, other Gainesville State students were no longer nonchalant about off-campus opportunities. When an upcoming event was posted, more students met the requirements to take part. And more people off campus wanted Gainesville State students to be a part of their activities. Boys from the facility rang bells to collect donations for the Salvation

Army. They took part in Gainesville's annual Christmas parade, smiling and waving from a float as residents smiled and waved back to them. The security fence remained, but as more students began taking part in supervised off-campus activities, and as more people interacted with them in those settings, other barriers began breaking down.

The feelings of hope that began with the football team had spread throughout the facility, Hawthorne said, and students were learning firsthand that there are people out in the free world who would give them a second chance. And that despite the bad choices that had brought them to Gainesville State School, they could go back out into society and make positive contributions.

"A lot of people are bubbling; everybody's excited," Williams said. "The kids are excited. When the staff and the teachers are excited and they're upbeat and positive, and when the kids are excited, everybody gets along better."[4]

+ + +

Up until this season, Styles had been an assistant coach for the football team. He had been there after the games when the players took their goodie bags from opposing teams and stepped back onto the bus for the return to their dreary prison lives. Although he had not been at the Faith game, he could tell what made that one different from the rest.

"These boys, a lot of them, just hadn't had anybody care about them," Styles said. "When they saw that, they brought that back. And then their peers heard that these people cared about them—really cared about them, not just throwing money at them or throwing a bag of stuff at them. They actually cared about them, and they showed it through their actions."[5]

Styles described previously feeling on edge at work, not knowing what might happen that day, always looking over his shoulder. How the question before had not been if there would be a fight, but where and when it would take place. But things had changed. Before, when his students would work on welding projects, he would have to watch their every move to make sure one would not stick a piece of metal in his pocket that could later be used as a makeshift knife. Now, leaders had stepped up from among the inmates. They were acting as overseers or trustees on projects, they were making sure their classmates were being responsible, they were doing exactly as instructed, then asking what else Styles wanted done.

Styles called the Faith game "a blessing," saying it made him and his peers feel good about working at Gainesville State. It was now, he said, "sort of like a real school."

+ + +

At Gainesville State, they kept playing the Faith Christian game over and over. Else and M. White laughed and looked at each other when asked to estimate how many times they had watched film of the game. "At least thirty times," White guessed.

Jordan Dunnington's father, Darryl, had turned the game film into a Tornadoes highlights film, complete with NFL Films–style music in the background. There were freeze-frames of each player, with his jersey number and name displayed on a graphic. Each player would receive a copy when he left the facility.

Players and nonplayers requested to watch the game during the television-watching privileges they earned. During recreation time, they would go outside and re-create plays from the game. Those who were at the game would tell those who were not there what it was like, how it felt, and that Faith Christian would be on the schedule again next year and they should do whatever it takes to be at that game. It would be, they told them, a night they would not forget.

"I don't care if I'm fifty years old," Else said, "I'm going to remember that spirit line."[6]

Back in his cell, when alone and feeling down, Castillo would look at his copy of the picture of him and his teammates giving Williams his on-field shower. The photo represented more than a story from that game. In that photo, Castillo could see stories back three years to the day he had been incarcerated. That picture, and those stories, motivated him to keep his calm, to control his anger, to keep making the right decisions he had learned to make inside the facility. That picture reminded him that whether he wins or loses is not as important as that he never quits—not just in football, but in life. He would tell himself to keep going, to keep setting high goals, to keep trying to achieve more and more. He would not let a slipup stop him. The photo reminds him, he said, to "learn from the mistakes that you did."[7]

"Those kids that were in that game," Lucinda Scott said, "I think it absolutely changed their lives. They think they have a chance. That there's something out there. That everything we've been preaching is really true."[8]

+ + +

The coach who prepares for everything was caught unprepared.

As the attention the game received grew, there was a growing sense of energy and inspiration on the Faith campus. Students, teachers, and administrators alike felt affirmation for their actions. "Anyone who has had a kid and gone through Christmas can relate to just how much better it is to give than to receive," Hogan said. "If you've ever been a blessing to anybody, not expecting anything in return, and felt how that would warm your heart. Anybody who has ever stopped on the side of the road and lent a helping hand to somebody in need, and with them having no way to pay you back. There's something about humanity that strives and wants to do good. That same experience is what has created energy and inspiration in us."

And the experience had come from a story Hogan had not anticipated would go beyond The Jungle's parking lot. "I was really surprised, because I feel like it shouldn't be that big of a deal that Christians take actions and do things like this," he said.

Yet it had become a big deal, and Hogan admitted to feeling overwhelmed. He had received more than five hundred e-mails of support and more media interview requests than he could accommodate. Suddenly it was rare that he could spend more than ten uninterrupted minutes on his usual duties as athletic director. However, he believed God had provided him with a platform, and he wanted to take advantage of every good opportunity while the opportunities existed. He preaches to his players, after all, to be doers.

The biggest surprise came when a representative of NFL commissioner Roger Goodell called to invite Hogan and his wife to the Super Bowl. Goodell was so moved by an account of the Gainesville State–Faith game that he pointed to that game as an example of how football can positively shape values. Goodell asked Hogan to come to one of the world's grandest sporting events and tell how he and his school used football to provide hope. "Coach Hogan is truly making a difference," the commissioner said, "and we wanted to salute him and help spread his story."[9] Hogan also made appearances on ESPN, *The 700 Club*, and local television shows. There were dozens of interviews with radio and print media.

Hogan had thought that winning a state championship would bring this platform, which is one reason he still carried the disappointments of the Regents loss in the semifinals two seasons ago and the Reicher loss in the state-championship game the previous season. But here he was talking about a season in which his team had finished 9–3 and lost in the second round of the playoffs. He could review his own highlights of the season: the Gainesville State game, how his players had prayed with the North Side players, how they had served and talked with the John Curtis players, how they had wanted to reach out to the family and friends of the Grace Prep player. The impact of those events had made this, Hogan would say, the most successful season of Faith football. Now, here he was with this unexpected platform, and because of one seemingly meaningless game against a winless team, people from all over the United States and abroad were wanting to know the secret of Faith football.

There is no secret, he says. From the four football priorities listed on each week's scouting report to the priorities demonstrated when a star player is pulled from a game by his own coach for attitude, everything taught in Hogan's program conveys the purpose of showing his players—the next generation of businessmen and husbands and fathers—how to see themselves and others as God sees them.

Be 'Sold Out.' Determine the few things in life that truly matter to you, and sell out to being great in those areas. *Your life is only enriched when you live it for a purpose bigger than yourself.* Live for yourself, and you'll never be satisfied. Become part of a purpose beyond yourself, and you will perform at a higher level; you will find true identity and find pure motivation. *Don't compartmentalize.* Be who God called you to be in all areas of your life. Don't change based on circumstances or surroundings, or you will feel empty, restless, and irritable. Live a regret-free life by always giving your all. *Meet with God as a lifestyle.* If you don't spend regular time in prayer and Bible study, you will make no spiritual impact on those around you. *It's all about relationships.* Long after your final game has been played, and even as the final scores blur in your memories, the relationships you built—and the tools you used in developing those relationships—will remain a part of your lives.

What took place that night on Faith's home field when Gainesville State visited was an opportunity for which the coaches and players had been preparing, even if they did not know what type of opportunity they were preparing for. All the lessons taught and learned on that field, on the adjacent practice field, in the locker room, and in conversations outside the field house caused them to look beyond a football game and deliver hope to fourteen players. And, without even considering it possible, deliver a message to countless others who would read about their game: that if a high school football field in Texas can be a place where positive impact is made in a real-life way, then so can any office cubicle, or meeting room, or an unplanned meeting in line at a store, or a father-son drive in the car. That the ability to make a dramatic impact comes as the result of steady faithfulness through smaller opportunities.

The genuine changes that took place on that football field may be surprising to those drawn in by the story, but not to Kris Hogan. He believes everything that is needed to be successful in football is also required to be successful in life. Tenacity. Overcoming adversity. Flexibility. The ability to adapt. Teamwork. Commitment. Perseverance. He says the list goes on and on.

"The great thing is," Hogan concluded, "all of that is encompassed in life's most important thing: relationships. It's just an incredible package."

That is why he is a high school football coach. And that is why a player such as Greg Wright could stand in Faith's empty locker room—his football career complete but everything football had prepared him for just beginning—and shrug at the attention. At least, Wright hoped, that attention would allow others to see that Faith football is "a little bit different."

"It's not just football," he said. "If it was just a football team, none of this would happen."

It's not just about football at Faith. It's about everything that Lion head stands for. And that is why they play.

Epilogue

The Faith players—especially the seniors on the 2007 team—said they had a sense that after they left high school, it would be difficult to establish relationships similar to the ones they had developed in their locker room. Perhaps that is why five of those players—Alex Nerney, Weston Clegg, Grant Hockenbrough, Jeff Kallal, and Brent Reeder—plan to be together on the University of Arkansas campus in the fall of 2010.

Nerney turned down a football scholarship offer from the United States Air Force Academy in order to pursue his dream of playing at Texas A&M University. However, he did not land a spot on the team as a walk-on and spent a year at a local community college (while hanging around the Faith team as much as possible) before transferring to Arkansas, where he made the Razorbacks' roster. He will be eligible to play in 2011 after sitting out one season because of NCAA transfer rules. Nerney and his father have improved their relationship, talking by phone at least three times per week.

Clegg attended Covenant College in Georgia on a soccer scholarship. But when the program joined the NCAA's Division III, it had to enter a transitional period that would have prevented the team from competing in postseason competition for essentially the rest of Clegg's college career. When the coach who recruited Clegg left for another school, Clegg decided to transfer to Arkansas. He plans to play on the Razorbacks' club soccer team.

Hockenbrough, who had scored the Faith soccer team's state championship–winning goal, entertained several soccer scholarship offers but attended a community college and trained in hopes of finding a place to play football. He did, at Hardin-Simmons University. After one season there, Grant decided to join his friends at Arkansas.

Kallal, also now at Arkansas, had hoped to play football at Hardin-Simmons, but he injured his shoulder lifting weights and decided to attend Texas A&M. There, he teamed with Daniel Ackerman and Brock Jameson to win the school's intramural dodgeball championship before transferring to Arkansas.

Curtis Roddy received a football scholarship from the Colorado School of Mines but had to quit football after one year because of knee problems. He remained at the school to study geological engineering and is now engaged to his high school sweetheart.

Landon Anderson received a baseball scholarship to Dallas Baptist University. Two juniors from the '07 football team also received baseball scholarships: Josh O'Neal and Pierce Shivers, both to Cisco College.

Clayton Messinger did indeed graduate as Faith's salutatorian. He is studying biomedical engineering at Texas A&M and serving as a counselor at a Christian retreat for incoming freshmen.

Tommy Rost played rugby at Sam Houston State University but, after enduring a semester of early-morning soreness from rugby, decided to switch to intramural softball.

Jordan Dunnington drew interest from the Air Force Academy and a few small college programs for football, but after visiting Kenya on Faith's annual missions trip during spring break of his senior year, he determined that God wanted him to pursue missions-related work instead of college football. Jordan attends Baylor University, where he is majoring in public relations and leading a hip-hop ministry.

Tanner Gesek, who caught coaches' attention as a scout-team running back his junior season, started at running back alongside Dunnington his senior year and rushed for almost a thousand yards. He enrolled at Wheaton College in Illinois with intentions of playing football, but he decided to run track instead. He is also heavily involved in music at Wheaton and was elected sophomore class president.

Greg Wright is studying mechanical engineering at Texas Tech University and working as a counselor at a Christian camp for incoming freshmen. He is considering trying out as a punter for Tech's football team.

Chance Cochran attends Arizona State University. He remains close friends with Hockenbrough and Clegg and stays in contact with some of his former Faith coaches.

Dexter Cheneweth did not play football his senior season, although he attended games and cheered for his former teammates. He is attending Dallas Baptist, along with Landon Anderson. "I don't have a sports scholarship," Dexter reported with a laugh, "but I do play kickball."

Peter Ashton has matured both as a football player and a student.

He started at quarterback and free safety his sophomore and junior seasons, making first-team all-state on defense as a junior. He entered his senior season being recruited at quarterback by major college programs. Peter was recently diagnosed to have none of the five learning disabilities he had previously been diagnosed with and has become mostly an A and B student.

Nathan Alcantara had hoped to walk on to the baseball team at Southeastern Oklahoma State University but did not make the team in his first attempt. He hasn't given up on playing baseball but has earned his pilot's license in the meantime. Like so many former Lions athletes, he says leaving Faith has shown him how unique and special the situation there was and that what he misses most is the relationships he had with Faith's coaches.

+ + +

The 2009 season was a struggle at times for a young Lions team, with Ashton the only returning starter. Faith finished 6–6 but did make the playoffs and, as it did the year before, advanced to the second round of the playoffs.

Again, one of the season's highlights had nothing to do with a final score. In 2008, Faith players had prayed with players from the North Side team when one of the Steers' players was injured on the field. In 2009, when the teams met again, North Side coach Chris Killian presented Coach Hogan with a letter of appreciation from his school that declared the Faith family "Honorary North Side Steers" and gave Hogan a football with a note of thanks signed by the injured player, Martin Rodriguez.

During that night's game, in an eerie twist, a Faith player was injured with what later was diagnosed as a concussion. As trainers and both head coaches surrounded the player on the field, players from North Side, a public school in Fort Worth, took a knee along their sideline. Visible from the Faith stands over the players' shoulders was a sign made by the Steers' cheerleaders that read, "North Side thanks Grapevine Faith for your prayers & support." When a stretcher was rolled onto the field, North Side players and coaches huddled briefly on their sideline, then jogged across the field to the Faith side. There, both teams prayed for the injured Faith player in a move that drew applause not only from fans on both sides of the stadium but also from game officials on the field.

Faith and Gainesville State met again in the final week of the regular season. Mark Williams had left as head coach to become an assistant coach, of all places, at Grapevine High School, just five minutes from Faith. Assistant coach Walt Scott had been promoted to replace Williams. During the 2009 season, the Tornadoes came into the Faith game with one victory to their credit—defeating A+ Academy of Dallas 20–0 in non-district play to end a thirteen-game losing streak.

The night before hosting Gainesville State, Faith football players painted "GSS" in one of their home field's end zones and painted two Tornadoes logos next to the Lion head at midfield. After finding out what particular needs Gainesville students had, Faith asked its fans to bring gloves and socks for Gainesville State students.

Because of the attention the previous year's game received, the second meeting was a big event. About four thousand—an overflow crowd—attended the game. The pre-game spirit line, which had been about forty yards long the year before, was 150 yards long—running along the back of one end zone, the length of the field, then curving toward the home stands. Among the fans in attendance were Dallas Cowboys coach Wade Phillips, Cowboys players Jason Witten and Jon Kitna, and Disney star Cody Linley.

As a part of the pre-game ceremonies, Mack White took part in the coin toss. Mack was the Gainesville State student manager referred to as "M. White" in the final three chapters of this book. Soon after being released from Gainesville State, Mack was taken in by a Faith family that is helping him transition back into the free world. Mack has started a modeling career. He also has an active role in the production of *One Heart*, the feature film about the first Faith–Gainesville State game, which is planned to release in fall 2011. Mack has had opportunities to speak in schools and youth prison facilities about his life story and the importance of making right decisions.

Although the teams' second meeting did not have the surprise element of the first game, it still was a night filled with emotion. Faith won—28–22 this time—and again played many of its backup players much of the night. But Tornadoes players again left the field feeling like winners after scoring a touchdown on the game's, and their season's, final play.

As testimony to the ongoing impact of the previous year's game, Gainesville State superintendent Gwan Hawthorne said that of the ten players from that game who had left the facility, not one had been returned to any part of the Texas Youth Commission system.

Afterword

This book has said a lot already about my teams and my coaching style. If there's one thing I'd add, it's that I desire for my thoughts, actions, and lifestyle to reflect the attributes of Jesus Christ, thereby glorifying the name of God. That is my personal mission statement, and it's to this end that I design my life. Coaching high school football in Texas is just one part of that work.

When David Thomas approached me about following our team for the 2007 season, I was truly honored, and I agreed with a sense of anticipation as the season approached. When the season was over, and I was able to see some of David's observations in print, I became genuinely excited. I realized immediately the potential impact his writing could make, and that is what excites me about life: making an impact.

I know God called me to use the platform of football to build the next generation of husbands, dads, business owners, voters, and leaders. This book represents the Lord's work in expanding that platform. He chose to reach down and explode the work of the Gainesville State game, to further broaden our platform and influence for His glory. From ESPN, NBC, *The 700 Club*, and hundreds of speaking opportunities, to Australian radio stations, the platform has grown far beyond what I had ever imagined.

The greatest experience of the process is simply a confirmation of principles I already know and teach every day. God has created us all for a purpose. It is impossible to understand your purpose apart from your Creator. When you truly embrace Jesus Christ as your personal Lord and Savior, you have only to seek His will for your life, and then be faithful to the call. It's been my experience that His plans for our lives are so much richer than we could ever imagine or create with our limited resources.

I pray this book serves as an exhortation to you, and possibly a source of reference as you work to make an impact for both time and eternity.

Kris Hogan

Acknowledgments

As a writer, the Acknowledgments section is one of my favorite parts of a book to read. Who a writer thanks and how he or she thanks them reveals a writer's heart. My heart is grateful to many people who helped make this book possible.

First, I must thank my wife, Sally. I could not even attempt to list all the different roles she played in *our* journey to publication. She helped convince me that this book needed to be written, then went so far above and beyond to make sure it was completed. After all these years, I still think it's neat—sorry to use "neat," but we met in the '80s—that God allowed me to marry my best friend.

My kids, Ashlin and Tyson, granted Dad permission to miss a few practices and games. Their payback, I hope and pray, is that because of the lessons I learned during my season with the Faith football team, I am a better dad.

When my parents drove an aspiring thirteen-year-old sportswriter fifteen minutes to the newspaper office so he could turn in his handwritten stories and chase his dream, I wonder if they imagined that one day they would be holding a book with his name on the cover. Life has thrown some curveballs at us since this book process began, and I am so thankful that my parents can hold this book in their hands. Thanks for fighting so courageously, Mom and Dad. I love you both.

Chip MacGregor is the world's best literary agent. Your offer to represent the manuscript was this book's first major victory. Your belief in these words and this author meant much. Your friendship means more.

Tyndale House Publishers sports its own incredible team. Carol Traver, thanks for championing this book and for your patience with a rookie author. Cara Peterson is a writer's dream editor. Thank you for helping me say what I meant to say! I have been energized by the sales team's enthusiasm for this project. The entire Tyndale roster has been a pleasure to work with.

My brother, Brad, is an amazing Web site designer. (See www
.RememberWhyYouPlay.com to sample his work. How's that for a shameless plug?) But you are a better brother than Web site designer.

Celeste Williams is the best boss I've ever had. Thanks for telling me I needed to write a book, and thanks for letting me.

Dallas Rysavy and Schuyler Dixon, in addition to being great friends, have been invaluable as sounding boards.

Steve Riach, producer of the coming feature film *One Heart*, generously shared his preproduction interviews, helping me better tell the entire story surrounding the Faith–Gainesville State game. I know that *One Heart* will touch and inspire many.

There were so many other friends who kept asking about the book, kept praying it would find its way into print, and kept encouraging me. Thank you all so much.

From Gainesville State School, I appreciate the help of Mark Williams, Walt and Lucinda Scott, Gwan Hawthorne, Karen Bates, Chris Styles, and Dottie Luera. Please know that the hope your players felt from the support of the Faith fans that night was built upon the foundation your school had established in those students.

I tell Dana Stone, Faith's assistant to the athletic director, that she is the person who truly runs the athletic department. Dana has the ability to juggle three or four tasks at once yet still look up at me from her desk and answer all my questions with a smile.

Of course, I owe more gratitude than I could ever repay to Kris Hogan and the rest of the Faith coaches. I am not sure why you allowed a nosy reporter and his recorder to shadow you for an entire season, but I am grateful you did. In addition to all the football lessons, you taught me life lessons. Throughout my time with you, I kept thinking that you are the type of coaches I want my children to play for.

Finally, I want to express my appreciation to the Faith Lions—the players. I asked you to share with me a football season. Instead, you shared a season of your lives. I will never forget those of you who hugged me after the state-championship game, most with eyes still moist, and apologized that you didn't provide a better outcome for the final chapter of that season. I am still amazed that amid all of the disappointment and pain you felt, you could be so selfless. Perhaps nothing better illustrates why you guys will always be champions in my book.

2007 Varsity Roster

NO.	NAME	POSITION	GRADE	HEIGHT	WEIGHT
3	**Alex Nerney**	WR/DE	12	6-3	190
4	**Jordan Dunnington**	RB/CB	11	5-7	155
5	**Brent Reeder**	WR/SS	12	5-11	170
6	**Landon Anderson**	QB/FS	12	5-10	165
8	**Weston Clegg**	WR/CB	12	5-10	160
10	**Peter Ashton**	QB/FS	9	5-11	175
12/66	**Greg Wright**	RB/LB/P	11	6-0	200
14	**Justin Huffman**	RB/LB	11	5-10	170
20	**John Elder**	OL/DL	12	5-10	170
21	**Pierce Shivers**	WR/SS	11	5-10	175
22	**Grant Hockenbrough**	RB/LB/K	12	5-10	175
33	**Gage Garrett**	OL/DL	10	6-4	210
34	**Josh O'Neal**	WR/DE	11	6-2	185
44	**Garrett Cox**	RB/LB	11	5-8	170
50	**Jacob Pruett**	OL/LB	11	5-11	165
51	**Steven Little**	OL/DE	12	6-1	220
55	**John Ashton**	OL/DL	11	5-11	210
56	**Clayton Messinger**	OL/DL/K	12	5-11	195
60	**Jeff Kallal**	OL/DT	12	6-0	230
63	**Mike Samuels**	OL/DT	11	6-0	180
64	**Curtis Roddy**	OL/DT	12	6-3	285
65	**Tommy Rost**	OL/DT	12	5-11	230
68	**Daniel Ackerman**	OL/DL	12	6-1	220
80	**Nathan Jordan**	WR/CB	12	5-10	155
81	**Brock Jameson**	WR/CB	12	5-10	170
84	**Nathan Alcantara**	WR/LB	11	6-0	165
88	**Tanner Gesek**	RB/CB	11	5-10	165

Head Coach: Kris Hogan
Assistant Coaches: Matt Dowling, Steve Ford, Doug Hutchins, Andy Postema,
    Axel Rivera, Matt Russell, Drew Sells, Brandon Smeltzer
Trainer: Auggie Gomez
Managers: Chris Palmara, Chris Wicker

Notes

CHAPTER 8

1. NIV.
2. Proverbs 23:7 (NKJV): "As he thinks in his heart, so *is* he."
3. 2 Timothy 1:7 (NLT).

CHAPTER 9

1. Included by permission of Tori Guinan.

CHAPTER 11

1. Reference to Romans 12:17, 19.

CHAPTER 21

1. David Thomas, "Two Teams Share United Feeling: For One Team, Playing Host Was a Matter of Faith," *Fort Worth Star-Telegram,* January 25, 2009.
2. Matthew 25:35-36, 40 (NIV).
3. Preproduction interview, *One Heart* movie, March 4, 2009.
4. Ibid.
5. Ibid.
6. Ibid.
7. Ibid.
8. Included by permission of Kris Hogan.

CHAPTER 22

1. Preproduction interview, *One Heart* movie, March 5, 2009.
2. Preproduction interview, *One Heart* movie, March 4, 2009.
3. Ibid.
4. Ibid.
5. Preproduction interview, *One Heart* movie, March 5, 2009.
6. Preproduction interview, *One Heart* movie, March 4, 2009.
7. Ibid.
8. Ibid.
9. Rick Reilly, "There Are Some Games in Which Cheering for the Other Side Feels Better Than Winning," *ESPN.com*, December 23, 2008, http://sports.espn.go.com/espnmag/story?section=magazine&id=3789373.
10. David Thomas, "Unique Fan Support Lifts Players' Spirits," *Fort Worth Star-Telegram*, November 9, 2008.

CHAPTER 23

1. David Thomas, "Two Teams Share United Feeling: For the Visitors, Being Cared about Was an Inspiration," *Fort Worth Star-Telegram,* January 25, 2009.
2. Ibid.
3. Ibid.
4. Ibid.
5. Ibid.
6. Ibid.
7. Preproduction interview, *One Heart* movie, March 4, 2009.
8. Ibid.
9. David Thomas, "Two Teams Share United Feeling: For One Team, Playing Host Was a Matter of Faith," *Fort Worth Star-Telegram,* January 25, 2009.